CHANGING PRACTICES IN EVALUATING TEACHING

Changing Practices in Evaluating Teaching

*A Practical Guide to Improved Faculty
Performance and Promotion/Tenure Decisions*

Peter Seldin

Pace University

and Associates

Foreword by Pat Hutchings, Senior Scholar

The Carnegie Foundation for the Advancement of Teaching

Anker Publishing Company, Inc.
Bolton, Massachusetts

CHANGING PRACTICES IN EVALUATING TEACHING
A Practical Guide to Improved Faculty Performance and Promotion/Tenure Decisions

ISBN 1-882982-28-2

Composition by Delaney Design

Cover design by Deerfoot Studios

Anker Publishing Company, Inc.
176 Ballville Road
P.O. Box 249
Bolton, MA 01740-0249
www.ankerpub.com

ABOUT THE AUTHOR

Peter Seldin is distinguished professor of management at Pace University, Pleasantville, New York. A behavioral scientist, educator, author, and specialist in the evaluation and development of faculty and administrative performance, he has been a consultant to nearly 300 colleges and universities throughout the US and in 26 countries around the world.

A well-known speaker at national and international conferences, Seldin regularly serves as a faculty leader in programs offered by the American Council on Education, the American Association for Higher Education, and the American Assembly of Collegiate Schools of Business: the International Association for Management Education.

His well-received books include: *The Teaching Portfolio, Second Edition* (1997), *Improving College Teaching* (1995, with associates), *Successful Use of Teaching Portfolios* (1993, with associates), *The Teaching Portfolio, First Edition* (1991), *How Administrators Can Improve Teaching* (1990, with associates), *Evaluating and Developing Administrative Performance* (1988), *Coping With Faculty Stress* (1987, with associates), *Changing Practices in Faculty Evaluation* (1984), *Successful Faculty Evaluation Programs* (1980), *Teaching Professors to Teach* (1977), and *How Colleges Evaluate Professors* (1975).

He has contributed numerous articles on the teaching profession, student ratings, educational practice, and academic culture to such publications as *The New York Times, The Chronicle of Higher Education*, and *Change*. For his contributions to the scholarship of teaching, in 1998 he was awarded an honorary doctor of education from Columbia College (Columbia, South Carolina).

ABOUT THE CONTRIBUTORS

William E. Cashin is emeritus professor of counseling and educational psychology at Kansas State University. From 1975 until 1996 he was consultant, then director of the university's Center for Faculty Evaluation and Development. Among his other responsibilities, he wrote IDEA papers and consulted with over 300 colleges and universities about student ratings, faculty evaluation, and the improvement of teaching.

Deborah DeZure is director of the Faculty Center for Instructional Excellence at Eastern Michigan University. Her publications on innovative and effective approaches to college teaching and faculty development have appeared in *Academe, Change, The AAHE Bulletin, Thought and Action, CEA Forum,* and NCTE publications, among others. She served as editor of *To Improve the Academy* (1997) and is on the editorial boards of *The International Journal of Academic Development, Journal of Excellence in College Teaching,* and *Issues and Inquiry in College Teaching and Learning.*

Mary Lou Higgerson is professor of speech communication and recipient of the outstanding teacher award at Southern Illinois University, Carbondale, where she serves also as the executive director for the undergraduate experience. Her books include *Communication Skills for Department Chairs* (1996), *Complexities of Higher Education Administration* (1993, coauthored with Susan Rehwalt), and *The Department Chair as Academic Leader* (1999, coauthored with Irene Hecht and Walter Gmelch). Higgerson is a regular presenter for the American Council on Education's National Leadership Development Seminars for Department Chairs.

Devorah A. Lieberman is a professor in the department of communication studies and director of teaching and learning in the Center for Academic Excellence at Portland State University. She is associate editor of *To Improve the Academy* and serves on the editorial board for *The Journal of Excellence in College Teaching.* Her areas of research involve assessment, student learning, Techno-CATs, and intercultural communication.

Michele Marincovich is assistant vice provost and director of the Center for Teaching and Learning at Stanford University. She is a past president of the Professional and Organizational Development (POD) Network in Higher Education and a frequent presenter in the US and abroad. Her most recent publications include *Disciplinary Differences in Teaching and Learning* (1995, coedited with Nira Hativa) and *The Professional Development of Graduate Teaching Assistants* (1998, coedited with Jack Prostko and Frederic Stout).

Joseph C. Morreale is associate vice president for planning, assessment, research, and academic support and professor of public administration (public finance) at Pace University in New York City. He is also senior scholar at the American Association for Higher Education and coauthor of *Post-Tenure Review: Practices, Policies, and Precautions* (1997) and *Post-Tenure Review: A Guide Book for Academic Administrators of Colleges and Schools of Business* (1997).

Joan DeGuire North has plowed the fields of academic administration as dean of the College of Professional Studies at the University of Wisconsin, Stevens Point, for over a decade. Previously, she served in administrative posts in two private colleges, directed the faculty development segment of a national grant, and was an early pioneer in the faculty development movement. She was the founding president of the Professional and Organizational Development (POD) Network in Higher Education in the early 1970s. She has written on post-tenure review, campus support for teaching, and faculty vitality.

Clement A. Seldin is associate professor in the department of teacher education and curriculum studies, School of Education, University of Massachusetts. He is recipient of several teaching awards including the university's highest faculty honor, the Distinguished Teaching Award. His research on parent/teacher conferencing and selectivity in teacher education has appeared in many professional journals. His teaching focus is social foundations of American public education. In addition, he serves as the Massachusetts director to the New England Educational Research Organization.

John Zubizarreta, a Carnegie Foundation/CASE Professor of the Year for South Carolina, is professor of English, director of honors and faculty development, and dean of undergraduate studies at Columbia College. He has earned several regional, national, and international awards for excellence in teaching and scholarship. In addition to his teaching responsibilities and his research and criticism in American and comparative literatures, he has also published variously on pedagogical issues, technology, teaching improvement, and teaching portfolios.

Table of Contents

FOREWORD

The evaluation of teaching is often treated as a problem to be managed. There are reasons for this: vexing technical issues, practical constraints, interpersonal politics and institutional policies. But the process for judging teaching—the methods, the occasions, the sense of purpose that shapes what we do and don't do—is also an opportunity to enact our core values as academics. This volume must be read, therefore, not only a practical resource but a statement, or set of statements, about what it means to be committed to and accountable for instructional excellence.

One thing that's clear is that it means something different today than in the past. Peter Seldin's opening chapter gives an overview of changes in the evaluation of teaching over the last two decades. His report pinpoints particulars in telling ways, both in terms of what we do and do not attempt. But it's interesting to think as well about the larger context of change and how this volume might look had it been written twenty years ago. I think it would not, for instance, have featured such a range of approaches. We would have read about student ratings, no doubt, which were and continue to be an essential component of the evaluation of teaching—and the one we know most about. But the role of peers is much more clearly in the picture at this point. And consider, too, the several strategies featured here that employ technology, and the attention to portfolios, which are dealt with by several of the volume's authors. Portfolios, in fact, reflect another emergent theme in our thinking about teaching these days: that ensuring the quality of teaching is not someone else's job but, as described in Chapter 5 and elsewhere, a process through which faculty can take responsibility for their own work and professional development throughout a career.

Also reflecting current developments is the volume's focus on colleagueship as an essential ingredient in the evaluation of teaching. Parker Palmer, among others, has written movingly about a "hunger" among faculty for conversation and colleagueship around this important aspect of faculty life. Certainly I have seen the same in the several projects I have been involved with over the last decade, and particularly in the project on peer collaboration and review of teaching sponsored by the American Association for Higher Education. There's no reason to presume this hunger was not felt in previous decades, but what has changed, I believe, is our awareness that colleagueship is not only a nice byproduct but a reason for choosing this or that approach to the evaluation of teaching, and a principle that can help shape how we undertake whatever methods are chosen. To put it differently, the evaluation of teaching is not simply a matter of achieving certain kinds of technical validity but as, Mary Lou Higgerson and Joan DeGuire North make clear, a matter of "climate," and of commitments to mutual trust, respect for differences, and a dedication to quality and improvement.

What's also notable in this volume and in other recent work on the evaluation of teaching is the focus on student learning. While it is true that the most established practice in the evaluation of teaching, the use of student ratings, relies on students, what's new, I think, is an interest in trying to get more directly and explicitly at the impact of what we do on their learning. A number of forces have been at work in moving us toward this mindset but central certainly is the phenomenon of student outcomes assessment, especially that aspect of assessment that focuses on the classroom, which K. Patricia Cross and her several collaborators over the years have done so much to bring into the mainstream. That is to say, though many faculty have been skeptical about external mandates for assessment at the institutional level, the principle that we might be more purposeful about whether our students are learning what we think we're teaching has caught fire in many settings; indeed, to talk about teaching without talking about learning has become a kind of anathema. This view does not, it should be said, show up in Peter Seldin's survey of changing practices very prominently (evidence of student achievement continues to be taken into consideration only minimally), but one can nevertheless see signs of change, as illustrated for instance in Devorah Lieberman's account of faculty's interest in classroom assessment and in Michele Marincovich's wonderful ideas about how to make better use of information from students about their educational experiences and learning. Indeed, the models and examples cited by these two authors are steps toward an area of work that is growing in prominence—the scholarship of teaching and learning, by which I mean a range of strategies and occasions through which faculty can systematically investigate their own practice and its impact on student learning in ways that not only improve the faculty member's own practice but contribute to the work of others. It will be interesting indeed to see if such work shows up in a sequel to this volume five or ten years down the road.

In his penultimate chapter, Peter Seldin describes the various slings and arrows that plague teaching evaluation programs. I would add another to his list—an odd one for academics to fall into, actually—which is a kind of know-nothing attitude, an insistence that nothing is known about effective teaching or how to evaluate it, and that personal opinion is all we have to draw on. That's simply not the case, as this volume illustrates, and those wishing to build practice on the solid ground of what is currently known and done will get a very good start in the chapters that follow.

Pat Hutchings, Senior Scholar

The Carnegie Foundation for the Advancement of Teaching

PREFACE

In their rush to make judgments on tenure, promotion, and retention, many colleges and universities are embracing seriously flawed teaching evaluation programs. Inadequate, biased, or worse, such programs yield a harvest of faculty resistance and, not infrequently, court challenges that reverse administrative decisions.

One compelling reason, then, for institutions to develop more effective and equitable approaches to the evaluation of teaching is to provide a sounder basis for personnel decisions.

Another important reason is that evaluation of teaching, when done well, helps identify areas of instruction that need fine tuning. As a result, the institution, the faculty member, and his or her students can benefit.

Changing Practices in Evaluating Teaching offers college and university faculty members and administrators ready-to-use and research-based information, the kind that is required to foster truly effective and equitable teaching evaluation at their institutions.

This book reveals changes and emerging trends in evaluating teaching by comparing current policies and practices with those used in 1978 and 1988, thereby providing a 20-year view of evaluation practices. Further, it addresses cutting-edge topics in the evaluation of teaching, such as post-tenure review, the use of electronic assessment tools, and the World Wide Web. And the book offers numerous suggestions for improving evaluation methods, avoiding common problems, and dealing with difficulties.

Changing Practices in Evaluating Teaching explains how to gain genuine faculty and administrative support; avoid common weaknesses in teaching evaluation by students, peers, and self; evaluate teaching by examining student learning; successfully combine disparate sources of data; establish a climate conducive to evaluation; and how to structure and use classroom visits, rating forms, electronic classroom assessment, and teaching portfolios.

The book supplies case studies, examples, tables, web sites, and exhibits which further enhance its utility. Special materials include useful forms which can be used directly in teaching assessment. They cover evaluation in many areas, including student assessment of instruction, peer observation, self-appraisal, portfolios, and annual teaching activity lists.

In short, *Changing Practices in Evaluating Teaching* offers college and university faculty and administrators pragmatic, hands-on information about state-of-the-art techniques, important trends, and the use and abuse of specific evaluation strategies.

Earlier books on teaching evaluation have taken a broad, how-to approach and have been geared primarily to institutions that are just setting up their evaluation programs. This book has a different thrust. It studies the transformation of teaching evaluation over the past two decades; it points out implications for the future; it provides institutions with a chance to compare practices; and it specifies the key elements of existing systems that must be improved in order to strengthen the overall system.

This book is written for presidents, provosts, academic vice presidents, deans, department chairs, instructional development specialists, and faculty. As the essential partners in improving teaching evaluating systems, they will be able to take new bearings from the changes and trends noted in this book. The practical suggestions and recommendations presented will be valuable to these administrators and faculty whether they are in public or private institutions. The language used is straightforward and nontechnical.

The book distills not only the literature but also the broad-based, personal experience of each contributor. The contributors are nationally prominent educators who have done seminal work in the improvement of teaching evaluation. In addition to being experts in their fields, almost all contributors have held teaching as well as administrative positions, and consequently, have been on both sides of the evaluation of teaching.

Overview of the Contents

In Chapter 1, Peter Seldin discusses his 1998 study of policies and practices of 598 liberal arts colleges in evaluating teaching for faculty tenure, promotion, and retention decisions. He compares the 1998 study with the 1978 and 1988 studies and offers eight tables on key changes and trends.

In Chapter 2, William E. Cashin spells out key uses and misuses of student ratings of teaching, discusses the research on which variables seem to bias ratings and which do not, and outlines 38 specific recommendations on what to do and what not to do in using student ratings to evaluate teaching.

In Chapter 3, Michele Marincovich argues that providing a peer or professional consultation service about results of student ratings is a vital step to teaching improvement. She details consultation options and presents a model for reconceiving the framing and implementation of student evaluations.

In Chapter 4, Deborah DeZure discusses key sources of peer observation bias and shows how to reduce them. She details critical issues and decisions and outlines effective and equitable ways to evaluate teaching through classroom observation.

In Chapter 5, Peter Seldin weighs reasons for using self-evaluation for personnel decisions and for improving teaching, cites barriers to their effectiveness, and offers two successful, evidence-based models which rely on self-reflection and self-evaluation.

In Chapter 6, Joseph C. Morreale argues that under post-tenure review, there must exist consequences—including the possibility of dismissal-for-cause—for continuing poor performance as a teacher by a tenured faculty member. He describes three post-tenure review models and offers numerous real-world examples of how post-tenure review can and should be used to improve teaching.

In Chapter 7, Devorah Lieberman describes how to use electronic classroom assessment to simultaneously evaluate student learning and the quality of teaching. Based on a six-component model, she demonstrates how this innovative technique can instantly provide valuable feedback to instructors about the effectiveness of specific teaching strategies in helping their students meet specific learning objectives.

In Chapter 8, Clement A. Seldin examines the World Wide Web and demonstrates how this resource can be used to improve the evaluation of teaching. He identifies 14 current web sites that offer comprehensive, immediately useful data and provides for each the title, URL, and a description of its contents.

In Chapter 9, John Zubizarreta explains why the teaching portfolio is an especially good vehicle for evaluating teaching. He offers concrete examples of the evidence that might be included, differentiates it from traditional end-of-the-year activity reports, and provides field-tested models of rating forms that can be used by evaluators in making decisions about the quality of evidence included in portfolios submitted for personnel decisions.

In Chapter 10, Joan DeGuire North argues that administrative courage is required to evaluate the complexities of teaching. She delineates the new perspectives—teaching as learning; the teacher as person; faculty personal reflections; depth, not comparisons—that are needed by knowledgeable academic administrators engaged in evaluating teaching effectiveness.

In Chapter 11, Mary Lou Higgerson discusses how and why so many department chairs (and other academic administrators) fail to encourage the kind of organizational and academic climate needed for effective teaching evaluation—and how to change the climate to make it more conducive to teaching evaluation. She offers an original case study to further illustrate how the chair's approach to evaluation alters the outcome of the process.

In Chapter 12, Peter Seldin describes how to plan and implement a viable teaching evaluation program, what should be evaluated, and who should do the evaluating. Also explored are reasons why evaluation programs often fail, a proven approach to revise a failing system, and characteristics of successful evaluation programs. Field-tested teaching evaluation forms are included in the chapter appendix.

In Chapter 13, Peter Seldin summarizes chapter-by-chapter key points and recommendations for faculty and administrators to bring about much needed improvement in teaching evaluation programs.

Peter Seldin

Pleasantville, NY

March 1999

CHAPTER 1

CURRENT PRACTICES
–GOOD AND BAD–
NATIONALLY

Peter Seldin

No group is more reluctant to admit that there are good teachers and bad teachers than college teachers themselves. This reluctance is often grounded in dubious assumptions about characteristics of teachers and students and about the nature of teaching and learning. But rarely are those assumptions confronted by practical experience, careful observation, or thoughtful reasoning.

Some faculty members oppose ratings by students, peers, or administrators on the grounds that the characteristics of effective teaching are too elusive to measure. They question how effective teaching can be evaluated when no one truly knows what effective teaching is.

These faculty members unwittingly dismiss the huge number of scholarly investigations that are sorting out effective and ineffective teaching behaviors. Seldin (1998a) notes that more than 15,000 studies have been published on one phase or another of teaching effectiveness. From this body of research arise reasonably consistent findings on what constitutes effective teaching.

No one doubts that we are short many answers to the teaching-learning process, just as we still have missing pieces to the Alzheimer's disease puzzle. But we do have some of the answers. And, as Hildebrand (1975, p. 31) points out, ". . . the concept of effective teaching is more exact than those of beauty, love, morality, femininity, normality, perversion, good taste, God, and many more." True, these concepts are difficult to define and measure, but they are in our everyday vocabulary, and we don't hesitate to use them simply because they lack neat definitions.

Even though no single list of teaching qualities has yet been developed to everyone's satisfaction, research studies dating from early in the century to the present have arrived at reasonably consistent findings about the characteristics of good teaching. What are those characteristics?

Eble (1988, p. 21-22) summarizing the research points out that:

Most studies stress knowledge and organization of subject matter, skills in instruction, and personal qualities and attitudes useful to working with students.

If personal characteristics are emphasized . . . good teachers will be . . . those who are enthusiastic, energetic, approachable, open, imaginative, and possessed of a sense of humor.

If characteristics of mastering a subject matter and possessing teaching skills are emphasized, good teachers will be those who are masters of a subject, can organize and emphasize, can clarify ideas and point out relationships, can motivate students, can pose and elicit useful questions and examples, and are reasonable, imaginative, and fair in managing the details of learning. Such characteristics as stupidity, arrogance, narrowness, torpor, cynicism, dullness, and insensitivity are commonly associated with bad teaching, as are shortcomings in command of subject matter or in teaching skills.

Beidler (1997), named the 1983 US Carnegie Professor of the Year, offers some personal observations on the qualities that make a good teacher. Among others, he says that good teachers:

1) Really want to be good teachers

2) Take risks

3) Have a positive attitude

4) Never have enough time

5) Think of teaching as a form of parenting

6) Try to give students confidence

7) Try to keep students—and themselves—off balance

8) Listen to their students

Employing factor analysis, a method of statistical analysis which establishes the tendency of responses to cluster, Eisenberg (1996) analyzed 18 studies dealing with effective teachers. She found a heavy cluster response on the following points: instructor knowledge, organization/clarity, stimulation/enthusiasm, active learning, effective communication, and instructional openness.

Seldin (1997a) suggests that his experience and his study of others' experience has led him to conclude that effective teachers:

1) Treat students with respect and caring

2) Provide the relevance of information to be learned

3) Use active, hands-on student learning

4) Vary their instructional modes

5) Provide frequent feedback to students on their performance

6) Offer real-world, practical examples

7) Draw inferences from models and use analogies

8) Provide clear expectations for assignments

9) Create a class environment which is comfortable for students

10) Communicate to the level of their students

11) Present themselves in class as "real people"

12) Use feedback from students and others to assess and improve their teaching

13) Reflect on their own classroom performance in order to improve it

Developed by Miller (1992), this definition of effective teaching is one with which many students, faculty, and academic administrators will probably agree:

> Effective teachers personify enthusiasm for their students, the area of competence, and life itself. They know their subject, can explain it clearly, and are willing to do so—in or out of class.
>
> Class periods are interesting and, at times, alive with excitement. They approach their area of competence and their students with integrity that is neither stiff nor pompous, and their attitude and demeanor are more caught than taught.

How Do Colleges Evaluate Professors?

Since the benchmarks of effective teaching have been cited repeatedly in innumerable research studies and position papers, an obvious question is: How do colleges determine the presence or absence of these qualities in a teacher?

To learn just what policies and practices are in actual use in evaluating teaching and other aspects of faculty performance, Seldin (1998b) conducted a nationwide survey early in 1998. Its purpose was threefold:

1) To examine critically the wide range of practices and emerging trends in the evaluation of faculty teaching, research, and service performance

2) To suggest which practices are in need of improvement

3) To provide colleges and universities with comparative data to open the door to improvement in evaluation procedures

To assure wide coverage, all the accredited, four-year, undergraduate, liberal arts colleges listed in the *1997 Higher Education Directory* (HEP, 1997) were surveyed. Only university-related liberal arts colleges were excluded to pare the population to more manageable size. Of 740 academic deans, 598 (81%) responded, an unusually high response rate, suggesting perhaps the seriousness with which faculty evaluation is looked upon by the deans.

Some of the respondents also attached sample evaluation forms used at their colleges or sent back comments. Although these materials don't lend themselves to formal analysis, they are noted when appropriate in the discussion of the data.

The questionnaire used in the study was first developed and used by the American Council on Education in 1967 and revised by the Educational Testing Service in 1977. It was designed to gather information on institutional evaluation of faculty performance in connection with tenure, promotion in rank, and retention.

It is anticipated that complete findings of the 1998 study will be reported in other educational publications. This chapter is confined to the significant changes in the evaluation of overall faculty performance and of classroom teaching.

Each question about the evaluation of overall faculty performance called for a response on a four-point scale: 1) major factor, 2) minor factor, 3) not a factor, or 4) not applicable. The answers were tallied and, when appropriate, t-tests were computed to look into the response differences.

Evaluating Overall Faculty Performance: Findings

In considering a professor for tenure, promotion in rank, and retention, institutions today choose and weigh a wide range of factors. The questionnaire offered the academic deans 13 criteria in connection with the evaluation of overall faculty performance. Table 1.1 shows the academic deans' responses to each factor as a "major factor" or "not a factor."

Almost to a person, the academic deans chose classroom teaching as the most important index of faculty performance. Far behind, by more than 30 percentage points, was student advising. Although classroom teaching holds first place in the appraisal of faculty performance, other factors were not neglected.

TABLE 1.1

FREQUENCY OF USE OF FACTORS CONSIDERED IN EVALUATING OVERALL
FACULTY PERFORMANCE IN LIBERAL ARTS COLLEGES, 1998

FACTORS*	MAJOR FACTOR	NOT A FACTOR
Classroom teaching	97.5%	0.7%
Student advising	64.2%	2.5%
Campus committee work	58.5%	1.7%
Length of service in rank	43.8%	18.9%
Research	40.5%	13.4%
Publication	30.6%	11.4%
Personal attributes	28.4%	26.9%
Public service	23.6%	9.5%
Activity in professional societies	19.9%	5.5%
Supervision of graduate study	3.0%	74.1%
Competing job offers	3.0%	80.1%
Supervision of honors program	3.0%	63.2%
Consultation (government, business)	2.0%	51.5%

* In descending order by "major factor" scores

The deans reported that other factors were also of major importance.
For example, four other items (student advising, campus committee
work, length of service in rank, and research) were marked as a "major
factor" by at least 40% of the deans, and another three (publication,

personal attributes, and public service) were cited as "major factors" by at least 23% of the deans.

There are a few differences within the liberal arts colleges. For example, 43.8% of the deans called length of service in rank a "major factor" whereas 18.9% dismissed it as "not a factor." Similarly, 28.4% of the academic deans viewed personal attributes as a "major factor," but 26.9% reported it "not a factor."

In analyzing the responses, numerical weights were assigned so that "major factor" carried a one, "minor factor" a two, and "not a factor" (or "not applicable") a three.

This method of summary ratings yields a reasonably accurate picture. Weights of each factor were added, and the sum was divided by the number of responses to yield an arithmetic mean for each. Thus, the lower the mean, the greater the importance. This ranking process, used by the American Council on Education in an earlier study, simplifies the identification of important factors.

Table 1.2 summarizes the relative importance of factors considered by the deans in evaluating overall faculty performance. Analyzing the data from this vantage point confirms the unmistakable conclusion that classroom teaching is the most important factor in assessing performance. Its exceptionally low mean score is compelling evidence of its prominence on almost every liberal arts campus.

Next in importance are student advising, campus committee work, and research. Liberal arts colleges devote considerable attention to a professor's on-campus activities. They are considered tangible evidence of a faculty member's contribution to the institution's efforts to keep its students content and in school. (In fact, several deans wrotethat their institutions had recently begun "Advisor of the Year" awards.) The emphasis on campus committee work seems to reflect a trend toward decentralization and a broader sharing of the institution's nonteaching load.

TABLE 1.2

FACTORS CONSIDERED IN EVALUATING OVERALL FACULTY
PERFORMANCE IN LIBERAL ARTS COLLEGES, 1998

FACTORS*	MEAN (N=598)
Classroom teaching	1.02
Student advising	1.34
Campus committee work	1.41
Research	1.70
Length of service in rank	1.72
Publication	1.77
Public service	1.81
Activity in professional societies	1.82
Personal attributes	1.93
Supervision of graduate study	2.24
Supervision of honors program	2.32
Consultation (government, business)	2.45
Competing job offers	2.73

*Ranked according to 1998 scores

But, at the same time, it seems clear that liberal arts colleges also prize the high public visibility of published research and public service. The importance of staying in the public eye lends credence to the often-heard observation that professors are paid to teach but are rewarded for their research and publication.

The statistical trends were underlined by comments from many deans. A dean of a college in Maine wrote, "Student advising is taken very seriously here. It's next in importance to teaching." A dean of a college in Colorado said, "Our institution's survival depends directly on keeping our student enrollment up. That's why our faculty evaluation system focuses on factors that impact directly on students: teaching and advising." The dean of a California college saw it somewhat differently: "Student advising is important here. But so is serious discipline-based research."

Length of service in rank still merits major importance in a professor's overall evaluation at almost half of the liberal arts colleges. Institutions relying on it would probably argue that a positive correlation exists between the number of years in rank and the faculty member's overall contribution to the college. That argument is open to challenge by younger faculty with fewer years of service but rapidly expanding reputations.

"Personal attributes," an elusive criterion, for years has enabled some deans and department chairs to ease targeted faculty out of a job or to deny them promotion or tenure. It remains an often-cited major factor. As a dean from New York said, "To go along, you've got to get along. Some faculty just don't fit in." A different perspective on personal attributes came from a dean of a California college: "Diversity is the name of the game in the 1990s."

For virtually all deans, near the bottom of the list of factors in the overall evaluation of faculty performance are supervision of graduatestudy, supervision of honors programs, consultation, and competing job offers. In 1978 and 1988, Seldin (1989) conducted a nationwide survey of "major factors" used in liberal arts colleges in evaluating overall faculty performance. The surveyed colleges as well as the questions and the four-point scales were identical to those employed in the present study. It should also be noted that although some instiutions had been accredited and others had closed or merged since the earlier studies, the effect of the few differences was negligible.

TABLE 1.3

LIBERAL ARTS COLLEGES CITING "MAJOR FACTORS" IN EVALUATING
OVERALL FACULTY PERFORMANCE, 1978, 1988, AND 1998

FACTORS*	1978 (N=680)	1988 (N=604)	1998 (N=598)
Classroom teaching	98.8%	99.8%	97.5%
Student advising	66.7%	64.4%	64.2%
Campus committee work	48.8%	54.1%	58.5%
Length of service in rank	49.9%	43.9%	43.8%
Research	24.5%	38.8%	40.5%
Publication	19.0%	29.4%	30.6%
Personal attributes	38.4%	29.4%	28.4%
Public service	13.7%	19.5%	23.6%
Activity in professional societies	17.0%	24.9%	19.9%
Supervision of graduate study	2.2%	2.6%	3.0%
Competing job offers	3.1%	1.8%	3.0%
Supervision of honors program	2.5%	2.4%	3.0%
Consulting (government, business)	1.2%	2.4%	2.0%

* In descending order by 1998 scores

Table 1.3 shows the frequency with which "major factors" were cited in those earlier studies and compares it to the 1998 findings.

Certain patterns and trends have emerged over the past 20 years. First, even a cursory examination of this table reveals that things have not changed very much in the evaluation of overall faculty performance. In fact, of the 13 factors only four—research, publication, personal attributes, and public service—changed by 10% or more from 1978 to 1998.

Research, publication, and public service jumped in popularity since 1978, while personal attributes fell. Second, most of the shift in popularity of those four factors took place between 1978 and 1988. Third, the heavyweight importance of classroom teaching, student advising, campus committee work, and length of service continues to be strong.

Fourth, there is growing reliance on traditional measures of academic repute: research, publication, and public service. Fifth, consistently at the bottom of the list in each of the three studies are supervision of graduate study, competing job offers, supervision of honors programs, and consulting.

Similar general stability also turns up in the data in Table 1.4, which reports t-tests of differences in mean scores of factors considered in overall evaluation. The data indicate significant difference at the .01 level of confidence between the mean scores of only one factor—consulting—in 1988 and 1998. It had a higher mean score in 1998 compared with 1988, indicating a decline in its overall importance. (Comparable statistical base data for factors in 1978 are, unfortunately, unavailable.)

The strong similarity between the 1988 and 1998 mean scores suggest that despite increasingly strident demands from legislative and institutional governing boards to hold faculty accountable for academic performance, only limited change has resulted in evaluation of overall performance.

TABLE 1.4

T-TESTS OF DIFFERENCES IN MEAN SCORES OF FACTORS CONSIDERED IN EVALUATING OVERALL FACULTY PERFORMANCE, 1988 AND 1998

FACTORS*	1988 (N=604) MEAN SCORE	1998 (N=598) MEAN SCORE	T
Classroom teaching	1.01	1.02	- 0.59
Student advising	1.37	1.34	0.79
Campus committee work	1.46	1.41	1.56
Research	1.67	1.70	- 0.83
Length of service in rank	1.68	1.72	- 0.90
Publication	1.76	1.77	- 0.36
Public service	1.87	1.81	1.67
Activity in professional societies	1.77	1.82	- 1.64
Personal attributes	1.93	1.93	- 0.01
Supervision of graduate study	2.26	2.24	0.48
Supervision of honors program	2.36	2.32	1.37
Consulting (government, business)	2.35	2.45	- 2.91**
Competing job offers	2.70	2.73	- 0.99

Note: Test was t-test for differences in independent proportions.

* Ranked according to 1998 scores

** Significant at a .01 level of confidence

Study Highlights: Overall Faculty Performance

1) Classroom effectiveness continues as the most important index of overall faculty performance.

2) Student advising and campus committee work are still widely cited as major factors.

3) Research, publication, and public service, the hallmarks of academic repute, have gained importance in evaluating overall faculty performance.

4) Length of service in rank still merits high, if somewhat declining, importance.

5) Supervision of graduate study, competing job offers, supervision of honors programs, and consulting continue to be at the bottom of the list in importance in evaluating overall faculty performance.

Evaluating Teaching Performance: Findings

Almost all liberal arts colleges designate classroom teaching effectiveness as the most important factor in overall faculty evaluation. It is reasonable to assume, then, that deans take considerable pains to locate relevant sources of information on teaching competence. How do they assess such competence? What information sources do they use?

To find out, the questionnaire asked the deans to indicate the frequency with which each of 15 possible sources of information were used on their campuses to evaluate faculty teaching performance. The deans had four possible responses and, again, each was assigned a numerical weight: "always used" (1), "usually used" (2), "seldom used" (3), and "never used" (4). Table 1.5 displays the sources of information and their frequency of use by deans in the 1978, 1988, and 1998 studies.

The evidence points to significant changes in the ways liberal arts colleges assess information sources when evaluating teaching performance. Of the 15 sources, four—systematic student ratings, self-evaluation, classroom visits, and course syllabi and exams—changed by

TABLE 1.5

LIBERAL ARTS COLLEGES CITING INFORMATION SOURCES AS "ALWAYS USED" IN EVALUATING TEACHING PERFORMANCE, 1978, 1988, AND 1998

INFORMATION SOURCE*	1978	1988	1998
Systematic student ratings	54.8%	80.3%	88.1%
Evaluation by department chair	80.3%	80.9%	70.4%
Evaluation by dean	76.9%	72.6%	64.9%
Self-evaluation or report	36.6%	49.3%	58.7%
Committee evaluation	46.6%	49.3%	46.0%
Colleagues' opinions	42.7%	44.3%	44.0%
Classroom visits	14.3%	27.4%	40.3%
Course syllabi and exams	13.9%	29.0%	38.6%
Scholarly research/publication	19.9%	29.0%	26.9%
Informal student opinions	15.2%	11.3%	15.9%
Alumni opinions	3.4%	3.0%	9.0%
Grade distribution	2.1%	4.2%	6.7%
Long-term follow-up of students	2.2%	3.2%	6.0%
Student examination performance	2.7%	3.6%	5.0%
Enrollment in elective courses	2.7%	1.2%	1.5%

*In descending order by 1998 scores

20% or more since 1978. And, more significantly, they all changed in the same direction. Each of these four sources of information is used more widely today. It would seem that the information-gathering process is becoming more structured and systematic, and that more colleges are reexamining and diversifying their approach to evaluating classroom teaching.

The predominate sources of information continue to be ratings by students, the department chair, and the academic dean. However, their relative importance has shifted considerably since 1978.

In this period, student ratings have become the most widely used source of information to evaluate teaching. No other source of information approaches its degree of usage. Whereas in 1978 they trailed evaluation by department chair by nearly 26 percentage points and evaluation by dean by 22 percentage points, they are now ahead, nearly 18 percentage points and 13 percentage points respectively. Student ratings are now the most widely used source of information on teaching effectiveness. A dean in Massachusetts wrote, "Student feedback is the most important factor in our determination of teaching effectiveness." A dean in Nebraska said, "We rely heavily on student ratings. The only direct, daily observers of a professor's teaching are the students in the classroom."

And a California dean said, "If I trust only one source of data on teaching performance, I trust the students."

Since evaluations from chairs and deans continue to have a major, though declining, impact, one might ask how sound are the judgments of these administrators? What are they based on? How are their evaluations constructed? It has been argued by many that administrators render sound judgments. They point to the analogous situation of clinical medicine, where experienced physicians often respond to obscure symptoms with a correct diagnosis, but would be at a loss to explain the leap from symptoms to diagnosis.

Department chairs and deans have ready access to a faculty member's teaching load and classroom enrollment data. But in the absence of personal classroom visits, administrators are forced to fall back on secondary sources of information about a professor's effectiveness as a teacher.

The key question is, which sources of information do administrators rely on for their judgments? In addition to student ratings, impressions of teaching competence are probably derived, at least in part, from the professors' self evaluation. It has steadily gained popularity as a useful tool in the assessment of teaching performance. There is mounting recognition that there is value in a reflective, candid self-evaluation and explanation of a faculty member's teaching objectives, methodologies, and shortcomings. The deans say, however, that to be useful in personnel decisions, the self-appraisal must be accompanied by solid evidence of accomplishment. A dean from Florida put it this way: "Self-evaluation provides insights into course and instructional objectives as well as classroom competency. But to be truly useful, it must be accompanied by hard evidence and illustrative material."

There is substantive evidence that administrators also rely on committee evaluation and colleagues' opinions. In many liberal arts colleges, faculty committees and colleagues' opinions continue to play pivotal roles in personnel decisions. For 20 years, with little change, committee evaluation and colleagues' opinions have each been cited by nearly one-half of the liberal arts colleges as "always used" as a source of information in evaluating teaching effectiveness.

It may be that administrators' and faculty committees' impressions of a professor's classroom competence are partly based on the professor's record of scholarly research and publication. This record was cited as "always used" by more than one quarter of the deans. How relevant are research and publication to classroom teaching? Arguably, if they provide insights into the professor's teaching effectiveness, they can be useful measuring rods. But the number of such textbooks, journal articles, and monographs offering such insights is quite modest.

In all three studies—1978, 1988, and 1998—alumni opinions, grade distribution, long-term follow up of students, student examination performance, and enrollment in elective courses were at the bottom of the list as important sources of information.

Table 1.6 shows the 1998 distribution of dean responses to each of 15 sources of information considered in evaluating faculty teaching performance as "always used" or "never used." Perhaps not surprisingly, liberal arts colleges report some internal variation. For example, committee evaluation is cited as "always used" by 46% of the colleges. But more than 34% of the colleges cited committee evaluation as "never used." Similarly, although about 40% of the colleges reported classroom visits as "always used," some 31% reported it as "never used." And, although scholarly research/publication was cited by nearly 27% of the colleges as "always used," nearly 49% reported it as "never used." It is clear that liberal arts colleges lack a uniform approach to the sources of information on which teaching effectiveness is based.

However, despite the divergence in some practices, there is considerable accord among the liberal arts colleges regarding the key sources of information in teaching evaluations. For example, systematic student ratings are reported as "always used" by 88% of the colleges and "never used" by fewer than 3%. And, chair and dean evaluations as well as self-evaluations are "always used" by a hefty majority of institutions, whereas only a modest number "never used" them.

It is clear that liberal arts colleges have partly dismantled and reconstructed their procedures for assessing the teaching performance of their faculty. The gathering process has broadened over the years, becoming more structured and systematized.

These changing procedures are indicated in the t-tests of differences in mean scores of sources of information considered in evaluating teaching performance, 1988 and 1998, as reported in Table 1.7. (Comparable statistical base data for 1978 are, unfortunately, unavailable.)

Analysis of Table 1.7 indicates significant differences at the 0.01 level of confidence between 1988 and 1998 mean scores of seven sources of information—systematic student ratings, self-evaluation or report, course syllabi and exams, committee evaluation, classroom

TABLE 1.6

FREQUENCY OF USE OF SOURCES OF INFORMATION CONSIDERED IN
EVALUATING TEACHING PERFORMANCE, 1998

SOURCES OF INFORMATION*	ALWAYS USED	NEVER USED
Systematic student ratings	88.1%	2.5%
Evaluation by department chair	70.4%	10.2%
Evaluation by dean	64.9%	16.4%
Self-evaluation or report	58.7%	13.4%
Committee evaluation	46.0%	34.3%
Colleagues' opinions	44.0%	19.2%
Classroom visits	40.3%	31.1%
Course syllabi and exams	38.6%	21.6%
Scholarly research/publication	26.9%	48.5%
Informal student opinions	15.9%	48.8%
Alumni opinions	9.0%	74.1%
Grade distribution	6.7%	78.4%
Long-term follow-up of students	6.0%	76.6%
Student examination performance	5.0%	79.1%
Enrollment in elective classes	1.5%	84.3%

* In descending order by "always used" score

visits, informal student opinions, and alumni opinions. Each source recorded a lower mean score in 1998, indicating an increase in importance. It seems clear that liberal arts colleges are gathering information from more sources, and doing so more systematically, for teaching evaluations.

Significant difference at the 0.05 level is found between the 1988 and 1998 mean scores of one source of information: evaluation by department chair. It recorded a higher mean score in 1998, indicating a decrease in importance.

Classroom visits have won increased popularity as an evaluative tool. Today there is considerable recognition that classroom visits can and should play a role in a multisource evaluation process. From the comments of the deans, it seems clear that the most successful institutions using classroom visits do so in a common way: They rely on several extensively trained observers who make several visits to dilute the possibility of individual bias by the observer or atypical performance by the professor. Pre- and post-observation meetings are held between the visitors and the faculty member. The entire process is characterized by careful planning, appropriate training, open communication, prompt feedback, and mutual trust.

Despite its steadily increasing popularity, however, classroom visits as a tool in personnel decisions remains controversial. A supporter, an Oregon dean, wrote, "Classroom visits are essential to knowing what's going on behind the closed classroom door." An opponent, a New Jersey dean, argued, "When a professor knows he's being observed for tenure or promotion purposes, his performance may depend more on his nerve than on his teaching skill."

Teaching judgments are increasingly derived from an analysis of course syllabi and examinations. Central to this approach is whether such instructional materials are current, relevant, and suitable to the course and the students. There is greater use of handouts, reading lists, homework assignments, and student-learning experiences to help appraise the professor's teaching effectiveness. All of this is consistent with the trend to locate more sources for, and give more structure to, information gathering.

TABLE 1.7

T-Tests of Differences in Mean Scores of Information Considered in Evaluating Teaching Performance, 1988 and 1998

SOURCES OF INFORMATION*	1988 (N=604) MEAN SCORES	1998 (N=598) MEAN SCORES	T
Systematic student ratings	1.25	1.14	3.16***
Evaluation by department chair	1.27	1.36	- 2.09**
Evaluation by dean	1.42	1.50	- 1.47
Self-evaluation or report	1.79	1.53	4.47***
Colleagues' opinions	1.75	1.73	0.28
Course syllabi and exams	2.02	1.82	3.79***
Committee evaluation	2.05	1.84	3.02***
Classroom visits	2.19	1.89	5.09***
Scholarly research/publication	2.24	2.19	0.63
Informal student opinion	2.45	2.30	2.96***
Alumni opinions	3.05	2.91	2.88***
Grade distribution	3.04	3.02	0.38
Long-term follow-up of students	3.07	3.05	0.39
Student examination performance	3.07	3.05	0.39
Enrollment in elective courses	3.21	3.29	- 1.20

Note: Test was t-test for differences in independent proportions.

 * Ranked according to 1998 scores

 ** Significant at a .05 level of confidence

 *** Significant at a .01 level of confidence

Table 1.8 shows the percentage of institutions using rating forms (whether completed by students, colleagues, or administrators) and the percentage conducting research on the instruments used. More than 76% of the colleges used rating forms of one kind or another in 1998, an increase of about 1% since 1988 and 14% since 1978.

What is still disheartening, however, is the persistent minimal research by the colleges on the validity of the forms used to evaluate their faculty. Only 14% of the colleges engaged in such research in 1998, and this figure has barely increased over the past 20 years. Without a supportive research base, an evaluative source of information risks being dropped and replaced by a more fashionable evaluative tool.

Study Highlights: Teaching Evaluation

1) Systematic student ratings have become the most widely used source of information on teaching effectiveness in liberal arts colleges.

2) The department chair and dean are still major sources of information, but with sharply diluted power.

3) Self-evaluation, classroom visits, and course syllabi and exams have gained currency in the assessment of classroom teaching.

4) Committee evaluation and colleagues' opinions continue to play major roles.

5) Alumni opinions, grade distribution, long-term follow up of students, student examination performance, and enrollment in elective courses continue to carry little weight in evaluating teaching performance.

6) In altering their teaching evaluation practices, liberal arts colleges are gathering information from more sources, and doing so more systematically.

Why has faculty evaluation—especially the evaluation of teaching—been transformed in recent years? Part of the answer is found in the demand for faculty accountability which has pressured colleges to

TABLE 1.8

FREQUENCY OF USE AND RESEARCH ON RATING FORMS TO EVALUATE
FACULTY TEACHING PERFORMANCE, 1978, 1988, AND 1998

	1978 (N=567)	1988 (N=604)	1998 (N=598)
Do you use special rating forms?	62.8%	75.3%	76.4%
Has your institution conducted research on the validity of these rating forms?	10.0%	13.7%	14.4%

more closely examine the cost-effectiveness of each department and the performance of each professor.

But more of the answer is found in administrative and faculty displeasure with the inadequacies of evaluation systems used in the past. Factual information, especially about teaching, has been skimpy at best. The result has been a growing chorus of complaints from those who serve on tenure and promotion committees that they are given little solid information about classroom teaching performance.

It is likely that many of the shifts in evaluative emphasis have been influenced by the burgeoning teaching portfolio movement. Portfolios are factual descriptions of a professor's teaching strengths and accomplishments. They include documents and materials which collectively suggest the scope and quality of a professor's teaching performance. They get at both the individuality and complexity of teaching (Seldin, 1997).

Portfolios often include student ratings, classroom observation reports, syllabi and other teaching materials, and self-evaluations— all items which the national surveys have shown rising steadily in frequency of use. They provide evaluators with hard-to-ignore information on what professors do in the classroom, why they do it, and how well they do it. The result? Evaluators are less inclined to look at teaching performance as a derivative of student ratings.

It is clear that evaluation methods—especially those connected to teaching—are changing. When current practices are compared to those in place in 1978 and 1988, the shifts become clear. Some factors are getting new weight and others less. But what is unresolved as yet is which of the shifts represent improvements and which are experimental question marks. More certain is the likelihood that a direct outgrowth of improved evaluation practices will be improvement in teaching performance.

REFERENCES

Beidler, P. G. (1997). What makes a good teacher? In J. K. Roth (Ed.), *Inspiring teaching: Carnegie professors of the year speak.* Bolton, MA: Anker.

Eble, K. E. (1988). *The craft of teaching* (2nd ed.). San Francisco, CA: Jossey-Bass.

Eisenberg, R. (1996). Personal correspondence.

HEP. (1997). *Higher Education Directory* (15th ed.). Falls Church, VA: Higher Education Publications.

Hildebrand, M. (1975). How to recommend promotion for a mediocre teacher without actually lying. In C. S. Scott and G. L. Thorne (Eds.), *Professorial assessment in higher education.* Monmouth, OR: Oregon State System of Higher Education.

Miller, R. I. (1992). Personal correspondence.

Seldin, P. (1989) How colleges evaluate faculty. *AAHE Bulletin, 41* (7): 3-7.

Seldin, P. (1997a, July). *Improving college teaching: Learning to use what we know.* Paper presented for the International Conference on Improving College Teaching, Rio de Janeiro, Brazil.

Seldin, P. (1997). *The teaching portfolio: A practical guide to improved performance and promotion/tenure decisions* (2nd ed.). Bolton, MA: Anker.

Seldin, P. (1998a, February). *The teaching portfolio.* Paper presented for the American Council on Education, Department Chairs Seminar, San Diego, CA.

Seldin, P. (1998b, June). *Changing practices in faculty evaluation.* Paper presented for the AAHE Assessment Conference, Cincinnati, OH.

CHAPTER 2

STUDENT RATINGS OF TEACHING: USES AND MISUSES

William E. Cashin

There probably are more studies of student ratings of teaching than all of the other data used to evaluate teaching combined. As of this writing, the ERIC database contains 2,175 references under the term, "student evaluation of teaching performance," ERIC's primary descriptor. I prefer to use the term "student ratings," because for many people the word "evaluation" connotes finality, the end; it implies that we have the answer. I strongly suggest that student ratings are primarily data, a means to an end. In combination with other kinds of data (e.g., peer ratings, administrator ratings, self report, and teaching portfolio materials), these data can be used by evaluators—usually faculty committees or administrators—to make a judgment about how effectively a faculty member has taught.

Although we use past performance as the basis for the evaluation, usually our real concern is to predict future performance. This certainly is the case for retention, tenure, and promotion decisions. To estimate how effective a faculty member's teaching will be, not just in a particular course or even a few courses but in general, requires that we collect data from a variety of courses over two or more years. Even in instances where our purpose in collecting the data is to improve instruction, we use past problems to improve future teaching. (Annual salary increases may be the only exception to this future orientation where our focus is at least in part to reward past performance—even so, we hope that quality performance will continue.) In all cases, effective evaluation of teaching requires the use of more than student rating data. This, of course, leads us to the primary misuse of such data.

MISUSES OF STUDENT RATINGS

I am going to argue that—with one major exception—there are relatively few misuses of student rating data other than not following the recommendations in the uses section that comes later in this chapter.

Too Much Reliance on Student Data

Many colleges and universities rely heavily, if not solely, on student rating data as the only systematic source of data collected to evaluate teaching. This conclusion is based not just on the experience of those active in the field of faculty development, but on a survey of over 40,000 department chairs (US Department of Education, 1991). Ninety-seven percent of the chairs indicated that they used "student evaluations" to assess teaching performance. The lowest use of student evaluations was still 92% of the 10,000 plus chairs from two-year institutions. The next four sources of data used were department chair evaluations (84%), peer evaluations (53%), self evaluations (47%), and dean evaluations (40%). With the exception of self evaluation, my question is: "What data do chairs, peers, and deans use to make their evaluations?" Some suspect that it is mostly secondhand student data, either from seeing student ratings, or having read students' open-ended comments, or just talking to students. I suggest that there is a lot more to teaching than what students see in the classroom. As a result, we need more than student rating data to accurately—and therefore fairly—evaluate teaching. We need information in seven areas:

1) Subject matter mastery

2) Curriculum development

3) Course design

4) Delivery of instruction

5) Assessment of learning

6) Availability to students

7) Administrative requirements

Most students know next to nothing about the first three, and perhaps the last. So, let me repeat: We need more than student data. In an earlier IDEA paper (Cashin, 1989), I suggested some possibilities.

Is Any Use of Student Ratings a Misuse?

Most college professors enjoy being rated by students about as much as most college students enjoy taking final exams. And many professors complain about the perceived problems with student ratings with the same frequency and fervor that students complain about the—perhaps real—faults in our exams. Some college professors argue that student ratings should never be used to evaluate them. A few will grant that student ratings may be useful to the individual instructor when used privately to improve teaching, although when we ask faculty, most say they prefer to use student open-ended comments.

Faculty allege a multitude of flaws in student ratings. As far back as 1976, Aleamoni listed eight concerns that faculty voice about student ratings. He then reviewed research indicating that these criticisms of student ratings were not supported by the research. Later, Aleamoni (1987) expanded his list to 15 "myths" about student ratings, again concluding that they were not supported by the research. Here are a few of the myths that many faculty give credence to (in parentheses I have cited reviews of the literature that indicate that the belief is false):

- Students cannot make consistent judgments (not so, see Feldman, 1977)

- Only excellent researchers can judge teaching because research and teaching are linked (no, see Feldman, 1987)

- Student ratings are only popularity contests (wrong, see both Cohen, 1981; Feldman, 1989)

- Ratings are biased by the gender of the students and instructor (wrong again, see Feldman, 1992, 1993)

- Grades bias student ratings (incorrect, see Feldman, 1976)

Dissenters can almost always find one, or even a few, individual studies that support their objections, but they tend to ignore reviews of the literature citing many studies that found contrary results. Occasionally, the popular media publish one or two studies that conclude that the prevailing wisdom is in error (e.g., *Change*, 1997, September/October; and *The Chronicle of Higher Education*, 1998, January 16). Personally, I don't believe that one swallow makes a summer, let alone one study that might not have met the acceptance criteria of most scholarly journals. In the main, past and present reviewers continue to conclude that student ratings tend to be statistically reliable, valid for most uses, relatively free from bias or the need for control, and useful both to improve instruction and to make personnel decisions. However, regarding personnel decisions, there is almost universal agreement that data from a variety of sources, not just student ratings, are required to accurately evaluate teaching.

USES OF STUDENT RATINGS

My position is that when used properly, student ratings are one excellent source of data both for summative evaluation, to make personnel decisions; and for formative evaluation, to improve teaching. (Please note that improvement does not imply any deficiency; moving from the 98th to the 99th percentile is still improvement.) Most of what follows is an elaboration and update of IDEA Paper No. 22, *Student Ratings of Teaching: Recommendations for Use* (Cashin, 1990a). To avoid too many references, generally I will only cite references not contained in that IDEA Paper. I recommend to the interested reader Braskamp and Ory (1994) and Centra (1993) and would add two general books on improving teaching. both of which have a chapter on student ratings, McKeachie's (1999) *Teaching Tips: Strategies,*

Research, and Theory for College and University Teachers and Davis' (1993) *Tools for Teaching.*

General Considerations of Student Rating Systems

The first 18 recommendations concern the general principles and overall context for a student rating system.

1) Use multiple sources of data about a faculty member's teaching if you are serious about accurately evaluating or improving teaching. Based on my experience, there has been little diminution of the over reliance, or complete reliance, on student ratings as the only systematically collected data used to make personnel decisions. Those who counter that they also use chair, or peer, or dean's evaluations might do well to imagine themselves in court being questioned by the opposition's attorney. How convincing a case could they make for the reliability, validity, usefulness, or credibility of the information they used to make their evaluation? Or was their evaluation really the result of a personal opinion based on incomplete, haphazard, and perhaps biased information?

2) Use student rating data as one source of data about effective teaching. Although probably only 3% to 7% of departments do not include student ratings in their evaluation procedures, the widespread negative comments that are still heard from faculty about student ratings suggest that many faculty, and probably administrators, give the student rating data little or no weight; that is, they do not really use the student ratings. Quoting the research (e.g., Marsh & Dunkin, 1992) to such faculty and administrators seems to have little effect. When it comes to student ratings, or how to teach effectively for that matter, many of us seem perfectly content to rely on our personal experience—no matter how limited—rather than on the literature. Imagine what we would do to students in our academic field if they acted that way.

3) Discuss and decide upon the purpose(s) that the student rating data will be used for before any student rating form is chosen or any data are collected. Before an institution, department, or individual teacher develops or selects a student ratings system, we must first decide for what purpose or purposes the data will be used. The three purposes most frequently mentioned in the literature follow.

1) Evaluation/summative evaluation. The data are used by faculty committees and academic administrators as part of the data upon which to base personnel decisions: retention, promotion, tenure, or salary increases. Every institution makes personnel decisions, so evaluation is necessarily one purpose of any institutional student rating system.

2) Improvement/formative evaluation. Student rating results are used by the instructor to make changes that he or she thinks will help the students learn more effectively or efficiently (again remembering that improvement is appropriate for everyone except the absolutely perfect). Although an institution's rhetoric often states that the primary purpose of student ratings is for improvement, too often there is no systematic help provided by the institution for faculty whose student ratings suggest that improvement is needed.

3) Advisement. The data are used by students and advisors to help in selecting instructors or courses. My impression is that relatively few institutions actually publish student rating data to help advise students.

All three of these purposes are legitimate uses of the data. However, not all student rating items serve every purpose. Everyone involved—faculty, administrators, and students—should discuss and decide how the data will be used; that is, what information will go to whom, before any ratings are collected. Such discussion, if open, can do much to allay the reasonable concerns of the various parties involved and to enlist their cooperation.

4) Ensure that the student rating system is legal. Baez and Centra (1995) conclude that courts rarely question the appropriateness of an institution's criteria for faculty evaluation, and that faculty rarely succeed in challenging the use of a particular evaluation tool. Nevertheless, considering the increasingly litigious culture of higher education, it would be prudent to involve the institution's attorney in any development or revision of a student rating system.

5) Ensure that your student rating system is ethical. Personally, I think that ethical considerations should take precedence over legal ones, but the topic has rarely been specifically addressed in the literature. One notable exception is Ory (1990) who describes several scenarios involving ethical issues. He follows each scenario with specific recommendations, most of which are covered in this chapter. The point here is that developing an effective student rating system and following its procedures is not simply a professional obligation, but an ethical one. It certainly is not just a matter of personal choice for any given faculty member.

6) Collect data from at least ten raters, if possible, to obtain statistically reliable student rating data. The more raters there are, the more reliable the data. The more reliable the data, the more likely it is that the average we obtained for an item will be close to what we would get if we had a perfect measure. For example, the item reliabilities for IDEA are approximately .70 with 10 raters; .80 with 20 raters; and .90 with 40 raters (all references to the IDEA System are to Sixbury & Cashin, 1995). Data based on the ratings of fewer than ten raters should be interpreted with special caution, including generalizing about what might be an effective way to teach the same course at a later date. However, combining data from several classes of fewer than ten students from the same course but over different terms can yield a usable approximation of reliability if the combined number of raters is ten or more.

7) Collect data from at least two-thirds of the class to obtain representative student rating data. This recommendation is based primarily on experience and common sense. Even using this guideline, one-third of the students would not be represented in the ratings. Some have suggested requiring ratings from three-quarters of the class, but experience with the IDEA system suggests that many classes would not meet that cutoff. I advise that the instructor ask himself or herself: Which students were missing? Then keep that in mind when interpreting the data. If an instructor thinks that ratings from those students would substantially alter the averages, that should be included in the instructor's self report (see Chapter 5).

8) Sample across both courses and time to generalize from student rating data to an instructor's overall teaching effectiveness. For improvement it is acceptable to look at the data from one course, but for evaluation we need a much broader sample. I suggest as a minimum two courses from every term for at least two years.

9) For improvement, develop a student rating system that is flexible. Instructional goals vary widely from course to course, and so what is an effective method to teach one goal may not be effective in teaching another. In an introductory course stressing basic content, being well organized and clear are the teaching methods to be emphasized. But in courses where critical thinking skills like analysis, synthesis, and evaluation are the instructional goals, it is more important to establish rapport and involve the students in interactive tasks. Student rating systems need to accommodate this diversity. Cafeteria-type systems, like those of Purdue University or the University of Illinois, provide the maximum flexibility. (Recommendation 22 discusses what items to use to achieve flexibility.)

10) Provide comparative data, preferably for all the items. Student ratings tend to be inflated. The average student rating on a five-point scale is not 3.0—as one might think—but usually between 3.5 and 4.0. Also, average ratings vary widely from item to item. On the 20 IDEA teaching method items, the lowest mean is 3.4; the highest, 4.4. What should an instructor conclude who receives an average rating of 3.9 on these two items? Without comparative data, I do not believe that it is possible to meaningfully interpret student rating data.

11) Decide which variables, if any, might be biased; which variables, if any, require controls. Student ratings are correlated with variables other than the instructor's teaching effectiveness (recommendations 12–15 will discuss specifics). The institution needs to decide what, if anything, will be done about these variables that may require control.

12) Do not give undue weight to the instructor's age, sex, teaching experience, personality, or research productivity; the student's age, sex, level (freshman, etc.), grade point average, or personality; or the class size or time of day when it was taught. These show little or no correlation with student ratings. This includes gender despite an occasional study that suggests that women instructors receive lower ratings. Two reviews by Feldman (1992, 1993) found little difference. In fact, reviewing studies using actual ratings of real teachers (1993) rather than experimental studies of ratings of fictitious teachers (1992), Feldman found that women teachers received slightly higher ratings (r = .02) than men. Exception: If an instructor provides evidence in his or her self-report for the influence of these variables, or if we have such evidence, that evidence should be taken into consideration. The research, and this chapter, deal with general, not universal principles.

13) Take into consideration the students' motivation level when interpreting student rating data. Student motivation tends to show higher correlations with other student rating items than any other variable. Instructors are more likely to obtain higher ratings in classes where students had a prior interest in the subject matter (Marsh & Dunkin, 1992), or were taking the course as an elective.

14) Decide how you will treat student ratings for courses from different levels (e.g., freshman, graduate, etc.). Higher-level courses, especially graduate courses, tend to receive higher ratings. However, the differences tend to be small. My suggestion is first to see if you find these differences on your campus; if so, check to see if they remain after controlling for student motivation and also class size. If they do, then you need to use comparative data for different levels or institute some other control.

15) Decide how you will treat student ratings from different academic fields. There is increasing evidence that different academic fields are rated differently, but what still is not clear is why (Cashin, 1990b; Hativa & Marincovich, 1995). In general, more quantitative courses (e.g., math) tend to receive lower ratings than social science courses, which, in turn, receive lower ratings than humanities courses. If you find that this is true on your campus and decide that it is because these courses are more difficult to teach, then you should take academic field into consideration when interpreting the data, ideally by developing comparative data. However, if you think that certain fields are more poorly taught then you should not.

16) For improvement, develop a system that is diagnostic. The more diagnostic the system is, the more useful it will be for improvement. This means that the items included on the form should be descriptive of specific and concrete teaching behaviors. For example, "the instructor provided an outline for each class" is more specific than an item like "the instructor gave clear presentations." (See also recommendation 21.)

17) Develop a system that is interpretable. It is very important that the data be understandable to the average instructor and, equally important, to the administrators and committee members who will use the data to evaluate the instructor. Using words as well as numbers is one way to achieve this. Including a written explanation along with the numeric results is also desirable, although experience suggests that many faculty will not read it. The ideal solution is to have one or more faculty consultants on your campus (see Chapter 3) who are available both to help faculty understand their ratings and to suggest ways that they might improve their teaching if that is appropriate; as well as to train evaluators in the proper interpretation of the ratings. (See recommendations 35, 36, 37; also Franklin & Theall, 1990; Theall & Franklin, 1991.)

The Student Rating Form

Recommendations 18 through 29 concern decisions related to the student rating form(s) to be used.

18) For evaluation, use a few global or summary items or scores. Using global or summary items is what most student rating researchers (e.g., Braskamp & Ory, 1994; Centra, 1993) recommend for evaluation. Sample global items are:

- Overall, how effective was the instructor?

- Overall, how worthwhile was the course?

- Overall, how much did you learn?

Global student rating items tend to correlate more highly with student learning than do more specific items (Cohen, 1981; Feldman, 1989).

The students' ratings on these items will be like a final course grade; they give the instructor—or evaluators—some idea of how the students rated the instructor's teaching, but no information about why. However, such items do serve the purpose of evaluation which is to decide how well the instructor taught (not what he or she might do to improve—which is the focus of development). Using a form with only a few items has definite advantages. Such items apply to a wide variety of courses (probably to all courses), and so could be used as the basis of comparison across the institution, as long as the appropriate comparative data was available. Using such a short form would also avoid wasting the students' time and the institution's money.

19) Do not average all of the items into a single score. Everyone agrees that student rating items are multidimensional (e.g., Marsh & Dunkin, 1992). Because of this, it is highly likely that the teaching method items included on any given form are not all from the same dimension, but are a mixture of some of the dimensions. If we average all of the items—dimensions—into a single score, we imply that there is a single, correct way to teach—those teaching methods included in our form. Further, we imply that these methods should be used by every instructor in every course—no matter how that course's instructional objectives vary from those of other courses. Finally, we imply that each of these teaching methods should be weighted equally for all courses: freshman survey, senior seminar, graduate specialties. None of these assumptions is correct. A possible exception to this recommendation might be when the teaching methods items were all chosen specifically for the individual course.

20) Use a short evaluation form (or items) in every class, every term. This recommendation is a personal opinion. Using such a form provides documentation for those courses being taught effectively and can flag courses that unknowingly are being ineffectively taught—so more extensive, diagnostic data can be collected next term.

21) Use a long diagnostic form in only one course per term—the course that the instructor wishes to focus on for improvement. Most instructors would be doing well to improve one course a term. Using a diagnostic form in only one course a term focuses the instructor's efforts and avoids wasting student time gathering data that may not be used.

22) For improvement, do not use a single, standard set of items for every class: Provide a pool of items or some kind of weighting system. This is a corollary of recommendation nine on flexibility. Different course objectives—and probably different student learning styles—require different teaching methods (see Chapter 4). One solution to the flexibility problem is to use a pool of items as the cafeteria systems do. The instructor selects only items that fit his or her course and students. At the very least, any form can accommodate for especially relevant items by permitting the instructor to add some extra items. (Many forms do this, but experience suggests that most faculty make little use of the option.)

23) For improvement, use items that require as little inference as possible on the part of the student rater and as little interpretation as possible on the part of the instructor/evaluators. This is a corollary of recommendation 16 that improvement systems need to be diagnostic. Concrete items that describe specific behaviors tend to be most helpful to an instructor looking for suggestions about how to improve. However, this requires a large pool of items because different teaching methods are appropriate to different instructional goals.

24) Use a five-point to seven-point scale to rate the items. Scales with fewer than five points do not discriminate as well, but using more than seven points adds little. There is little consensus about other technical considerations (see Berk, 1979; or Doyle, 1983).

25) In the analysis of the results, report computations only to the first decimal place. Even reporting data to only the first decimal place yields 41 points on a five-point scale (1.0 to 5.0). Student rating data—as most of our classroom exam data—are rarely that precise, that is, a 4.0 is rarely different from a 3.9 or 3.8, and perhaps 3.7.

26) Do not overinterpret the data and allow for a margin of error. This is a corollary of recommendations 24 and 25. Depending upon the standard error of measurement of the items, scores within + or -.3 or more may not really be different. Combining the data into a limited number of categories, perhaps ten or fewer, rather than using all 41 points is both more understandable and more realistically reflects the level of precision of the data.

27) Use frequency distributions (what number or percent of the students rated the item "1" or "2," etc.). Frequency distributions are more understandable to most faculty than calculating a standard deviation for each item. Also, the distributions can convey useful information. If all of our ratings are high, we want to keep doing whatever we're doing. If they are all low, stop. But what if the distribution tends to be flat, the ratings tend to spread across all of the numbers about equally; or tends to be bimodal, with the ratings clustering at the two ends? Flat or bimodal distributions may mean that what we are doing works for one group of students but not for another. We probably need to keep doing what we are doing for the one group, and add something new for the other group. First, we have to figure out who the two groups are. The most common groupings are majors and non-majors.

28) For improvement, ask for open-ended comments as well as quantitative ratings. It is highly likely that several such items are used on every campus. Some sample items follow:

- Describe one or more things about the course that you found helpful. Please be specific and give examples.

- What suggestions do you have about how the course might be improved.

- Describe something that the instructor did not do that you personally would have found helpful.

The comments which the students make in responding to these kinds of questions can be particularly helpful for improvement (see Chapter 3). Often these comments will help explain why we received low ratings on one of the quantitative items. They can also provide suggestions about some changes we might make to help the students learn better. However, I would not substitute open-ended questions for quantitative ones. The two types complement each other.

Sometimes just reading the students' comments gives a negative impression while looking at the numerical ratings shows relatively high numbers giving a positive impression. Combining both qualitative and quantitative data is useful for improvement.

29) Use the open-ended comments only for improvement. My reasoning for this recommendation is that, especially for promotion and tenure decisions, there can be hundreds or even thousands of comments. To assess them accurately we must do a content analysis, classifying every response as to content and also making a judgment about how positive or negative the comment is. This is extremely time consuming. My belief is that usually only the individual instructor has the motivation to do this and so the comments should only be used by the instructor for improvement. To have evaluators simply scan the comments to gain a general impression often leads to their only remembering the more sensational comments, not the more representative ones.

Administration of Student Rating Systems

Recommendations 30 through 35 deal with administering the system. The proper administration of a student rating system and appropriate interpretation of the data are two neglected areas of research. For the most part we lack even descriptive data about what institutions typically do. Most of the following recommendations are based on what seems to make sense (see also Arreola, 1995).

30) For evaluation, develop standardized procedures covering all relevant aspects of your student rating system and monitor that the procedures are followed. When the student rating data are going to be used for personnel decisions, it is important that all the stakeholders have confidence that the data were gathered and treated fairly. However, developing standardized procedures without monitoring that they are followed is an empty gesture. Ory (1990) suggests that students be informed of the policies and provided a means to report violations of those procedures.

31) For evaluation, administer the ratings about the second to the last week of the term. Ratings should be collected near enough to the end of the term so that the students have a reasonably accurate perception of the total course and of what they have learned, but not so close to the end that the students are distracted by concerns about getting assignments in or what will be on the final exam. Avoid administering the ratings on the last day of class or on the day of the final exam.

32) Develop standardized instructions that include the purpose(s) for which the data will be used and who will receive what information, when. Ideally, these instructions will be both printed on the top of the students' form and read aloud by the proctor. Typically, institutions will say that the primary purpose is to improve teaching, even though the institution provides the faculty with little or no help specifically for improvement. If the primary purpose is evaluation (a legitimate purpose), say so.

33) Instruct the students not to sign their ratings. Some studies suggest that requiring signatures will inflate the ratings, so the conventional wisdom is not to have the students sign their ratings.

Also, tell the students if the instructor will be given their handwritten responses. By doing this, the students can print or leave blank the open-ended questions if they are concerned about confidentiality and possible retaliation from the instructor (which unfortunately happens). Some instructors have the open-ended questions printed on a separate sheet of paper which they let the students take home so students can type their comments if they wish. This also allows the students to give more thought to their responses. If we want the students to cooperate by giving us their honest feedback, we must do everything we can to ensure confidentiality.

34) The instructor may hand out the rating forms and read the standardized instructions, but the instructor should leave the room until the students have completed the ratings and they have been collected. When the instructor remains in the room, the ratings tend to be higher; that is, the ratings are probably inflated.

35) The ratings should be collected by a neutral party and the data taken to a predetermined location—often to where they are to be scored—and they should not be available to the instructor until the grades are turned in. Again, this is the conventional wisdom with which I strongly agree. Following these procedures does much to ensure people's confidence in the fairness of the system.

Interpretation of Student Ratings

Recommendations concerning how the data are interpreted may be the most important of all of the recommendations, but this area is the least studied.

36) Develop a written explanation of how the analyses of the student ratings are to be interpreted. Often using a sample report is a helpful way to explain the results. Indicate what comparative data are being used, if any. For some faculty it may be helpful to explain some of the statistical terms, for example, percentiles. For data from individual classes that will be interpreted in isolation—particularly if being used for evaluation—include the caveats about having at least ten raters and about having data from at least two-thirds of the class. Remind readers that if they want to generalize to the instructor's overall teaching effectiveness, they should have ratings from two or more courses from two or more years. Above all, remember that student ratings are only one source of data. Avoid simply presenting the instructor, or the evaluators, with a page or more full of numbers, leaving it to their ingenuity or imagination to figure out what the data mean.

37) Appoint a faculty member to serve as instructional consultant to help faculty (and evaluators) interpret the results and improve teaching. Give this consultant release time to develop the desirable skills and fulfill these consulting responsibilities. When successful, such consultants often offer campus-wide programs and workshops on topics of interest to the faculty.

38) Educate administrators and evaluators about how to interpret student rating data. Considering the possible complexity of student rating data, and the size of the research literature on the topic, and especially, the important uses the data are put to, I suggest that it is time that we not only recommend, but require, that administrators and other evaluators—and I would suggest all faculty who teach—be educated in the interpretation of student ratings. I might even go so far as to suggest that not only should they be educated, but their competence might be tested by having them interpret case studies using student rating data.

CONCLUSION

The proper use of student rating data can do much to improve the evaluation of teaching, both summative evaluation for personnel decisions, and formative evaluation for improvement. We know how to use student rating data appropriately.

Then why don't colleges and universities make better use of such data? I suggest that it is because, despite all of our rhetoric, US higher education is still primarily focused on creating knowledge and skills, not on teaching or helping students learn. If teaching were trees, the prevailing culture of US higher education would still be a desert (Arrowsmith, 1967). However, if we are interested in growing trees, the recommendations in this chapter should help.

ACKNOWLEDGMENTS

I would like to thank Kansas State University's IDEA Center (formerly the Center for Faculty Evaluation and Development) for permission to use material from IDEA Paper No. 22. I would also like to thank Michael Theall, University of Illinois, Springfield, for his helpful comments and suggestions to an early draft of this chapter.

REFERENCES

Aleamoni, L. M. (1976). Typical faculty concerns about student evaluation of instruction. *National Association of Colleges and Teachers of Agriculture Journal, 20,* 16-21.

Aleamoni, L. M. (1987). Student rating myths versus research facts. *Journal of Personnel Evaluation in Education, 1,* 111-119.

Arreola, R. A. (1995). *Developing a comprehensive faculty evaluation system: A handbook for college faculty and administrators on designing and operating a comprehensive faculty evaluation system.* Bolton, MA: Anker.

Arrowsmith, W. (1967). The future of teaching. In C. B. T. Lee (Ed.), *Improving college teaching* (pp. 57-71). Washington, DC: American Council on Education.

Baez, B., & Centra, J. A. (1995). *Tenure, promotion, and reappointment: Legal and administrative implications.* ASHE-ERIC Higher Education Report, No. 1. Washington, DC: School of Education and Human Development, George Washington University.

Berk, R. A. (1979). The construction of rating instruments for faculty evaluation. *Journal of Higher Education, 50,* 650-669.

Braskamp, L. A., & Ory, J. C. (1994). *Assessing faculty work: Enhancing individual and institutional performance.* San Francisco, CA: Jossey-Bass.

Cashin, W. E. (1989). *Defining and evaluating college teaching.* IDEA Paper No. 21. Manhattan, KS: Center for Faculty Evaluation and Development, Kansas State University. (This paper is now available on the Internet: www.idea.ksu.edu.)

Cashin, W. E. (1990a). *Student ratings of teaching: Recommendations for use.* IDEA Paper No. 22. Manhattan, KS: Center for Faculty Evaluation and Development, Kansas State University. (This paper is now available on the Internet: www.idea.ksu.edu.)

Cashin, W. E. (1990b). Students do rate different academic fields differently. In M. Theall & J. Franklin (Eds.), *Student ratings of instruction: Issues for improving practice.* New Directions for Teaching and Learning, No. 43 (pp. 113-121). San Francisco, CA: Jossey-Bass.

Centra, J. A. (1993). *Reflective faculty evaluation: Enhancing teaching and determining faculty effectiveness.* San Francisco, CA: Jossey-Bass.

Cohen, P. A. (1981). Student ratings of instruction and student achievement: A meta-analysis of multisection validity studies. *Review of Educational Research, 51,* 281-309.

Davis, B. G. (1993). *Tools for teaching.* San Francisco, CA: Jossey-Bass.

Doyle, K. O. (1983). *Evaluating teaching.* Lexington, MA: DC Heath.

Feldman, K. A. (1976). Grades and college students' evaluations of their courses and teachers. *Research in Higher Education, 4,* 69-111.

Feldman, K. A. (1977). Consistency and variability among college students in rating their teachers and courses: A review and analysis. *Research in Higher Education, 6,* 233-274.

Feldman, K. A. (1987). Research productivity and scholarly accomplishment of college teachers as related to their instructional effectiveness: A review and exploration. *Research in Higher Education, 26,* 277-298.

Feldman, K. A. (1989). The association between student ratings of specific instructional dimensions and student achievement: Refining and extending the synthesis of data from multisection validity studies. *Research in Higher Education, 30,* 583-645.

Feldman, K. A. (1992). College students' views of male and female college teachers, Part I: Evidence from the social laboratory and experiments. *Research in Higher Education, 33,* 317-375.

Feldman, K. A. (1993). College students' views of male and female college teachers, Part II: Evidence from students' evaluations of their classroom teachers. *Research in Higher Education, 34,* 151-211.

Franklin J., & Theall, M. (1990). Communicating student ratings to decision-makers: Design for good practice. In M. Theall & J. Franklin (Eds.), *Student ratings of instruction: Issues for improving practice,* New Directions for Teaching and Learning, No. 43 (pp. 75-93). San Francisco, CA: Jossey-Bass.

Hativa, N., & Marincovich, M. (Eds.). (1995). *Disciplinary differences in teaching and learning: Implications for practice.* New Directions for Teaching and Learning, No. 64. San Francisco, CA: Jossey-Bass.

Marsh, H. W., & Dunkin, M. (1992). Students' evaluations of university teaching: A multidimensional perspective. In J. C. Smart (Ed.), *Higher education: Handbook of theory and research,* Vol. 8 (pp. 143-233). New York, NY: Agathon. [Reprinted in R. P. Perry & J. C. Smart (Eds.), (1997). *Effective teaching in higher education: Research and practice.* (pp. 241-320). New York, NY: Agathon Press.]

McKeachie, W. J. (1999). *Teaching tips: Strategies, research, and theory for college and university teachers.* (10th ed.). Boston, MA: Houghton Mifflin.

Ory, J. C. (1990). Student ratings of instruction: Ethics and practice. In M. Theall & J. Franklin (Eds.), *Student ratings of instruction: Issues for improving practice.* New Directions for Teaching and Learning, No. 43 (pp. 63-74). San Francisco, CA: Jossey-Bass.

Sixbury, G. R., & Cashin, W. E. (1995). *Description of database for the IDEA Diagnostic Form.* IDEA Technical Report No. 9: Manhattan, KS: Center for Faculty Evaluation and Development, Kansas State University.

Theall, M., & Franklin J. (1991). Using student ratings for teaching improvement. In M. Theall & J. Franklin (Eds.), *Effective practices for improving teaching.* New Directions for Teaching and Learning, No. 48 (pp. 83-96). San Francisco, CA: Jossey-Bass.

US Department of Education. (1991, Winter). Assessing teaching performance. *The Department Chair: A Newsletter for Academic Administrators, 2* (3), 2.

CHAPTER 3

USING STUDENT FEEDBACK TO IMPROVE TEACHING

Michele Marincovich

Articles in such notable publications as *The Chronicle of Higher Education* (Wilson, 1998) and *Change* (Williams & Ceci, 1997) raising questions about the validity and fairness of student evaluations of teaching have created increasing interest in the evaluation of faculty's teaching. As director of the Center for Teaching and Learning at Stanford, I have found myself fielding inquiries from our faculty about the evaluation controversy and the campus's several student evaluation of teaching forms (which vary by school and even department). While I, too, am concerned about issues raised by the current controversy and am certainly pleased when faculty take an interest in teaching evaluation, for whatever reason, I would raise a very different question about the whole system of student evaluation of teaching on our campuses. For me, the real question is how can we more effectively use end-of-term student evaluation data and other sources of student feedback to improve teaching.

Admittedly, end-of-term student evaluation of teaching systems do not exist mainly or only to improve faculty teaching. Most can and do serve at least two other purposes (Cohen, 1980; Cashin, 1990): to provide accurate and reliable data on the quality of faculty's teaching to administrators who must make important decisions on the granting of renewal, tenure, or promotion (and maybe even on setting salary); and to give students information on faculty's teaching that will help them choose which courses to take. Menges (1990, 1999) reminds us that teaching evaluation data can play two other roles: providing information for accreditation reviews and encouraging students to be more thoughtful about their education. But important as these other purposes may be, the edifice of teaching evaluation seems a hollow one to me if the individuals being evaluated are not also learning how to be more effective teachers. In the same vein, I suspect grading would be even more distasteful to most faculty if they did not think that careful grading had at least some chance of improving how well a student is learning. Certainly in my experience, students seem to assume that one of the main reasons they should take time to fill out teaching evaluations is to help faculty get better. Student focus group interviews (Toward Greater Excellence in Teaching at Stanford, 1995) carried out by a faculty senate subcommittee (the Subcommittee on the Evaluation and Improvement of Teaching) indicated how important it was to students that faculty seek and use student feedback on their teaching.

Why am I assuming that there aren't changes in faculty teaching as a result of end-of-term student evaluations? Although some faculty apparently do learn from and act upon their evaluations, Centra (1993) argues persuasively that improvement occurs only under certain conditions—involving the acquisition of new knowledge that is valued by a teacher who knows how to make changes and is motivated to do so. These are conditions, I would argue, that most of us would easily concede are rarely achieved in the end-of-term student evaluation systems we are familiar with. In an ASHE-ERIC Higher Education Report, Keig and Waggoner (1994) further suggest that there are enough problems associated with summative student evaluation of teaching systems that an alternative, formative system of peer review is both necessary and desirable if the improvement of teaching is to be achieved.

In my own personal experience of having consulted with over 200 Stanford faculty on their teaching, I have been struck by how few of those eager to, or under pressure to, make significant improvements in their teaching have been able to conclude from their end-of-term student evaluation data what improvement strategies to pursue. Nor, in my experience, have such individuals pursued other avenues of student feedback that might bring them helpful information. Even among those who, with consultation, were able to make significant progress in their teaching—in some cases quite dramatic progress— almost none of them had achieved noticeable improvement when relying purely on their own reading and analysis of their student evaluation forms. They did not make progress until they took the rather unusual step of consulting with someone else. This is consistent with Cohen's (1980) often cited observation that faculty receiving "augmented feedback, or more specifically expert consultation," are much more likely to improve (p. 338). Brinko (1991) goes even further, stating that a meta-analysis Menges and she conducted concluded "that consultation quadrupled the effect of student ratings feedback" (p. 39).

Why do I say that it is a rather unusual step for a faculty member to consult with a teaching and learning center? Aren't there teaching and learning centers on a majority of our college and university campuses, and aren't most of these equipped to do one-on-one consultation with their faculty clients? Although there are hundreds of teaching centers in the US, and although most of these offer individual consultation to faculty (Graf & Wheeler, 1996), a recent telephone survey (Lichtenstein & Deitz, 1998) of such centers at 16 research universities indicated that many centers are still frustrated by their ability to reach the faculty that might need them the most. A 1995-1996 survey (Pihakis & Marincovich, in preparation) also indicated that even on campuses with teaching and learning centers, some centers are not empowered to do confidential work with faculty on their teaching evaluations in particular or do not have enough staff members to carry out that kind of work.

I would like to make the case, then, for specific steps that institutions, administrators, and faculty can take to improve the likelihood that the end-of-term student evaluations existing on almost all of our campuses will lead to real teaching improvement. I will also make the case for the use of other sources of student feedback that faculty can initiate themselves or with the help of a teaching and learning center. Note, however, that my perspective will be that of a practitioner, someone whose office's mission is to facilitate individual and institutional teaching excellence. Thus, I will not be talking about what must be done to improve the quality of the teaching evaluation forms themselves, nor about the responsible use of the data to make sound administrative decisions (see Chapter 2), absolutely crucial as both those issues are. It goes without saying that the more confidence faculty have in the reliability and validity of a teaching evaluation system, the more likely it is that they will pay attention to the resulting data.

Before I get into specific steps, however, I have to stress that there is an overarching institutional commitment that must be made before any other measures are to have an effect. And this is, quite simply, that a college or university's leadership must clearly signal the value that it puts on effective teaching and make that value unambiguous through its reward system. Boyer (1990) argued the importance of a new regard for and conception of teaching far more eloquently and extensively than I can in this chapter, so I will not belabor the point (see Chapter 6). But an observable institutional commitment to effective teaching and learning is the fulcrum upon which all my other suggestions leverage.

The Provision of Teaching Consultation Options

Given the body of evidence (Cohen, 1980; Levinson-Rose & Menges, 1981; Murray, 1984; Menges & Brinko, 1986; Wilson, 1986; Marsh & Roche, 1993) on the power of consultation to increase the likelihood of improvement as a result of student evaluations, probably the single most important step that institutions can take to increase the efficacy of their teaching evaluation system is to provide some sort of teaching consultation service. As the director of a teaching and learning center, I have seen repeated evidence of the effectiveness of professional teaching consultants in particular, but it is clear to me that other sources of consultation, particularly from peers, can be effective (see Chapter 4). Faculty who teach with teaching assistants and feel comfortable discussing their evaluations with their TAs have also mentioned to me how much they have learned from such conversations; some faculty have even found it useful to talk things over with a particularly mature and insightful undergraduate. In this section, however, let me dwell on teaching consultation professionals and peer consultants.

Teaching Consultation Professionals

Since not all campuses at this point have teaching improvement/faculty development centers or centers that offer teaching consultation services, institutions that currently have not made provision for access to teaching consultation should certainly consider doing so. While, as noted, I believe in the effectiveness of peer consultants, there is something to be said for at least one (or, even better, more) teaching consultation professionals on a campus. Like any other kind of professional, the dedicated teaching consultant will have (if not from the beginning, soon) a depth of experience, a familiarity with relevant literature, a network of colleagues, and a level of commitment that will benefit the whole campus. This expert will also be available to train faculty for effective peer consultation and to set up programs that will interest the faculty in the benefits of consultation.

When working with faculty, the consultant's most important contribution will be in helping clients to pick out those two or three aspects of their teaching in which improvement will have the greatest payoff for their students' learning and in helping to devise improvement strategies. Among my clients, the faculty who need to improve their student evaluations the most are usually those who are most confused and frustrated by their low ratings. Because almost all of them are dedicating time and effort to their teaching, they are usually genuinely perplexed by the students' criticisms. Moreover, even if they discern a need to be more organized or more enthusiastic, they are not sure how to exhibit those qualities. As a consultant, next to helping a client focus on the chief issues in their teaching, I feel that I often make the greatest difference by suggesting effective strategies for their particular situation.

Peer Consultants

Since almost no institution would have the required resources if professional teaching consultation were sought by any significant fraction
of its faculty, fortunately there is an alternative: peer consultation. The
peer approach has the additional advantage of offering faculty two
ways to learn about teaching—as the one who consults and as the one
who is consulted. I was particularly impressed with the peer review
efforts that occurred on my own campus as a result of Stanford's participation in the American Association for Higher Education (AAHE)
Peer Review of Teaching Project.

Led by Lee S. Shulman (now president of the Carnegie
Foundation for the Advancement of Teaching), Russell Edgerton
(now director of the education program of the Pew Charitable Trusts),
and Pat Hutchings (currently affiliated with both AAHE and the
Carnegie Foundation for the Advancement of Teaching), the Peer
Review of Teaching project began in 1994 with 12 institutions.
Coming from a variety of institutional types—public and private
research and comprehensive universities—these institutions committed a small core of energetic faculty from certain selected disciplines to
pilot new forms of peer interaction around effective teaching and
learning. Although there was no effort to focus the peer experience
particularly on the use of student evaluations of teaching, the Stanford
department of mechanical engineering (ME) pilot program developed
a very impressive peer consultation model that could easily be adapted elsewhere.

As it worked out over time, the ME Peer Review model
(Sheppard, Leifer, & Carryer, 1996; Sheppard, Johnson, & Leifer,
1998) begins with a group of faculty, usually eight or ten, who volun-
tarily commit themselves to a quarter or more of peer engagement
either as teaching mentors, mentees, or both. All participants first discuss and agree to, or modify, a general model of effective teaching
developed by the first pilot group in association with Stanford's
Center for Teaching and Learning and also agree to work in pairs or
triplets according to certain steps in the peer process. For the mentee,
the first step is to write a reflective memo about the course that their

peer review will focus on. The reflective memo is relatively short, two or three pages, and yet should contain the course design and rationale, a description of the main course components, the strengths and weaknesses of the course as the instructor knows them, expected course outcomes, and aspects of the course that the instructor would like to focus on in the review. The peer consultant or mentor starts his or her role with a review of the reflective memo and then conducts a structured interview (based on a set of questions developed by the pilot group and derived from the elements of effective teaching) of a sampling of students who took the course the last time it was offered. Students are not chosen in a rigorous, random fashion, but an effort is made to get a cross-section by sending an email invitation to a lunchtime discussion (lunch provided) to all students from the course who are still on campus. At least eight or ten students are assembled, with follow-up phone calls if necessary.

At the student interview, one peer conducts the discussion while a second, if possible (this is why peers are encouraged to work in triplets, not pairs), records student responses. Lasting 60 to 90 minutes, the interview can result in several pages of student comments. These are usually distilled, together with thoughts generated by the reflective memo, into a report that the mentor peer writes for and discusses with the mentee. Ideally, the mentor uses all the data available to make recommendations, with an emphasis on the specific and practical, for strengthening the course. The mentee not only has a sense of what might be improved in the course, he or she also has a very specific idea of how to proceed to do this.

The ME Peer Review process, as judged by participant satisfaction at Stanford, is collegial, effective, and efficient (using approximately six to ten hours on the part of the faculty peers). One junior faculty member enthused to me that it had jump-started his career at Stanford by providing him early on with immediately useful feedback that allowed him to feel confident and comfortable about his teaching responsibilities. The experience seems to have made him what Boice (1991) describes as a "quick starter," an outcome any professional teaching consultant would be proud to claim. I urge other campuses to try something similar to the ME Peer Review process, thereby tackling one of the main problems associated with consultation: its labor-intensive character.

Yet another AAHE peer review product, the course portfolio (Hutchings, 1995, 1996) could also be used in a peer setting in order to encourage faculty to build on their teaching evaluations. Similar to the teaching portfolio (see Chapter 9) but focused on a single course, the course portfolio features a faculty member's scholarly exploration of his or her design, development, implementation, and refinement of a chosen course. Such a compilation, especially when discussed with disciplinary and nondisciplinary peers, encourages a deep engagement with student learning and satisfaction, as judged not only by teaching evaluations but also by various measurements of student learning. While the course portfolio need not rely exclusively on student evaluations, such evaluations are one possible measure of success and one possible avenue to improvement. If course portfolios began to circulate among the various disciplines, they could go far to model how faculty might make use of their student evaluation data to make course improvements that would enhance student learning.

RECONCEIVING THE FRAMING AND IMPLEMENTATION OF STUDENT EVALUATIONS OF TEACHING

Crucial as the provision of teaching consultation services is, the mere availability of help will not motivate faculty to seek it out nor convince them of its importance. Only a concerted effort on the part of administrators to dignify the teaching evaluation system and to make its implementation both efficient and appealing is likely to influence faculty members. The easiest and most obvious step, of course, is simply to make it clear that evidence of successful teaching will be needed for promotion and pay raises. Even in my research-conscious university, our former dean of engineering, James Gibbons, had a tremendous impact on the use of my office by engineering faculty because he established and carried out a policy of serious attention to student evaluations of teaching in the appointments and pay-setting process. I suggest these additional steps:

Situate the Evaluation System Firmly within the Academic Context

At many institutions, including my own, the teaching evaluation system is run out of a registrar's office, an office well suited to the efficient generation, distribution, and processing of forms, but one not usually associated with scholarship, including the scholarship of teaching (Boyer, 1990). I am not arguing that teaching evaluation systems should instead be run out of teaching and learning centers. Although a few centers do successfully play this role (e.g., the measurement and evaluation division in the Office of Instructional Resources at the University of Illinois, Urbana-Champaign), most of us who run or staff centers feel that there is a conflict of interest between the administrative uses of teaching evaluation and our own commitment to confidentiality and improvement. What is important, however, is that the teaching evaluation system be framed within the academic and scholarly mission of the institution. At Yale, for example, the evaluation forms are distributed from the office of the dean of Yale College; a letter from the dean accompanies the forms, reminds faculty of their importance, and mentions the role of the faculty themselves in the adoption and modification of the forms. This sort of decanal imprimatur seems ideal to me. If it is decided that a registrar's office should do the actual distribution and processing of the forms, a letter or other materials from the academic dean could still accompany the forms to situate them in an academic/scholarly context.

Disseminate Research-Based Information on Student Evaluations

It has been observed (Keller, 1985) that faculty members in general make little use of the research on higher education that higher education itself produces. In my experience, this is especially true of the research on student evaluations of teaching. In this environment, administrators, teaching centers, and educational researchers can at least try to remind their constituencies of the careful research that is available to inform almost every decision that has to be made about a teaching evaluation system and the responsible use of data from it (see Chapter 2). My center has done workshops, newsletters, and sections of our teaching handbook on the topic of teaching evaluation and improvement, highlighting the relevant research. Before initiating a review of the teaching evaluation system in his school, our dean of humanities and sciences, in collaboration with the vice provost for undergraduate education, solicited and received from our center a background memorandum on teaching evaluation. Teaching centers should not only take full advantage of such opportunities when they arise but should also create opportunities whenever possible. Fortunately, there is now a legion of readable, recent, and useful books on this topic for our own and our colleagues' consumption (Seldin & Associates, 1990; Centra, 1993; Braskamp & Ory, 1994; Arreola, 1995; Richlin & Manning, 1995, among others).

Provide Interpretive Aids along with Evaluation Results

Even if a campus makes teaching consultation services available, as I have urged, it should still make sure that its teaching evaluation forms are not returned to the faculty without some explanatory material. Otherwise, many faculty—including those in the humanities who may or may not have had much exposure to statistical analyses or interpretations—may be unclear as to the significance of their data. The University of Minnesota (Flash, Tzenis, & Waller, 1995) has produced a particularly extensive handbook for those teaching on their campus and interested in learning as much as they can from their evaluations. After providing an interpretation of each item on the evaluation form, the handbook describes strategies for this teaching component that have been effective for other University of Minnesota faculty; it also provides both questions for self-reflection and a short bibliography.

Building on earlier research by Hildebrand, Wilson, and Dienst (1971) and Jacoby (1976), UC, Berkeley has gone a step further and has developed a web-based help system. Although the system was not intended to be used only in association with teaching evaluation data, faculty whose evaluations indicate that they could improve in some area of their teaching can turn to http://uga.berkeley.edu/sled/compendium and read about the approaches and techniques of faculty who have been very successful in this aspect of instruction. The electronic, nonlinear design of this system makes it easy for faculty to go quickly and directly to the area of teaching that they currently want to explore and to see as many or as few suggestions as they would like. Faculty on any campus would find this compendium useful (see Chapter 8).

At Stanford we have recently tried something a little different from the Minnesota publication mentioned earlier, which is potentially effective but lengthy. Cognizant of faculty's time pressures, our center produced a six-page guide for faculty and lecturers, sent out under the school of humanities and sciences dean's signature, on interpreting and following up on their teaching evaluation forms. We are eager to see whether a very short guide, produced as a result of faculty inspiration and under very close faculty guidance, influences professors' experience with their teaching evaluation forms. This guide has not been out long enough to know the results. A short brochure of improvement suggestions is also under development.

Provide Assistance in Interpreting Students' Written Comments

From the students' point of view, probably the most time-consuming part of filling in teaching evaluation forms is answering the forms' open-ended questions, and yet probably the most underused of all the data on the forms are the students' written comments. Since experts on teaching evaluation (Centra, 1993; Braskamp & Ory, 1994; Arreola, 1995) consider the closed, global items on teaching evaluation forms the most reliable for summative purposes, I am not urging that more use be made of student written comments in administrative decision-making. But if analyzed properly, they can be of great help for improvement purposes. Faculty often profess the greatest interest in these responses, and yet they can also find them contradictory or confusing. Unfortunately, very little has been written on the topic of analyzing students' written comments, and some teaching centers provide little or no help in making sense of the comments (Pihakis & Marincovich, in preparation).

Yet teaching centers can offer faculty significant help, both directly and indirectly, in understanding their student comments. First, centers can suggest methodologies for analyzing the student comments. Most faculty seem to read through each student's comments completely before going on to the next student's form. Reading the comments question by question, instead of form by form, is a small change that can make it more likely that helpful patterns will emerge. Even better, faculty might first organize students' comments by the overall rating that the student gave the faculty member (Lewis, 1991-92), using for this the rating from the global question that most forms contain on the faculty member's teaching overall or the value of the course overall. By reading together all the comments of students who gave them a high overall score, a middling score, and a low score, faculty are more likely to detect if the students who are less satisfied with the course identify certain common problems. Lewis (1991-92) suggests that one can go even further in organizing the student comments by grouping them into a matrix that uses the overall rating for one axis and characteristics of effective teaching (such as organization, enthusiasm, etc.) for the other axis. Or, one could put along the second axis certain themes especially appropriate to this course (e.g., the quality of problems in a problem-based learning course).

The University of Rhode Island's end-of-term form has an interesting approach that faculty might consider adding to their own institution's questionnaires. Questions 25a and 25b on the Rhode Island teaching questionnaire ask students to comment on "What made you rate the course as high as you did?" and "What kept you from rating the course higher?" Even if faculty can't add these questions to the forms they use, they might have these questions in the back of their minds as they try to make sense of their students' comments.

Finally, Morrison (1995) of the Higher Education Research Office of the University of Aukland has made an interesting suggestion regarding the processing of student comments. In an effort to develop a less labor-intensive means of providing their faculty with a qualitative analysis of their student comments, he first did a study "to determine the most common positive and negative qualities of university teachers. We now simply make a check mark against the appropriate category [for each student comment] and the resulting 'graph' becomes a visual record of responses" (p. 561). If other teaching consultants test this out, perhaps we will discover that most of us can be far more helpful to faculty in processing their student written comments than we ever imagined.

Strive for the Quick Processing and Return of Forms

If teaching evaluation data are to be taken seriously by faculty for improvement purposes and not just for administrative decision-making, then faculty must receive their results as close to the administration of the forms as possible. Too often weeks or even months pass before faculty know how students rated their courses or commented on their teaching. In my experience, if faculty are already deeply involved in the teaching of another course when the data from a previous course arrive, they are much less motivated to go back and learn what they can about the earlier course. They are already hard pressed and preoccupied by the challenges of their current teaching. (Recall Centra's [1993] emphasis on the importance of faculty being motivated to change if evaluation is to result in improvement.) A quick turnaround of the data, on the other hand, will give the faculty feedback when they are more likely to still have interest in it.

Create a Grace Period in the Evaluation of New Faculty

Pleased as I am when schools and departments at Stanford take student teaching evaluations seriously, I am not in favor of making student evaluation data from the first year of teaching an official part of a new professor's file or part of a student course guide. Teaching is highly contextual; the success of the teaching in any particular course can be affected by the subject matter, the students, other courses in the department, and even external factors (earthquakes and floods come to the minds of those of us in California institutions in recent years). Few of us are good teachers in the abstract, without regard to our setting. For this reason, faculty new to an institution deserve a settling-in period, a time when they should receive student evaluation feedback but not be penalized or paralyzed by it if they initially have a lot to learn. McKeachie (1979) warns us of how devastating "low ratings and critical comments" on student evaluations can be (p. 388).

The very fact that new faculty are given a period of time in which to benefit from their student evaluation data, without having to fear that it will be used against them, should drive home the point that one of the reasons for the collection of the data in the first place is to improve teaching. Too often young faculty receive the message that they must be successful right from the beginning. Even experienced teachers may still have to learn things about the characteristics and capabilities of the students at their new institution. There should be a safe period for this process.

Educate Students Regarding Their Role in an Evaluation System

As noted earlier, one reason for a student evaluation system is to give students information that will be helpful to them in choosing which classes to take (Cohen, 1980). On many campuses, this is achieved through a student-run course guide system. Perhaps the oldest and best known is the *Committee on Undergraduate Education Course Evaluation Guide* at Harvard. Stanford students have just revived a course guide system that existed on campus for many years, though, in tune with the times, they have made it web-based rather than hard copy. One of their challenges is to avoid some of the problems that contributed to the demise of the previous system. Essentially, student editors of that earlier guide tended toward the colorful, often choosing to print the student comments about a course that were the most attention-getting. As you can imagine, because faculty were free to release or not release their data to the guide, those who were embarrassed or disappointed by earlier comments often stopped participating. Soon a dwindling number of courses was covered, and the guide became of marginal value.

Students at any institution must realize that both in their individual comments and in a student course guide, it is the constructive criticism that is likely to do the most good. Just as students would highly criticize a faculty member who gave them harsh, blunt comments on their papers or homework, so too they should concentrate in their evaluation forms on tactful feedback that indicates why a change seems important and how it could be done. Faculty members are increasingly urged to be coaches and mentors to their students; in the area of teaching, students might themselves take on the attitude of coach and concentrate on direct, constructive, and practical feedback. To achieve this at Stanford, we have been exploring the possibility of training students in their evaluation role during their initial orientation period to the university. Brigham Young University has already begun a program to train students as evaluators.

Create Opportunities for Recognition and Reflection

Many campuses require that faculty write an annual review of their previous year's efforts. Although these are generally heavily weighted toward faculty's research accomplishments and publications, such reviews can also encourage reflection on one's teaching evaluations and plans for change or improvement. Course portfolios and teaching portfolios are particularly ideal vehicles for ensuring that student evaluations are put to thoughtful use rather than languishing in a faculty member's file cabinet or, worse, in a circular file. It is even better if department chairs use the annual review or a teaching/course portfolio to underscore to their faculty that their interest in evaluation results is not punitive but constructive (see Chapter 9).

For too many faculty, attention to teaching evaluations comes not when they are satisfactory or even outstanding but when they are troublesome. More than one teaching award-winning faculty member at Stanford has mentioned to me that his or her award brought no recognition from the department chair, not even a quick, congratulatory exchange in the hall or by phone. Presumably, if annual reviews covered teaching responsibilities and accomplishments, chairs would be more likely to give both the positive reinforcement that teaching accomplishment deserves and, perhaps, the constructive support that less-than-satisfactory evaluations should receive.

Disseminate and Use the Results of Reflection: The Power of Stories

We have all seen the tide of a committee's deliberations turned by the well-chosen and compelling anecdote. Influencing faculty's attitudes toward their own teaching evaluations is no different. It is important that faculty hear stories of professors who had significant teaching evaluation problems and solved them. I am never happier on our own campus than when award-winning teachers mention that they were not always so successful, that they had low ratings in the beginning but in fact went on to raise them, not through pandering to students or inflating grades but through better understanding students' learning needs or their own roles as teachers. Although our center's lecture series "Award-Winning Teachers on Teaching" was not set up specifically to provide such a forum, in fact it often has.

Even better, we can use the articles that exist, and encourage more such articles, in which faculty publicly grapple with the strengths and weaknesses of student evaluations of teaching in general or their own teaching evaluations. Elbow's (1992) thoughtful "Making Better Use of Student Evaluations of Teachers" should appeal not only to his fellow professors of English but to any faculty member or faculty committee struggling with the role of student evaluations on their campus. And faculty inside and outside of chemistry will appreciate Hoffmann and Coppola's (1996) meditation on approaching and learning from the student evaluations of their chemistry course.

We should also encourage faculty to talk more with students about how previous student evaluations have helped to shape their courses, thereby letting students know that previous evaluations were indeed read and paid attention to. One of Stanford's award-winning teachers indicated that when he discussed the design of a course at the first class, he would mention how evaluation feedback from previous students in the class had influenced his choice of textbook, topics, assignments, and other major elements of the course. He left little doubt that previous student evaluations had been carefully read and, if possible, acted upon.

USING MID-TERM EVALUATIONS AND OTHER SOURCES OF STUDENT FEEDBACK ON TEACHING

Although the literature on the evaluation and improvement of teaching stresses the importance of mid-term evaluation (Centra, 1993), too many teaching evaluation systems are entirely preoccupied with summative judgments. Most teaching centers can offer faculty various ways of obtaining formative (improvement-oriented) feedback, either on their own or with the help of the center. In addition to different kinds of written mid-term forms, many of us offer the so-called SGID (Small Group Instructional Diagnosis, Clark, 1979), a structured mid-term interview of a class with the students divided into small groups, which provides specific feedback on what the students like about a course, what they feel needs improvement, and their ideas on how to carry out the improvement. Although this method takes approximately 20 minutes of class time, it has the unique advantage of exposing students to what their peers think of a course's strengths and weaknesses. Any official teaching evaluation system should make sure that faculty know about the availability and the desirability of mid-term approaches. Yale is again a case in point; the Yale College dean's letter regarding the summative evaluation system also mentions that course improvement forms, intended for mid-term use, will be sent to the faculty by the registrar along with their preliminary class lists. Faculty should also know that professors who do mid-term evaluations can achieve higher end-of-term evaluations (Overall & Marsh, 1979; Cohen, 1980).

Although on my campus the SGID, the ME Peer Review, and faculty self-designed questionnaires have proved the most popular types of mid-term student evaluation, there are other models for obtaining useful student feedback. At a National Science Foundation–funded workshop for new (up to three years' experience) engineering faculty hosted at Stanford in August 1998 by three colleagues and myself, we found that these faculty responded positively to the suggestion of teaching circles or quality control circles. As described by Tiberius (1997), such circles involve the recruitment of student volunteers from a class who agree to meet with the professor regularly in order to convey feedback from themselves and their peers on how the class is going. The fact that the student volunteers are not representing simply their own reactions but are supposed to have canvassed their peers means that students can engage in a level of frankness to the faculty member that they may not feel comfortable or secure about as individuals. We should also not underestimate the benefit to the students of being such serious and influential participants in the instructional process.

Let me emphasize, however, that the results of any alternative student feedback system should remain formative and confidential. Otherwise, alternative student feedback systems may suffer the same fate the end-of-term student evaluations have. As Centra (1993) points out, the end-of-term student ratings began as formative feedback; they became summative when colleges and universities found themselves needing an objective and quantifiable source of data on teaching that would help them make sensitive and important personnel decisions.

Let me add one other final word of caution. Faculty who devise and follow up on their own methods of obtaining student feedback should be careful not to operate in a vacuum. Their sincere efforts to strengthen their classes can backfire if they respond casually to what they think they are hearing from their students. I have worked with several faculty who had earlier done their own mid-term questionnaires and had changed their courses significantly because of what they had thought were important student suggestions. In the end, however, they had invested serious amounts of time without getting any more favorable student end-of-term evaluations. For example, one junior faculty member had received complaints about being disorganized. Because one student had suggested that he give the class complete lecture notes, he invested literally hundreds of hours in doing comprehensive and even elegant notes. The students then complained that the class was boring because the professor was closely following the lecture notes he had given them. His student evaluations ended up no higher than when he had started out.

On the basis of my own experience, Boice's (1991) work on "quick starters," and the work of many other experts (Stevens, 1987; Centra, 1993; Brinko & Menges, 1997; Tiberius, 1997; Menges, 1999), I would offer the following guidelines to faculty who decide to solicit student feedback on their teaching:

- Specific, concrete, behaviorally oriented information is most useful in trying to improve your teaching (Murray, 1984; Wilson, 1986; Geis, 1991; Menges, 1999). If the questions on your institution's student evaluation forms do not provide this kind of information, you may need to acquire it through other types of student feedback.

- Don't go it alone unless you have already established a successful record for interpreting and acting upon your student feedback. Instead, consult a peer, your teaching and learning center, your teaching assistant(s), or a group of interested students. Check with them before you invest large chunks of your time in significant changes to your course.

- Take the tinkering approach (Stevens, 1987). Make small, modest changes and don't abandon a change the first time it doesn't seem successful. Tinker with it, making little adjustments, and see if it can be made successful after all.

- Although one student's suggestion can seem especially insightful or interesting, be aware of investing too much significance in any single opinion. Concentrate on the issues that seem problematic for a large number of students or for a subset of students with particular needs. Try especially hard not to take it to heart if only one or two students are particularly critical. Every teacher has such students at some time or other, and the reasons for their discontent may lie more with them than with you. The one exception is if only one or two students are brave enough to tell you that you are making racist or gender-discriminatory remarks. This kind of feedback must always be taken seriously.

- Start conversations with your colleagues about how they handle difficult situations that you're struggling with. You don't have to confess that something is a problem for you; just ask them, for example, how they know whether or not students are following them or whatever else you suspect may be hard for you. Although most faculty don't seem to begin conversations on teaching very often, most of them seem happy to engage in one once it's begun.

- Consult the sizable, and very readable, literature on teaching. Your teaching and learning center staff or any number of introductory books on teaching (three of my favorites are Davis, 1993; Lowman, 1995; and McKeachie, 1999) can help you think more broadly about your teaching situation and the options open to you.

CONCLUSION

Within a mere 20 to 30 years, the student evaluation of teaching on American college and university campuses has gone from a relatively rare, improvement oriented exercise to an almost universal, administratively oriented, end-of-term-focused system that materially affects the careers of junior and even senior faculty throughout the United States (Centra, 1993; Baiocco & DeWaters, 1998; Chapter 1, this volume). In the process, much of the power of students' ratings and comments to constructively criticize faculty and improve the teaching students receive has been lost. Let us reclaim that system for improvement purposes, so far as we can, by reemphasizing the possibilities of mid-term evaluation, employing other kinds of student feedback, and creating the conditions for faculty reengagement with the implications of their end-of-term student evaluations.

ACKNOWLEDGMENTS

I would like to thank the National Center for Postsecondary Improvement (http://www.stanford.edu/group/ncpi), directed by Professor Patricia Gumport of the Stanford School of Education, for permission to adapt parts of a paper (Marincovich, 1998), produced under center auspices, for this chapter.

REFERENCES

Arreola, R. A. (1995). *Developing a comprehensive faculty evaluation system: A handbook for college faculty and administrators on designing and operating a comprehensive faculty evaluation system.* Bolton, MA: Anker.

Baiocco, S. A., & DeWaters, J. N. (1998). *Successful college teaching: Problem-solving strategies of distinguished professors.* Boston, MA: Allyn & Bacon.

Boice, R. (1991). Quick starters: New faculty who succeed. In M. Theall & J. Franklin (Eds.), *Effective practices for improving teaching.* New Directions in Teaching and Learning, No. 48. San Francisco, CA: Jossey-Bass.

Boyer, E. L. (1990). *Scholarship reconsidered: Priorities of the professoriate.* Princeton, NJ: Carnegie Foundation for the Advancement of Teaching.

Braskamp, L. A., & Ory, J. C. (1994). *Assessing faculty work: Enhancing individual and institutional performance.* San Francisco, CA: Jossey-Bass.

Brinko, K. T. (1991). The interactions of teaching improvement. In M. Theall & J. Franklin (Eds.), *Effective practices for improving teaching.* New Directions for Teaching and Learning, No. 48. San Francisco, CA: Jossey-Bass.

Brinko, K. T., & Menges, R. J. (Eds.). (1997). *Practically speaking: A sourcebook for instructional consultants in higher education.* Stillwater, OK: New Forums Press.

Cashin, W. E. (1990, January). *Student ratings of teaching: Recommendations for use.* IDEA Paper No. 22. Center for Faculty Evaluation and Development, Kansas State University.

Centra, J. A. (1993). *Reflective faculty evaluation: Enhancing teaching and determining faculty effectiveness.* San Francisco, CA: Jossey-Bass.

Clark, D. J., & Bekey, J. (1979). Use of small groups in instructional evaluation. *POD Quarterly, 1,* 87-95.

Cohen, P. A. (1980). Effectiveness of student rating feedback for improving college instruction: A meta-analysis of findings. *Research in Higher Education, 13* (4), 321-341.

Davis, B. G. (1993). *Tools for teaching.* San Francisco, CA: Jossey-Bass.

Elbow, P. (1992). Making better use of student evaluations of teachers. *Profession, 92,* 42-47.

Flash, P., Tzenis, C., & Waller, A. (1995). *Using student evaluations to increase classroom effectiveness* (2nd ed.). Minneapolis, MN: The Faculty and TA Enrichment Program, University of Minnesota.

Geis, G. L. (1991). The moment of truth: Feeding back information about teaching. In M. Theall & J. Franklin (Eds.), *Effective practices for improving teaching.* New Directions for Teaching and Learning, No. 48. San Francisco, CA: Jossey-Bass.

Graf, D. L., & Wheeler, D. (1996). *Defining the field: The POD membership survey.* Valdosta, GA: POD Network.

Hildebrand, M., Wilson, R. C., & Dienst, E. R. (1971). *Evaluating university teaching.* Berkeley, CA: Center for Research and Development, University of California, Berkeley.

Hoffmann, R., & Coppola, B. P. (1996). Some heretical thoughts on what our students are telling us. *Journal of College Science Teaching, 25,* 390-394.

Hutchings, P. (Ed.). (1995). *From idea to prototype: The peer review of teaching: A project handbook.* Washington, DC: The American Association for Higher Education.

Hutchings, P. (Ed.). (1996). *Making teaching community property: A menu for peer collaboration and peer review.* Washington, DC: The American Association for Higher Education.

Jacoby, K. E. (1976, February). Behavioral prescriptions for faculty based on student evaluations of teaching. *American Journal of Pharmaceutical Education, 40* (1), 8-13.

Keig, L., & Waggoner, M. D. (1994). *Collaborative peer review: The role of faculty in improving college teaching.* ASHE-ERIC Report No. 2. Washington, DC: George Washington University.

Keller, G. (1985, January/February). Trees without fruit: The problem with research about higher education. *Change,* 7-10.

Levinson-Rose, J., & Menges, R. J. (1981). Improving college teaching: A critical review of research. *Review of Educational Research, 51* (3), 403-434.

Lewis, K. G. (1991-92). Making sense (and use) of written student comments. *Teaching Excellence, 3* (8), 1-2.

Lichtenstein, G., & Deitz, J. (1998). (Survey of 16 research university teaching centers regarding their current services and priorities). Unpublished survey.

Lowman, J. (1995). *Mastering the techniques of teaching* (2nd ed.). San Francisco, CA: Jossey-Bass.

Marincovich, M. (1998). *Ending the disconnect between the student evaluation of teaching and the improvement of teaching: A faculty developer's plea.* National Center for Postsecondary Improvement, Deliverable #4010.

Marsh, H. W., & Roche, L. (1993). The use of students' evaluations and an individually structured intervention to enhance university teaching effectiveness. *American Educational Research Journal, 30* (1), 217-251.

McKeachie, W. J. (1979). Student ratings of faculty: A reprise. *Academe,* October, 384-397.

McKeachie, W. J. (1999). *Teaching tips: Strategies, research, and theory for college and university teachers* (10th ed.). Boston, MA: Houghton Mifflin.

Menges, R. J. (1990). Using evaluative information to improve instruction. In P. Seldin & Associates, *How administrators can improve teaching: Moving from talk to action in higher education.* San Francisco, CA: Jossey-Bass.

Menges, R. J. (1999). Appraising and improving your teaching: Using students, peers, experts, and classroom research. In W. J. McKeachie, *Teaching tips: Strategies, research, and theory for college and university teachers* (10th ed.). Boston, MA: Houghton Mifflin.

Menges, R. J., & Brinko, K. T. (1986). *Effects of student evaluation feedback: A meta-analysis of higher education research.* Paper presented at the 70th annual meeting of the American Educational Research Association, San Francisco, CA. (ED 270 408).

Morrison, A. A. (1995). Analyzing qualitative responses on student evaluations: An efficient and effective method. *Higher Education Research and Development Proceedings,* Vol. 18, 559-564.

Murray, H. (1984). The impact of formative and summative evaluation of teaching in North American universities. *Assessment and Evaluation in Higher Education, 9* (2), 117-132.

Overall, J. U., IV, & Marsh, H. W. (1979). Midterm feedback from students: Its relationship to instructional improvement and students: Cognitive and affective outcomes. *Journal of Educational Psychology, 71,* 856-865.

Pihakis, J., & Marincovich, M. (In preparation). Making use of students' open-ended comments on teaching evaluation forms.

Richlin, L., & Manning, B. (1995). *Improving a college/university teaching evaluation system: A comprehensive, developmental curriculum for faculty and administrators* (2nd ed.). Pittsburgh, PA: Alliance Publishers.

Seldin, P., & Associates. (1990). *How administrators can improve teaching: Moving from talk to action in higher education.* San Francisco, CA: Jossey-Bass.

Sheppard, S. D., Leifer, L., & Carryer, J. E. (1996). Commentary on student interviews. *Innovative Higher Education, 20* (4), 271-276.

Sheppard, S. D., Johnson, M., & Leifer, L. (1998). A model for peer and student involvement in course assessment. *ASEE Journal of Engineering Education, 87* (4), 349-354.

Stevens, E. A. (1987). *The process of change in college teaching.* Unpublished doctoral dissertation. Palo Alto, CA: Stanford University.

Tiberius, R. (1997). Small group methods for collecting information from students. In K. T. Brinko & R. J. Menges (Eds.), *Practically speaking: A sourcebook for instructional consultants in higher education.* Stillwater, OK: New Forums Press.

Toward greater excellence in teaching at Stanford. (1995). Final report of the C-AAA Sub-Committee on the Evaluation and Improvement of Teaching. Stanford University.

Williams, W. M., & Ceci, S. J. (1997, September/October). How'm I doing?: Problems with student ratings of instructors and courses. *Change,* 13-23.

Wilson, R. C. (1986). Improving faculty teaching: Effective use of student evaluations and consultants. *Journal of Higher Education, 57* (2), 196-211.

Wilson, R. (1998, January 16). New research casts doubt on value of student evaluations of professors. *The Chronicle of Higher Education,* A12-14.

CHAPTER 4

EVALUATING TEACHING THROUGH PEER CLASSROOM OBSERVATION

Deborah DeZure

There is both good news and bad news about peer observation of classroom teaching. On the one hand, many institutions are now using peer observation of teaching as part of their evaluation of instruction, augmenting the heavy reliance on student evaluations of teaching and the increasing use of teaching portfolios. A survey by Seldin (1998, p. 6) indicates that 40.3% of colleges and universities now use peer classroom observation for summative evaluation, up from only 5% 25 years ago. As a result, there is increased interest in assessing and ensuring its effectiveness as a reliable and valid tool for high-stakes decisions, such as tenure and promotion. There is also more research to guide us, although much of it is on peer observation for purposes of formative evaluation, that is, when the primary purpose is to improve teaching rather than evaluate it for purposes of personnel decisions (Keig & Waggoner, 1994).

The bad news is that research on current practice indicates that too often peer classroom observation is neither a reliable nor a valid tool as it is currently used. The safeguards to control for sources of bias are often not in place, and practices are often idiosyncratic and unsystematic, resulting in inequities in how peer observation is conducted for faculty, even within the same department (Centra, 1993). Peer observation of teaching, nonetheless, offers critical insights needed to provide a fuller and more accurate picture of instructional effectiveness.

The goal of this essay is to identify the sources of bias and unreliability in current practice and to suggest an array of approaches to maximize the effectiveness of peer observation. These approaches are not intended to be prescriptive. Instead, they are intended to provide options and stimulate informed discussions. Ultimately if the process is to succeed, it will be necessary to adapt these options to fit the institutional culture, disciplinary paradigms, departmental policies, and available resources. To assist in these efforts, this chapter identifies key decisions to make when designing an approach to peer observation of classroom teaching that will reflect and serve unique institutional contexts and needs.

WHAT DOES RESEARCH TELL US ABOUT PEER CLASSROOM OBSERVATION?

Peer classroom observations are useful, offering insights we cannot obtain if we rely solely on self-assessment or student evaluations. Numerous studies indicate that student evaluations continue to be our most valid and reliable tool to assess many aspects of instruction, but they are not adequate measures of content and its related dimension— pedagogical content knowledge—or ethical standards of practice. (See Chapter 2; see also Cashin, 1994; Chickering & Gamson, 1994; Feldman, 1994a, 1994b, 1996; Lowman, 1996; Marsh & Dunkin, 1997.) Faculty continue to be the best judges of these and several other dimensions of teaching effectiveness. Keig and Waggoner (1994) indicate that faculty should assess the goals, content, and organization of course design; the methods and materials used in delivery; and evaluation of student work, the instructor's grading practices, and the instructor's adherence to ethical standards. These echo Cohen and McKeachie's (1980) ten criteria of effective teaching that colleagues are best able to judge: mastery of course content, selection of course content, course organization, appropriateness of course objectives, instructional materials, evaluative devices and methods used to teach specific content areas, commitment to teaching and concern for student learning, student achievement, and support for departmental instructional efforts.

Further, research tells us that peer classroom observation is not very reliable as widely practiced. Centra (1993) indicates that "when colleague ratings of teaching are based solely on classroom observations, only slight inter-rater reliability can be expected" (p. 117). In Feldman's (1989) meta-analysis comparing colleague evaluations of teaching with other groups, the correlation of colleagues and students was .55, higher than correlations of colleagues and administrators (.48), administrators and student evaluations (.39), colleagues and self-evaluations (.15), and administrators and self-evaluations (.08).

What Are the Primary Sources of Bias?

There are many sources of bias that undermine equitable peer observation of teaching: disagreement about what constitutes good teaching, both in the discipline and in higher education; interpersonal relationships between the observer(s) and the instructor and its related issue of who selects the observers; reputation of the instructor being observed; disagreement about what to observe; lack of consistency in the process (e.g., observation instruments, recording methods, reporting methods, number of observers, criteria for selection of the course being observed); and lack of training of observers (Centra, 1993; Goodwin & Stevens, 1996).

How Can Reliability Be Increased?

First and foremost, reliability can be increased through the training of observers, including what criteria to use, how to apply them, observational skills, record-keeping, and how to provide constructive criticism. Second, it is useful to base conclusions on more than one observation by more than one observer. Third, the process should be based on consensus about what constitutes good teaching in the discipline with a focus on shared criteria for teaching effectiveness including the elements colleagues can best judge. Fourth, the process should be consistent for all instructors and observers. Fifth, the rules of the game should be known to all (the instructors, the observers, the reviewers or personnel committee, and the department administrator should all know the purposes and the processes that will be used). Sixth, the instructor should have input into the process at several stages (e.g., the selection of observers, selection of class to be observed, interpretation of the classroom experience after the observation, input into the written report). And seventh, a validated observation instrument should be used. Each of these dimensions offers a rich opportunity for improving the process.

ESTABLISHING A PROCESS FOR PEER CLASSROOM OBSERVATION: KEY ISSUES AND DECISIONS

Although the following issues are discussed separately, they are by no means discrete decisions. They are highly interdependent and subject to changing dynamics within departments and institutions. For example, the decision as to how many people to include in the pool of possible observers will affect the decision about how many observers should attend each observation. University-wide policy decisions and contractual negotiations may also impact these decisions, requiring them to be redefined in response to changing institutional conditions.

There is no single right way to approach peer classroom observations because the approaches will inevitably represent compromises among competing needs and possibilities. Departments and faculty do not have unlimited resources or time. Departments may have to choose between using more than one observer per observation (one aspect of good practice) or conducting more than one observation for each evaluation (also an aspect of good practice). Both are good, but may not be possible. Nonetheless, through careful deliberation, units can establish their priorities, make informed choices, and develop a process that can be implemented consistently. In doing so, they will establish the basis for equitable treatment and improved, if not optimal, effectiveness.

1) Planning a Process for Peer Classroom Observation

As with any other institutional change that has a direct impact on faculty, it is best to involve them in all steps of the decision-making process. Peer classroom observation, in particular, has a high impact on both those who will be evaluated and those asked to evaluate their colleagues. In some contexts, faculty have a long history with classroom observation in which there are well-established traditions. At other institutions, peer classroom observation will represent new opportunities and responsibilities that will be welcomed by some and resisted by others. Whatever the context, most faculty will want input and involvement in planning and decision-making (Hutchings, 1996).

Preliminary steps. Step one is to provide faculty and administrators with information to clarify why peer observation is useful and worth the time and effort as part of a comprehensive and multidimensional model of faculty evaluation (Arreola, 1995; Hutchings, 1995; Richlin & Manning, 1995; Seldin, 1980, 1995, 1998). Are there campus experts who can assist faculty in their research and deliberations on effective practice in faculty evaluation? Over 60% of American campuses now have instructional development centers and staff who have both resources and expertise to assist in providing this information (see Chapter 3). There are numerous external consultants who can be brought in to share their knowledge of the extensive body of research on faculty evaluation generally and peer classroom observation specifically. And last but not least, there are numerous published resources which offer rich and varied materials on faculty evaluation and peer classroom observations.

Step two is to decide the level at which these deliberations will occur. Should they occur at the college, department, or program level? Although they often occur at the department level for use within the entire unit, many academic departments have programs rooted in different disciplines, and faculty from each of these may want the process to reflect their unique disciplinary paradigms. Alternatively, the planning process may occur at the college or university level in order to establish a process that will be used across the disciplines with opportunities for departments or programs to adapt specified parts of the process, such as the observation protocols.

Step three is to decide who will develop the process. Are there groups with the legitimacy and expertise to take on this planning role (e.g., the personnel or instruction committee)? If not, how will individuals be appointed, and what will be the limits of their authority? How will they convey their ongoing deliberations to the rest of their colleagues, and how will consensus be reached? Is this planning process tied to institutional efforts to improve the evaluation of teaching? If so, are there considerations beyond priorities of the unit or department? Are there contractual and policy constraints? And what will be the projected timeline for these efforts?

Ongoing implementation and supervision of the plan. Many of us in higher education have been through planning processes that take enormous amounts of time and effort and result in reports that remain on shelves collecting dust. In the context of planning a process for peer observation, it is also useful to determine who will provide leadership and oversight in the future to ensure that the plans are implemented and maintained in ways consistent with the intention and the guidelines for practice in the department. The guidelines are ultimately rendered meaningless unless they are known and understood by all members of the department and used to shape practice. Thus, the planning committee may want to answer the following questions: Who will ensure that new and continuing faculty and administrators know and use the guidelines for peer classroom observation consistently? How will those guidelines be conveyed? Should personnel committees be given a protocol with guidelines to ensure that they follow and document the procedures they use for each observation? What, if any, consequences will follow for noncompliance with the established model on the part of the personnel committee, observers, or the instructors? What process will be used if an instructor wants to pursue a grievance because the guidelines were violated? Although deliberations on these questions should be deferred until after the model has taken shape, it is useful to identify such questions from the beginning to assure that the process includes a commitment to monitor implementation on an ongoing basis in the future.

2) Clarifying Purpose: Formative, Summative, or a Combined Model

In short, why are you doing it? Peer observation of classroom teaching may be used for formative or summative evaluation purposes. Formative assessments of teaching are used for the improvement of teaching. They are usually confidential between the instructor and the observer(s) and are often tied to recommendations for future development activities and opportunities for improvement. Summative assessments are used for evaluation for personnel decisions, including tenure, promotion, reappointment, or salary. They are often done with only limited confidentiality (i.e., the instructor, the department head or chair, and the personnel committee may share the results but bar others from them). The procedures should be consistent with contracts, accreditation, and grievance procedures. In some cases, the process will include elements of both formative and summative assessments (e.g., a process in which two final reports are prepared: a formative one that is for the instructor but does not become part of the permanent personnel file and a summative one that does). The decision about the purpose of classroom observation is a critical one and will define most other decisions that follow. It is important that both formative and summative assessments be valid and reliable. As a result, many of the following issues will apply to both; but the implications of error in summative evaluations are generally more serious and therefore may imply an even higher standard of practice than in formative assessments.

3) The Selection Process for Observers

The selection of observers involves several interrelated issues: 1) What is the possible pool of observers from which to choose? 2) Who selects the observers? and 3) How many observers are needed?

The possible pool of observers. The parameters of the pool determine both the kinds of expertise and perspectives that will be represented by the observers as well as the number of people available to share the responsibilities of observing. If the pool is very small, it may preclude the option to have more than one observer at each observation, which in turn affects reliability. Potential observers may be members of the personnel and/or instruction committee; all faculty within the program, department, or discipline; the department head; the program head; faculty outside the discipline; and even student observers either within the department or outside it to augment faculty observers. Brigham Young University has a pool of trained student observers who can be called upon to participate in classroom observations along with faculty observers.

On many campuses, the department administrator must conduct a classroom observation periodically and that is certainly advisable, but an administrator is not a peer in the sense implied here. If an administrator is included in the pool, it might be best not to rely solely on the administrator observation unless he or she is one of two or three observers. It is also advisable to include at least one faculty member with content area expertise because content is one of the dimensions of teaching for which we most need faculty input (Sorcinelli, 1984). In a team of two or three observers, it can be useful to have a faculty member outside the department or a student or alumnus who can provide input on the clarity of explanations to a novitiate or nonexpert.

Who should select the observers? Most commonly, the selection of observers is done by the personnel committee, department head or chair, or the instructor being observed. One model that is widely lauded as equitable and effective is to have the instructor select a list of four to five names from the observer pool; then the personnel committee or administrator selects from among those names. Or, conversely, the personnel committee or administrator selects a list of four to five names from the observer pool, and the instructor picks from that list. The advantage to this model is that it tends to reduce bias associated with interpersonal relationships with the instructor. The instructor can eliminate those he or she most distrusts, and the committee can eliminate the best friends and closest colleagues of the instructor. All parties feel that they have some control in the process and there is real choice for all.

How many observers should be used for each observation? In most circumstances, one observer is insufficient, although it is still common practice. A single observer invites trouble for many reasons. One observer cannot see it all. One observer has no one to challenge, validate, or offset his or her perceptions. One observer is more likely to be challenged on the grounds of personal bias. Once the number increases to two, it is more difficult to make claims based on personal idiosyncrasies of the observers. Two is certainly preferable to one from the perspective of reliability. For larger classes, three may be useful, but in medium to small classes, the presence of three faculty observers may have an inhibiting impact on classroom dynamics. From a practical perspective, it may be difficult to find three observers for all observations. Each part of the process will require compromises. In general, two will be a reasonable compromise in many departments.

How many times should the instructor be observed for each evaluation, and which courses should be observed? Although it is common practice to observe an instructor once per evaluation cycle, increasingly schools are moving toward multiple observations, either of the same course observed twice during a semester or different courses observed once during that semester. There are obvious advantages to multiple observations. One observation is simply a snapshot. The instructor can have a bad day or an unusually good one. The material or the instructional method may or may not be characteristic of the instructor. Like reliability on tests, more items increase the likelihood that the sampling of behavior is representative.

Consistency of observers. If the model requires more than one observation, should the same or different observers be used? There are advantages and disadvantages to each approach. A single observer has the advantage of assessing consistency and change across the observations, but it is more work for that observer. Different observers may also bring different expertise to bear. One observer may be a specialist in large lecture classes and another in lab settings. Assuming the two observers are willing to spend the time to discuss their experiences and compare notes with care, the differences will add richness and depth. The optimal situation may be to have two observers who attend both observations. But the disadvantage is that it is a very labor-intensive approach.

Which courses to observe, and who shall decide? Should the instructor, committee, observers, or administrator decide which courses to observe? Should it be a function of observers' availability during the instructor's courses or instructional or curricular considerations, such as desire to see the instructor teach one undergraduate general education course and one course in the major or one graduate course? Once again, there is no right or wrong answer, but fairness requires consistency. Committees should not be able to select the course that is most difficult to teach for one instructor and to provide the option to select his or her favorite course for another instructor. Defining who decides and the basis for the decision will help to ensure that the process is equitable for all instructors.

4) Observer Training

Observer training is essential whether the evaluation is formative or summative (Braskamp & Ory, 1994; Centra, 1993, 1996; Millis & Kaplan, 1995; Webb & McEnerney, 1997; Weimer, Parret, & Kerns, 1988). Training might be handled at the institutional, department, or college level. Training could be required or optional for all observers or required for at least one observer in any team of observers. Topics that are often included in training are dimensions of effective teaching; observational skills (of both instructors and students); use of protocols and forms; record-keeping (such as narrative models, keeping track of time on task); review of syllabi, exams, assignments, labs, and texts; constructive feedback; building consensus among reviewers; reconciling forms and narrative notes; and final report writing. Examples of institutions that use observer training include Texas A&M University, Appalachian State University (North Carolina), University of Maryland Asian Division, University of Arizona, and The Ohio State University.

Because training and observations are time-consuming and challenging, institutions may want to consider rewarding instructors who devote time to observer training either as trainers or participants. Rewards may take the form of released time; credit for department service; payment in bonuses; additional travel funds; or perks associated with office location, access to technology, or course schedule.

The time commitment may be considerable. Appropriate training may include attendance at more than one training workshop, often two hours each. The observation process itself can take up to four hours for each evaluation, including a pre-observation meeting (30 minutes); review of the materials (30 minutes); the observation (75 minutes); preparation of the report, including discussion with the other observers (60 minutes); and the post-observation meeting with the instructor (45 minutes).

Training can be compressed. The institution might develop a training video to share with faculty as they are identified as observers. The video can then be shown to small groups with discussion or given to faculty to watch at their own convenience. Training might be condensed into a single workshop or department meeting. At a minimum, a manual of instructions and guidelines for classroom observations should be available to all faculty. Two exemplary models of published guidelines include ones prepared by the Center for Teaching Effectiveness at the University of Texas at Austin (1996) and the University of Maryland Asian Division (Millis, 1994).

5) Announced Versus Unannounced Classroom Visits

This issue can be quite contentious. Announced visits permit specific pre-observation discussion and preparation on the part of both the instructor and the observers. Announced visits also allow the instructor to be seen at his or her best. Unannounced visits can be wasteful of the observers' time if they attend on exam days or when media is shown. Unannounced visits can also create a climate of distrust and fear. But despite all these reasons to use announced visits, some personnel committees prefer unannounced visits as a way to detect instructors who are unprepared for their classes. In balance, announced visits have the potential to be highly productive, and unannounced visits have the sole advantage of catching people who are underachieving. Nonetheless, many departments prefer unannounced visits or compromise on a combination of one pre-scheduled visit and one unannounced visit.

6) Length of the Observation

There are several models: the whole class; part of the class, including five to ten minutes before or after class to observe the transition; or part of a longer class including at least one coherent unit of instruction. In all these models, the minimum recommended observation is 50 minutes and includes at least a few minutes before or after class to observe the transition into or out of class and/or between topics.

Walking into a class late is both poor practice and inconsiderate, often disrupting the class and unnerving the instructor, particularly if the visit is unannounced. In such cases the observer may miss the introduction to the topic under discussion, any advanced organizers or instructions for the activity, and the tone that was established in these initial minutes.

It is equally problematic to have an observer leave when group work is initiated as if the instructor is no longer teaching. Supervision of student groups is not only a significant form of instruction, but also requires great skill to be done well. Observers should stay in the room and document the role of the instructor during group work as an important and active part of his or her instructional style.

Given the proliferation of instructional technology, observers may want to examine the online component of a course (e.g., a class computer conference, electronic bulletin board, email communications from the instructor, or the course web site that augments classroom instruction). (See the resources section, Chapter 8.) The instructor should be encouraged to identify his or her uses of instructional technology and provide observers with access to online course materials.

7) Expectations for Participation by Observer(s) during Class

Many of us have heard of situations in which the observer intrudes himself or herself into a class by offering alternative explanations or answers or even standing up and joining the instructor in front of the class as if team teaching. Collegial as this may appear, it is not appropriate in an evaluation context. At most, the instructor should introduce the observers to the class, explain why they are there, and move on. This can also be done at the previous class to alert students in advance. If the instructor doesn't explain that they are there to do observations required of all faculty in the department, students may assume that they are there for remediation purposes. It will clear the air about any questions students may have. And, over time, it will be pro forma in the department: Students will expect observations as a normal occurrence and form of quality control on the part of the university.

Observers should not ask individual students how they feel about the course or instructor. In most institutions, student opinions are assessed through systematic student evaluations. The comments of individual students solicited during observations offer idiosyncratic and unreliable information. For example, if observers sit in the back of the room and lean over to ask students questions about the instructor, they would be speaking with students who are in the back of the room. These students are often the least engaged, and it would be inappropriate to generalize from their comments.

Observers may find it useful to listen in on the deliberations of student groups or rove among students in a lab or studio setting, but these activities should be as unobtrusive as possible.

Observers may find it useful to sit toward the back of the class so they can observe both the students at the back and the front of the room. It is a better vantage point to assess audibility, legibility of visual materials, and classroom dynamics across the entire class. It also removes the observers from the direct line of sight of most students, minimizing the impact of the visitors, their notetaking, and observational activities.

8) A Pre-Observation Meeting of Instructor and Observer(s)

The pre-observation meeting should be initiated by the observers, and all observers should be in attendance. The meeting should take place in a neutral and confidential space.

The form and content of this meeting will differ if the observation is to be pre-scheduled or unannounced. If it is pre-scheduled, then the date for the observation should be selected before this meeting, enabling the instructor to prepare materials relevant to the observation of a particular class session. If the observation is unannounced, the pre-observation meeting will be more general, focusing on the course or courses taught by the instructor and more general statements about the instructor's goals and methods.

More specifically, the pre-observation meeting of a pre-scheduled observation may include discussion of the following: 1) the instructor's course goals in the context of program goals, objectives for the class, instructional methods used to accomplish those goals, who are the students in the class, how the instructor will assess student learning and track student progress, and graded student work and grade distributions; 2) the materials relevant to the course: syllabus, exam(s), assignments, labs, computer conference, course home page or electronic bulletin board, texts, or resources made available; 3) the observer form and criteria for evaluation as well as modifications or adaptations of the observer form for the teaching methods of the instructor; 4) a meeting time for a post-observation meeting and a timetable for the written report that will be submitted to the personnel committee, administrator, and instructor (Wilkerson, 1988).

If the class is very long, it may be useful to discuss how long the observers will visit and which portion of the class might include a coherent unit of instruction. If the observation is for formative purposes, the instructor will often identify areas about which he or she is concerned or which need improvement. In summative evaluations, instructors do not generally focus on their weaknesses (Millis, 1994; Sorcinelli, 1984).

9) The Classroom Observation

There are numerous decisions and deliberations related to the classroom observation itself. These include decisions about what constitutes good teaching in the discipline, the best ways to evaluate instruction through observation, what the observer(s) will look for, the method of recording observations, and the content of the instruments.

What constitutes good teaching in the disciplines? One of the most difficult and complex tasks is to reach consensus on what constitutes good teaching in the discipline. There are many ways to be an excellent and effective instructor with different methods serving different goals. Different disciplines have different epistemologies and paradigms that influence both the selection of content and methods (Murray & Renaud, 1995). The disciplines and their paradigms are changing at an unprecedented pace as are the methods used to teach them. The goal of reaching consensus about what constitutes good practice in the discipline may be very difficult, with the optimal result being a deeper appreciation of diversity in instructional styles and a healthy respect for the varied approaches faculty use in instructional decision-making. Having said that, there is a rich body of research on effective teaching across the disciplines and norms of effective teaching within disciplinary contexts. These discussions should be informed by this substantial and growing body of literature (Feldman, 1994a, 1994b, 1996; Lowman, 1996; McKeachie, 1997; Marsh & Dunkin, 1997; Murray, 1997).

With the shift from the teaching paradigm to the learning paradigm in higher education, it is likely that there will be an increased emphasis on documenting the role of the instructor in promoting student learning outcomes. At the present time, it is assessed indirectly from low inference teaching behaviors such as clarity, organization, and content knowledge rather than assessed directly through measures of student learning, but the latter may be on the horizon as mandated program assessment clarifies program elements in need of improvement and as approaches to assessment become increasingly more sophisticated.

What are the best ways to evaluate practice through observation? There are forms (checksheets with scaled responses and/or open-ended questionnaires), focused narratives or open-ended questions on a few topics, a combination of a checksheet and a narrative, or an open narrative, that is, the infamous blank sheet of paper. Checklists and focused narratives used in combination all render useful and reliable information. The least reliable model is use of an open narrative—a blank sheet of paper—that offers no sense of priorities for the observation and no consistency among observations. Forms and checklists attempt to standardize observations, prompting the observer to look for certain things. Many items can be observed and recorded. However, the disadvantage is that the checklist may distract the observer from watching what is happening. The categories may not be appropriate to that particular class or instructional method, and the checklist may imply a prescriptive list of preferred behaviors so that instructors who don't demonstrate all items may be seen as deficient. This can be alleviated by a response choice for "not applicable" as well as "not observed."

A narrative format allows the observer to go with the flow of events and record them in a linear fashion, including narrative detail. The method allows the observer to note unusual or repetitive behaviors on the part of students or the instructor, and it allows transcription of verbatim dialogue. The disadvantage is the time it takes. Only a limited amount of things can be observed and recorded and those may reflect observer bias.

Both checklist and narrative forms can also include tracking time by indicating what is happening at timed intervals, although this is easier to do with narrative approaches because they allow more accurate reporting to the instructor about the amount of time allocated to specific activities, including student questions and answers.

A combination of checklist, open-ended questions, and open narrative is both common and useful. It is generally advisable for observers to familiarize themselves with the checklist criteria before the observation and to spend the time during class observing behavior that can be checked off after the class.

Another alternative is to videotape the class using two video cameras, one recording the students and one recording the instructor. Observers can then view the tapes running simultaneously on a split screen. The video can be used when providing feedback to the instructor and offers a permanent record that can be reviewed by additional observers and the instructor if there is disagreement. This is an unusual, costly, and labor intensive option for summative evaluation that is used when other options are not available. Videotaping is more commonly used for formative evaluation to improve instruction and is often accompanied by consultation with an instructional expert.

Methods used to record observations. There is a plethora of forms and checklists to use for classroom observations that are widely available in books and articles on faculty evaluation (Arreola, 1995; Centra, 1993; Chism, 1999; *Guidelines for Observing an Instructor's Case-Teaching Approach and Behavior,* 1995; Helling, 1988; Millis & Kaplan, 1995; Center for Teaching Effectiveness, 1996; Richlin & Manning, 1995; Webb & McEnerney, 1997). (Also, see the resources section, Chapter 8.) These forms can be used intact or adapted. Although these forms may work well for a majority of faculty in some disciplines, they may not work well for other faculty or other disciplines. One option is to collect a range of forms that reflect different instructional styles and beliefs about teaching and make them available so that instructors can select the form that best reflects their instructional methods. Alternatively, a department might adopt a single form or checklist on which the last few items include alternatives that represent a range of instructional methods. In the first option, the instructor selects a form in advance of the observation, and the observers come prepared to use it; in the second option, the form is simply modified for use based on the instructional style that is used the day of the observation. This latter example is clearly more appropriate when the observation is unannounced.

What is included on the observer forms? In general, there are generic questions that fit all teaching styles (e.g., establishes positive rapport with students, begins and ends class on time, organization and presentation skills such as speaks clearly and audibly, demonstrates sensitivity to diverse students, promotes active learning and student engagement, and supports underprepared students). There are often questions that reflect specific teaching methods (e.g., lecture, case study discussions, group inquiry, labs, studios, student performances, or clinical settings). There are also questions that reflect goals of general education: promotes higher-order critical thinking, encourages writing across the curriculum. Open-ended sections may focus on content or the degree to which students appear to follow and understand the material. Finally, there may be an area that invites observations about notable or unusual elements or verbatim quotes.

What should the observer look for? The list is long, and the observer must maintain priorities. The observer will want to pay particular attention to the following:

1) The class environment, both as a physical space with light, sound, heat, cleanliness, and comfort, and as an interpersonal experience with power relations signaled by the physical organization of desks, chairs, podium, or lectern

2) Indicators of student involvement and engagement: attendance, participation in answering and asking questions, notetaking, inappropriate activities such as sleeping or reading noncourse material

3) The instructor's ability to convey the course content through explanations, examples, stories, demonstrations, use of media, problems and answers to questions

4) The range of instructional methods and how they support student understanding of the content

5) Student-instructor rapport through indicators such as participation, active listening, body language, informal discussion with the instructor before and after class, and willingness of students to ask questions

6) A global rating for overall effectiveness

Research on instructional effectiveness consistently cites the following dimensions: presentation style, enthusiasm, sensitivity to student level of knowledge and progress, openness to questions, and clarity and organization (Murray, 1997). Feldman's 1988 study indicated that faculty gave their highest ratings to knowledge of subject, enthusiasm, sensitivity to class level of knowledge and progress, preparation and organization of class, and clarity (Centra, 1993).

Much of this research and many of the forms reflect the long-standing hegemony of lecturing. We are beginning to see research that advocates more active modes of learning in which the instructor may do less dissemination of information and more coaching or organizing of the environment to promote discovery-based learning and peer instruction. Care should be taken to use observation protocols that do not privilege lecture as the sole or best approach and that can be adapted to other modes of instruction.

There are elements of instruction that are crucial to assess but which cannot be observed directly in class, including fairness, grading, ethical standards, and professionalism. (See Braxton, Bayer, & Finkelstein, 1992, and Rodabaugh, 1994, for specific norms of unacceptable teaching behaviors.) These have to be assessed through a careful examination of course materials and graded student work provided by the instructor.

10) Communication Immediately Following the Observation

It may be several days before the observers can provide formal feedback to the instructor. For that reason, it is useful to have a brief five-minute meeting with the instructor immediately following the observation to 1) get immediate clarification or obtain materials referred to during the class, 2) provide a chance to ask the instructor if this was a typical class and to ask if any additional clarification would be helpful in interpreting what was observed, and 3) thank the instructor and offer some word of interpersonal support while taking care not to offer premature feedback that is either praise or criticism. These additional inquiries should be made in person, not by email, because the tone of email is easily misunderstood, particularly in the context of an instructor's performance anxiety. If this step is omitted, an instructor often experiences a sense of isolation and alienation from his or her colleagues. Even the briefest of comments at the end of the session provides a form of closure in a situation that is often fraught with high anxiety.

11) Post-Observation Meeting to Provide Feedback

It is best to have the post-observation meeting within three to seven days. In some institutions, the timing is defined by contract. The instructor and all observers should be present at the meeting. It should occur in a neutral space. It is advisable for the instructor to receive a copy of the preliminary written report at least one day before the post-observation meeting.

During the meeting, the observers discuss their observations, making direct reference to their feedback forms and narratives as well as their written report. They may ask the instructor for his or her assessment of the class and to respond to the written report. The session provides an opportunity for the observers to provide constructive honest feedback. Such feedback identifies both strengths and weaknesses and helps the instructor to envision specific ways to improve or provides referrals to units or individuals on campus that can assist in these efforts. Constructive feedback emphasizes description rather than evaluation, is specific rather than general, and focuses on behavior that is observable. If there are several observers, they should determine in advance who will provide the feedback and what the priorities will be. There is always more material to discuss than time allows or than an instructor can process in one session. Choices must be made, and it is best to make them in a deliberative and carefully planned manner that balances praise with criticism in a tactful and empathetic manner (Millis, 1994).

12) The Final Written Report

In some institutions, the written report that is shown to the instructor during the post-observation meeting is truly the final report. Any amendments on the part of the instructor or the observers are considered addenda and do not change the text of the document. At other institutions, the written report is a preliminary draft that can be modified as a result of the discussion at the post-observation meeting. These approaches reflect different assumptions about the role of the report and the conception of evaluation as a process.

The model that considers the written report as the final document does not leave room for instructor input or clarification except as a response to the report. The model that considers the written report to be a preliminary draft treats the document as a work-in-progress that needs the input of the instructor for completion. One of the goals of the latter approach to performance evaluation is to reframe evaluation as something that happens with a person, not to a person. For this reason, use of a preliminary written report followed by a final written report may be advisable. Access to the preliminary written report does not imply that the instructor necessarily agrees or accepts all that is in it; it does imply that the instructor has had an opportunity to comment on its contents before it is considered a final document. This model is more collaborative and collegial and does not compromise the integrity or objectivity of the process. Quite the contrary, it may increase its validity, reliability, and stature because it is collaborative (Wilkerson, 1988).

Some institutions use classroom observations for both formative and summative evaluation simultaneously. In these cases, there may be two final reports, one written for formative purposes and one for summative purposes. The formative one is confidential between the observers and the instructor. The summative one, in contrast, goes to the personnel committee and department head or chair and becomes part of the instructor's permanent file.

If there are several observers, they should decide what viewpoint the document will present: 1) A single joint statement? 2) Discrete voices that may or may not concur? 3) Both joint and individual statements, noting differences and similarities in perceptions and observations?

The tone of written reports on classroom observations should be honest, with criticism that is stated gently, purposefully, and clearly, leaving no ambiguity. Comments should be phrased positively if possible, without harshness, sarcasm, or vitriol. Comments and conclusions should be based directly on observed teacher behaviors and teacher materials, not on teaching in general or on the instructor's personality. The report may link areas in need of improvement to opportunities for improvement, using action-oriented language when possible. If the instructor challenges the preliminary written report, but the observers continue to disagree with the instructor's input, it may be advisable to refer to the instructor's input in the final report.

If the instructor continues to feel strongly about these issues, he or she should have the option to submit a subsequent response to the final written report. Documenting the instructor's earlier input will anticipate that development and clarify its history.

Who sees the document? If the document is for summative evaluation, it may have only limited confidentiality and may be seen by members of the personnel committee and/or the department head or chair as well as the instructor. Equitable practice requires that the instructor receive a copy of the document as soon as it is available and be informed about who has access to it. All instructors should have the same opportunities and same restrictions.

13) What About Special Cases?

With higher education transforming itself at an unprecedented rate, special cases will increase as new pedagogies and new technologies proliferate. Current practice is to avoid conducting peer classroom observations in unusual class settings, relying primarily on more traditional settings in which to evaluate instructors. But instructors who, for example, team teach, teach in learning communities, or use interdisciplinary approaches should also have opportunities for classroom observations. The forms and procedures must be adaptable to accommodate these variations. The same is true for modes of instruction that use instructional technology and other innovative models such as problem-based learning, service-learning, and constructivist approaches.

CONCLUSION

One final point: Approaches to faculty evaluation that are both effective and equitable must also be adaptable to change and innovation. We know from the extensive body of research on master teachers that the best teachers are characterized by their risk-taking and experimentation. They are the ones who lead the way for us. We must be sure that our approaches to peer evaluation both support and promote their innovations by being equally forward-thinking and flexible.

References

Arreola, R. A. (1995). *Developing a comprehensive faculty evaluation system: A handbook for college faculty and administrators on designing and operating a comprehensive faculty evaluation system.* Bolton, MA: Anker.

Braskamp, L. A., & Ory, J. C. (1994). *Assessing faculty work.* San Francisco, CA: Jossey-Bass.

Braxton, J. M., Bayer, A. E., & Finkelstein, M. J. (1992). Teaching performance norms in academia. *Research in Higher Education, 33* (5), 533-569.

Cashin, W. E. (1994). Student ratings of teaching: A summary of the research. In K. A. Feldman & M. B. Paulsen (Eds.), *Teaching and learning in the college classroom* (pp. 531-542). Needham Heights, MA: Ginn.

Center for Teaching Effectiveness. (1996). *Preparing for peer observation: A guidebook.* Austin, TX: The Center for Teaching Effectiveness, University of Texas, Austin.

Centra, J. A. (1993). *Reflective faculty evaluation: Enhancing teaching and determining faculty effectiveness.* San Francisco, CA: Jossey-Bass.

Centra, J. A. (1996). Identifying exemplary teachers: Evidence from colleagues, administrators, and alumni. In R. J. Menges & M. D. Svinicki (Eds.), *Honoring exemplary teaching.* New Directions for Teaching and Learning, No. 65, (pp. 51-56). San Francisco, CA: Jossey-Bass.

Chickering, A. W., & Gamson, Z. F. (1994). Seven principles for good practice in undergraduate education. In K. A. Feldman & M. B. Paulsen (Eds.), *Teaching and learning in the college classroom* (pp. 255-263). Needham Heights, MA: Ginn.

Chism, N. V. N. (1999). *Peer review of teaching: A sourcebook.* Bolton, MA: Anker.

Cohen, P. A., & McKeachie, W. J. (1980). The role of colleagues in the evaluation of teaching. *Improving College and University Teaching, 28,* 147-154.

Dilts, D. A., Bialik, D., & Haber, L. J. (1994). *Assessing what professors do: An introduction to academic performance appraisal in higher education.* Westport, CT: Greenwood.

Feldman, K. A. (1989). Instructional effectiveness of college teachers as judged by teachers themselves, current and former students, colleagues, administrators, and external (neutral) observers. *Research in Higher Education, 30,* 137-189.

Feldman, K. A. (1994a). The association between student ratings of specific instructional dimensions and student achievement: Refining and extending the synthesis of data from multisection validity studies. In K. A Feldman & M. B. Paulsen (Eds.), *Teaching and learning in the college classroom* (pp. 543-576). Needham Heights, MA: Ginn.

Feldman, K. A. (1994b). Effective college teaching from the students' and faculty's view: Matched or mismatched priorities? In K. A Feldman & M. B. Paulsen (Eds.), *Teaching and learning in the college classroom* (pp. 335-364). Needham Heights, MA: Ginn.

Feldman, K. A. (1996, Spring). Identifying exemplary teaching: Using data from course and teacher evaluations. In R. J. Menges & M. D. Svinicki (Eds.), *Honoring exemplary teaching.* New Directions for Teaching and Learning, No. 65 (pp. 41-49). San Francisco, CA: Jossey-Bass.

Goodwin, L. D., & Stevens, E. A. (1996). The influence of gender on university faculty members perceptions of 'good' teaching. In D. E. Finnegan, D. Webster, & Z. F. Gamson (Eds.), *Faculty and faculty issues in colleges and universities* (pp. 272-286). Needham Heights, MA: Simon & Schuster.

Guidelines for observing an instructor's case-teaching approach and behavior. (1995, May 5). Cambridge, MA: Harvard Business School Press.

Helling, B. B. (1988, Winter). Looking for good teaching: A guide to peer observation. *Journal of Staff, Program, and Organizational Development, 6* (4), 147-158.

Hutchings, P. (Ed.). (1995). *From idea to prototype—The peer review of teaching: A project workbook.* Washington, DC: AAHE.

Hutchings, P. (1996). *Making teaching community property: A menu for peer collaboration and peer review.* Washington, DC: AAHE.

Keig, L., & M. D. Waggoner. (1994). *Collaborative peer review: The role of faculty in improving college teaching.* ASHE-ERIC Higher Education Report, No. 2. Washington, DC: The George Washington University, Graduate School of Education and Human Development.

Lowman, J. (1996, Spring). Characteristics of exemplary teachers. In R. J. Menges & M. D. Svinicki (Eds.), *Honoring exemplary teaching.* New Directions for Teaching and Learning, No. 65, (pp. 33-40). San Francisco, CA: Jossey-Bass.

Marsh, H. W., & Dunkin, M. J. (1997). Students' evaluations of university teaching: A multidimensional perspective. In R. P. Perry & J. C. Smart (Eds.), *Effective teaching in higher education: Research and practice* (pp. 241-320). New York, NY: Agathon.

McKeachie, W. J. (1997). Good teaching makes a difference—And we know what it is. In R. P. Perry & J. C. Smart (Eds.), *Effective teaching in higher education: Research and practice* (pp. 396-410). New York, NY: Agathon.

Millis, B. J. (1994). *Guide to good practices in class visits.* College Park, MD: University of Maryland.

Millis, B. J., & Kaplan, B. B. (1995). Enhancing teaching through peer classroom observations. In P. Seldin & Associates (Eds.), *Improving college teaching* (pp. 137-152). Bolton, MA: Anker.

Murray, H. G. (1997). Effective teaching behaviors in the college classroom. In R. P. Perry & J. C. Smart (Eds.), *Effective teaching in higher education: Research and practice* (pp. 171-204). New

York, NY: Agathon.

Murray, H. G., & Renaud, R. D. (1995, Winter). Disciplinary differences in classroom teaching behaviors. In N. Hativa & M. Marincovich (Eds.), *Disciplinary differences in teaching and learning: Implications for practice.* New Directions for Teaching and Learning, No. 64 (pp. 17-34). San Francisco, CA: Jossey-Bass.

Richlin, L. & Manning, B. (1995). *Improving a college/university teaching evaluation system: A comprehensive two-year curriculum for faculty and administrators.* Pittsburgh, PA: Alliance.

Rodabaugh, R. C. (1994). College students' perceptions of unfairness in the classroom. In E. C. Wadsworth & Associates (Eds.), *To Improve the Academy,* Vol. 13 (pp. 269-281). Stillwater, OK: New Forums Press and the Professional and Organizational Development Network in Higher Education.

Seldin, P. (1980). *Successful faculty evaluation programs.* Crugers, NY: Coventry.

Seldin, P. (1995). *Improving college teaching.* Bolton, MA: Anker.

Seldin, P. (1998, March). How colleges evaluate teaching: 1988 vs. 1998. *AAHE Bulletin, 50* (7), 1-7.

Shulman, L. (1993). Teaching as community property. *Change, 24,* pp. 6-7.

Sorcinelli, M. D. (1984). An approach to colleague evaluation of classroom instruction. *Journal of Instructional Development, 7* (4), 11-17.

Webb, J., & McEnerney, K. (1997). Implementing peer review programs: A twelve step model. In D. DeZure (Ed.), *To Improve the Academy,* Vol. 16 (pp. 295-316). Stillwater, OK: New Forums Press and the Professional and Organizational Development Network in Higher Education.

Weimer, M., Parrett, J. L., & Kerns, M. (1988). *How am I teaching? Forms and activities for acquiring instructional input.* Madison, WI: Magna.

Wilkerson, L. (1988). Classroom observation: The observer as collaborator. In E. C. Wadsworth, L. Hilsen, & M. A. Shea (Eds.), *Professional and organizational development in higher education: A handbook for new practitioners* (pp. 95-99). Stillwater, OK: New Forums Press and Professional and Organizational Network in Higher Education.

CHAPTER 5

SELF-EVALUATION: WHAT WORKS? WHAT DOESN'T?

Peter Seldin

A lmost all college teachers assess their classroom performance, partly by judging student reactions in the classroom and partly by seeing how well students perform on examinations. Some college teachers go even further by completing self-evaluation forms.

Self-evaluation has its proponents as well as its detractors. Braskamp and Ory (1994) argue that faculty can provide valuable information about their teaching by writing about their teaching goals and strategies. Arreola (1995) sees self-evaluation as a valuable part of a program of continuous assessment. Seldin (1998) agrees and says that a good searching and reflective self-evaluation can be of value: It frequently is the precursor of improved performance because it increases commitment to institutional goals.

On the negative side, self-evaluation is a faculty member's self-judgment. If the teacher is dull but generous, his or her services will be rated very highly. But if the faculty member is brilliant but self-effacing, he or she can end up with a poor rating. For that reason, Centra (1993) argues that self-evaluations are not a meaningful measure of teaching performance because they lack validity and objectivity. Donald (1997) also is opposed to self-evaluation and, like Centra, warns strongly against its use in personnel decisions.

SELF-EVALUATION AND ITS RELATIONSHIP TO STUDENT RATINGS AND TEACHER CHARACTERISTICS

The research literature on self-evaluation is thin and inconclusive. Some studies show that instructors rated highly by students give themselves higher scores than do instructors rated less highly by students (Doyle & Crichton, 1978; Marsh, Overall, & Kesler, 1979; Braskamp & Ory, 1994). Student and self-evaluations provide a similar profile of instructor strengths and weaknesses (Feldman, 1989). But doubt is cast on this general agreement by Centra (1993) who suggests that the instructors previously had been student-rated and may have lowered their self-ratings as a result.

Some studies have found that faculty give themselves higher ratings than their students do (Arreola, 1995), especially on their rapport with students and on the frequency and quality of their feedback to students (Centra, 1993). Superior teachers tend to be more accurate in their self-evaluations than mediocre or poor teachers (Sorey, 1968; Centra, 1973; Barber, 1990).

Several interesting differences between self-evaluation and student evaluation have been found in the natural sciences. Faculty members thought the pace of their courses were slower than the students thought they were and disagreed with the students' contention that they put a great deal of effort into the course. Centra (1993) says this may be due to these teachers either having higher expectations than most for students or reacting to the large amount of subject matter they believed should be covered and learned in their courses.

Teacher self-evaluations appear not to be distorted by teacher characteristics such as age, sex, tenure status, teaching load, or number of years of teaching experience (Doyle & Webber, 1978; Feldman, 1989).

SELF-EVALUATION FOR PERSONNEL DECISIONS

Some institutions use self-evaluation as one component in a multi-component evaluation system. This has the obvious advantage of adding another piece of evidence to the collective judgment. In a widely distributed position paper, the American Association of University Professors (1974) concluded that giving faculty members the opportunity to evaluate their own teaching effectiveness (and, in addition, to add their interpretation of student ratings and classroom visitation) would improve the review process.

Self-evaluation is widely popular today as a component in the assessment of teaching performance. There is considerable recognition that faculty members can and do produce not only insights into their own course and instructional objectives but also solid clues to their classroom teaching competency. Perhaps that is why the Carnegie Foundation for the Advancement of Teaching (1994) found that 82% of four-year colleges and universities reported that they used self-evaluation in evaluating faculty teaching performance.

Regrettably, many of the colleges and universities using self-evaluation for tenure, promotion, or retention decisions rely on faculty activity sheets ("brag sheets"). The problem is that the data on these activity sheets are vague and self-serving. They show what professors did rather than how well they think they did it. They are self-reports rather than self-evaluations. They lack credentials for personnel decisions.

What can a professor in a self-evaluation contribute that will benefit a multisource evaluation system? In specific terms, a teacher's self-evaluation needs to address his or her objectives, activities, accomplishments, and failures during the year. The self-evaluation form must be structured to uncover teaching specifics. A standardized format for the information is mandatory. Illustrative material and hard evidence of accomplishment are needed. Clear, simple, factual, candid self-evaluations can assist the task of personnel review committees and administrators to come up with fair judgments of teaching performance.

Wergin (1992) suggests that faculty can present evidence that reflects:

1) Clarity and coherence of their teaching philosophy

2) Course objectives

3) Course syllabi and teaching strategies

4) Testing and evaluation procedures

5) Approaches to evaluating the course

6) Adaptations in their teaching as a result of assessment

Braskamp and Ory (1994) offer additional types of evidence that can be collected to describe and judge teaching:

1) What students learned from the course

2) Evidence that reflects the scholarship of teaching, such as command of the subject matter, accuracy, and relevance of material taught

3) Fairness of exams and grading

4) Efforts to improve performance, such as workshop attendance and self-reports of lessons learned

5) Teaching honors and awards received

When all the data on the standardized form are carefully examined and judiciously interpreted, self-evaluation can be a welcome addition to the evaluation process. It offers a basis for colleague, promotion committee, and administrator judgment. But self-evaluation should never be used as the sole basis for tenure, promotion, retention, or salary decisions.

SELF-EVALUATION FOR IMPROVING PERFORMANCE

At many colleges and universities, self-evaluation is found to be more useful to improve teaching than to aid personnel decisions. The reason may be that asking the instructor for a searching self-reflection, with no fear of retribution regardless of revelation, opens the instructor to more self-recognition and provides a fresh basis for the improvement of teaching skills. Self-evaluation thus has the potential for a positive effect on teaching as the instructor develops self-recognition and is thereby enabled to respond more effectively to students and others.

Despite this obvious benefit, however, self-evaluation by itself holds limited promise to teaching improvement. Some teachers simply do not know how to evaluate their performance. Others can identify strengths and weaknesses but are at a loss at how to proceed from there. And still others are taken in by illusions of themselves as superb teachers.

How can self-evaluation be harnessed to improve teaching performance? How can students, faculty colleagues, instructional improvement specialists, and others offer the kind of constructive help that teachers can embrace and that can hone teaching skills?

In general, the approach is by videotape recording of teaching behaviors in the classroom, a friendly discussion on teaching with faculty colleagues or instructional improvement specialists, and a sympathetic comparison and discussion of student and self-rating.

Videotape Recording

As teachers watch their taped classroom performance, they tend to become more aware of their teaching strengths and weaknesses. Most people have selective memories, and teachers are no exceptions. They tend to recall classroom highlights. Watching a videotape replay can bring out important but forgotten details and bring teaching strengths and weaknesses into sharper focus.

Some teachers are able to watch a videotape and recognize immediately how to improve their teaching. But most teachers need faculty colleagues or instructional improvement specialists to help analyze their teaching and to suggest modifications.

Seldin (1998) reports that teachers who view videotapes of their classes as part of a group failed to catch their strengths and weaknesses unless the replay was stopped at selected points and the teachers' attentions were directed to specific teaching behaviors. He also found that analyzing a videotape seemed capable of inducing change only when teachers could compare their performance with a "good teaching" model. This suggests that guide sheets or checklists may be of considerable help to instructors in identifying and assessing aspects of their classroom instruction.

By using two cameras, some institutions simultaneously record both the teaching and the student reaction. Then, using a split screen, tape excerpts of teacher and students are shown and discussed with faculty colleagues or instructional improvement specialists.

One caution: Because they are inherently self-confrontational, videotape replays also have the potential for harm. Teachers who submit to videotaping over their objections or those who have teaching limitations beyond remedy may be adversely affected.

Discussions about Teaching Effectiveness

Some teaching-improvement specialists are convinced that the process of strengthening teaching is dependent not only on cognitive knowledge and skills but also on the personal makeup of the teacher. To change personal makeup, and thereby improve teaching, the teacher must be made to confront cherished (and unchallenged) assumptions, values, and attitudes. In the process of clarifying an instructor's teaching attitude, for example, improved performance may result.

The trouble is, this evolution of teaching attitude is not always readily achievable. Many teachers are reluctant to discuss their pedagogical methods with others. They avoid seeking peer advice in the handling of some teaching problems. Their insecurity easily overwhelms their desire for problem resolution.

There are several reasons for such reticence:

1) Teachers tend to see themselves as part of a special discipline rather than in the teaching profession.

2) Since most teachers enter the teaching profession without the benefit of formal training, they tend to shrink from discussing its rationale.

3) Most teachers do not really understand and, therefore, do not support team-teaching in higher education.

4) The hallowed tradition of classroom autonomy leaves scant room for teaching discussion.

One method of meeting these problems is the in-depth interview in which the teacher is asked probing questions about his or her teaching. It routinely runs one to three hours and is conducted by a trained faculty member or instructional improvement specialist.

Typically, the interview includes such questions as:

- Where did you do your graduate work?

- How did you decide to become a teacher?

- What do you enjoy most about teaching? Least?

- How effective are you as a teacher?

- If you were not a teacher, what would you like to be?

- What is the one criticism that you are most fearful of receiving from a student? From a colleague?

- If this were your last term teaching, would you do anything different? Is so, what?

- What is your greatest strength as a teacher? Weakness?

- What do you consider your greatest accomplishment as a teacher in the last three years? Your greatest failure?

- What is the most important thing a student can learn from you?

At times, instead of a face-to-face interview, a small group of teachers is assembled and asked to reflect on each question and conduct a discussion about each answer. The value of group discussion is the dilution of personal misgivings about revealing innermost thoughts and concerns about teaching. Each participant learns that his or her colleagues share the same doubts and qualms. By sharing, each emerges from the discussion more aware, more knowledgeable, and more self-confident as a teacher.

Student Ratings and Self-Ratings

There is value in having the teacher complete the same evaluation form as his or her students. In this approach, the evaluation form is given first to the students to complete, then to the teacher. Then the teacher is asked to redo the evaluation form with the ratings he or she anticipates will be given by the students.

Thus, the ground is prepared for the teacher's self-evaluation, the evaluations by the students, and the accuracy of the teacher's perceptions about how the students feel about his or her teaching. A careful and honest analysis of the triad can be fruitful to the teacher desiring to improve (Aleamoni, 1987; Seldin, 1998). A jarring discrepancy in the three ratings should signal the need for close scrutiny. Confronted by such discrepancy, the instructor may find it helpful to spend part of a class period in open discussion with the students.

Will a teacher's performance improve with the realization that the students' view of his or her teaching is dimmer than that of the instructor? For most teachers, the answer is yes, especially if the teacher's self-rating is far apart—whether favorable or unfavorable—from the students' ratings.

GUIDING QUESTIONS FOR SELF-EVALUATION

Experience suggests the wisdom of allowing the teacher who is engaged in a searching and reflective self-evaluation to write his or her own answers to direct, open-ended, written questions. This format gives the instructor the opportunity to explain in detail the objectives, strategies, and circumstances of his or her classroom performance.

Guiding questions are needed both to encourage the modest teacher to state accomplishments and to discourage the pretentious teacher from inflating them. The following examples may help.

Discipline and Classroom Approach

- What is your greatest asset as a teacher? Your greatest shortcoming?

- Within your discipline, which area do you regard as your strongest? Your weakest?

- Which teaching approach works best for your discipline? Why?

- Do you change methods to meet new classroom situations? Can you give an example of this?

- What is your primary goal with respect to students?

Instructor-Student Rapport

- How would you describe the feelings between you and your students?

- How would you describe the atmosphere in your classroom? Are you satisfied with it?

- How do you encourage students to seek your help when necessary?

- Do your students consider you sarcastic?

- What kinds of student do you most enjoy teaching? What kind of student bothers you?

Knowledge of Discipline

- How would you judge your content mastery in the courses you teach?

- In what ways have you tried to stay current in your field? What could you do to broaden and deepen your knowledge of the discipline?

- If you were to teach another subject, what would it be?

Course Organization and Planning

- How effectively do you use class time?

- When did you last revise your approach to a particular course? Why? Can you give a recent example?

- What is the one thing you most want your students to learn? Why is that so important to you?

Questions about Teaching

- What is the best thing that could happen to you in a class? Worst?

- How do you feel about having some of your colleagues visit your classes?

- What is the one thing you would most like to change about your teaching? What have you done about changing it?

- What do you like most about teaching? Least?

- What kind of activities take place in your classroom? Why?

- How would you describe your attitude toward teaching? Has it changed in recent years? In what ways?

- What would you most like your students to remember about you as a teacher ten years from now? Why?

A checklist of questions for instructors preparing for a new semester was developed by Cleary (n.d.). The following items are excerpted from that checklist.

- What is the value of the course and my way of teaching it?

- How heavy a workload can I reasonably impose?

- Should I encourage group or collaborative effort on assignments?

- Where do I draw the line between acceptable absenteeism and abuse?

- Would it help to weave more contemporary or real-world material into the course?

- Have I relied for too many years on the same dogeared notes or tired, dated textbook?

- How available will I be—should I be—outside of class?

- How promptly do I grade and return assignments?

- What have I learned about myself or the course that needs changing this year?

USING A SELF-EVALUATION INSTRUMENT

Self-evaluation has two quite different purposes. And each purpose is best served by a specially tailored evaluation instrument. If the purpose of self-evaluation is for administrative decisions, such as promotion, tenure, salary, and retention, the form should contain general and summary items and be judgmental in character. For example, several questions should be devoted to the comparative effectiveness of the teacher (see forms in Chapter 12).

But if the purpose of self-evaluation is for teaching improvement, the form should include diagnostic questions. Unfortunately, too many colleges and universities use the same self-evaluation form as a blanket to cover both purposes. The result is that the form serves neither purpose well.

The standardized forms should produce answers to questions such as:

1) Is the teacher's self-evaluation consistent with information obtained from other sources?

2) Does the self-evaluation reflect similar strengths and weaknesses that turn up in other assessment forms?

3) Does the self-evaluation offer adequate explanation of contradictory information obtained elsewhere?

At many institutions, the annual report is the most common type of self-evaluation. Faculty members are required to describe their teaching, scholarship, and service activities each year. Typically, the information is used by academic administrators to help allocate merit pay or determine faculty salary increases. (See resource section in Chapter 12 for a typical annual activity list for the teaching component of a faculty member's report.)

MODELS OF SELF-EVALUATION

Those who do not learn from their mistakes are doomed to repeat them, the philosopher Santayana warns. Similarly, colleges and universities which have decided to embark on a program of assessing teaching that includes self-evaluation (or further develop an existing one) can avoid some mistakes by learning from the experience of others.

Although self-evaluation is a recognized component of effective teaching, the procedures employed and the results achieved are often flawed. Among the reasons: questions inappropriate to the purpose (summative or formative); self-evaluation imposed by the chair or dean triggering high anxiety which contaminates the data; self-evaluation conducted as a one-time only activity; lack of uniform self-evaluation format; and resultant data neither objective nor comprehensive.

Following are two evidence-based successful models which rely on a core of self-reflection and self-evaluation. Care must be taken, of course, to adapt the models to local needs.

Faculty Growth Contracts

Self-evaluation plays a key role in a faculty growth contract. The contract is prepared by the faculty member in writing and spells out certain items in specific terms:

1) The teacher's academic goals for the year

2) The plan to achieve each goal

3) The budget required to achieve the goals

Thus, the faculty growth contract offers a systematic approach to charting the direction of professional growth and self-assessing the year's performance.

Establishing performance goals is the most critical aspect of the growth contract. Generalities are to be avoided. It is particularly important to state explicitly the timing and scheduling, support, and reward payoffs, feedback systems, and future development procedures. In addition, the list of goals should be accompanied by a specific yardstick for measuring their achievement.

For example, the goal "to be a good teacher" is too vague to suggest appropriate methods of evaluation. An improvement would be "to obtain from students and faculty colleagues, opinions on the effectiveness of my teaching in the business and society course."

The latter statement is specific enough to suggest means of

assessing accomplishment. Such assessment might read, for example, "All students in my business and society course will be asked to complete the McKeachie student evaluation form on teaching effectiveness at the conclusion of the spring and fall 1999 semesters. In addition, the management department chairperson will be asked to observe two sessions of my business and society class. Using the university classroom visitation appraisal form, the chair will evaluate my teaching performance and will develop a narrative description based on the visit. We will then discuss the chair's opinions as well as student ratings of my teaching. After that, I will prepare a written statement detailing areas in need of improvement and the measures needed to correct teaching weaknesses."

Agreed upon goals must be challenging, significant, and attainable within the specified time period. The importance of realistic goals cannot be overstated. Goals beyond the realistic reach of a faculty member will serve only as a demotivating influence. Excessively modest goals will inevitably fall short of contributing to faculty growth.

Should fresh circumstances force a renegotiation of goals, they should be rewritten with the same diligent attention to specifics as the original set of objectives.

Since it is individually tailored, the growth contract tends to turn the teacher inward to reflect on his or her strong and weak points as a teacher, and often suggests further improvement steps for the next academic year. At the same time, the contract produces at year's end tangible evidence on the degree of achievement and failure.

The contract rests on the double assumption that instructors know their shortcomings and are also intent on overcoming them. To write the contracts, the instructor first has to identify his or her strengths and weaknesses.

Then comes a detailed list of institutional and community responsibilities as well as long-range personal and professional goals. Last is an assessment of current responsibilities and desired changes during the growth contract (Seldin, 1976; Wergin, 1992; Braskamp & Ory, 1994).

Depending on the size of the academic unit, each faculty member works closely with the dean or department chair in the development of a personally tailored set of goals for professional growth. As each instructor grows, so does the entire teaching staff.

Teaching Portfolios

What is a teaching portfolio? It is a factual description of a professor's teaching strengths and accomplishments. It includes documents and materials which collectively suggest the scope and quality of a professor's teaching performance.

Why would very busy faculty members want to prepare a portfolio? They might do so in order to gather and present hard evidence about their teaching effectiveness to tenure and promotion personnel committees. Or they might do so in order to provide the needed structure for systematic self-assessment—including reflection, appraisal, and analysis—about areas of their teaching needing improvement (Seldin, 1997).

Braskamp and Ory (1994) describe two key characteristics of a portfolio:

First, faculty organize it around principles: It is more than random information . . . thrown into a box. For example, faculty can use career development as an integrative theme. Second, the work included . . . represents best work. Best work does not necessarily mean the most highly rated (such as high student ratings . . .) but the most useful work in terms of self-learning, career advancement, and responsiveness to the institution's collective goals. In sum, (portfolios) are not brag sheets but thoughtful and reasoned self-assessments.

An important point: The portfolio is not an exhaustive compilation of all of the documents and materials that bear on teaching performance. Instead, it presents comprehensive but selected information on teaching activities and solid evidence of their effectiveness.

Being selective does not mean constructing a biased picture of one's teaching but rather providing a fair and accurate representation of it. Even an occasional flop is worthy material for a portfolio if it reveals a process of genuine adjustment and growth.

Because the portfolio is a highly personalized product, no two are exactly alike. Both the content and organization differ widely from one faculty member to another. The items chosen depend on the teaching style of the professor, the purpose for which the portfolio is prepared, the discipline, and any content requirements of a professor's department or institution.

Even though portfolios differ considerably from each other, there are certain items which seem to appear consistently. A review of more than 400 portfolios has led Seldin (1998) to conclude that the following items are often selected for inclusion:

1) Student evaluation data

2) Statement of current teaching responsibilities

3) Reflective statement by the faculty member discussing his or her teaching objectives, strategies, and methodologies

4) Syllabi for all courses taught

5) Participation in seminars and workshops intended to improve teaching

6) Teaching goals

How time consuming is the preparation of a portfolio? Most teachers can complete their portfolio to second draft stage in 12 to 15 hours spread over several days. And a large part of that time is spent in thinking, planning, and gathering the documentation for the appendices. They already have much of the material on hand, such as departmental annual reports, syllabi, student ratings, or letters of invitation or thanks. These items comprise the basics of the portfolio. (See Chapter 12.)

How much information is needed to represent a faculty member's teaching performance fairly and completely? Experience suggests that a selective document of eight to ten pages plus supporting appendix material is sufficient for the vast majority of professors.

The appendices must be of manageable size if they are to be read. Typically, the appendices and the narrative section of the portfolio are housed in a single three-ring binder.

Braskamp and Ory (1994) say that the process of developing a teaching portfolio is as important as its content. During the process of deciding how to most effectively document their teaching, instructors are forced to review their strengths and weaknesses and rethink their philosophy of teaching and their plans for the future.

Experience suggests that preparing a portfolio can help professors unearth new discoveries about themselves as teachers. The following topics may assist in the process of self-reflection: What new strategies have you tried in the last year? What did you learn from them? What do your syllabi say about your teaching style? Describe a teaching success in the past year. Why did it work? Describe a teaching flop. Why did it not work (Rehnke, 1994)?

If the portfolio is ultimately to be embraced, a climate of acceptance must first be created. The following guidelines should be helpful:

1) Start small

2) Field-test the portfolio at the institution

3) Find faculty volunteers but don't force anyone to participate

4) Encourage some high visibility professors to take part

5) Include faculty who are new to teaching and others who are new to the institution

6) Use the carrot, not the stick, approach

7) Keep everyone informed every step of the way about what is going on (Seldin, 1996)

SUMMARY

Faculty are a particularly good source for providing evidence about their own teaching. Unfortunately, many of the colleges and universities which use self-evaluation rely on vague and self-serving faculty activity sheets. Far more credibility and trustworthiness is warranted by a system of self-evaluation that uncovers specific aspects of teaching, such as instructional responsibilities; reflective statements about teaching goals, strategies, and objectives; representative instructional materials; recent student and peer evaluations; and descriptions of steps taken to improve one's teaching. Such thoroughly documented self-reflection is highly recommended for both individual and institutional purposes.

REFERENCES

Aleamoni, L. M. (1987). *Techniques for evaluating and improving instruction.* New Directions for Teaching and Learning, No. 31. San Francisco, CA: Jossey-Bass.

American Association of University Professors. (1974). Committee C. Statement on teaching evaluation. *AAUP Bulletin, 60* (2), 166-170.

Arreola, R. A. (1995) *Developing a comprehensive faculty evaluation system: A handbook for college faculty and administrators on designing and operating a comprehensive faculty evaluation system.* Bolton, MA: Anker.

Barber, L. W. (1990) Self-assessment. In J. Millman & L. Darling-Hammond (Eds.), *The new handbook of teacher evaluation.* Newbury Park, CA: Sage.

Braskamp, L. A., & Ory, J. C. (1994). *Assessing faculty work: Enhancing individual and institutional performance.* San Francisco, CA: Jossey-Bass.

Carnegie Foundation for the Advancement of Teaching (1994). *National survey on the reexamination of faculty roles and rewards.* Princeton, NJ: Carnegie Foundation for the Advancement of Teaching.

Centra, J. A. (1973). Self-ratings of college teachers: A comparison with student ratings. *Journal of Educational Measurement, 10* (4), 287-295.

Centra, J. A. (1993). *Reflective faculty evaluation: Enhancing teaching and determining faculty effectiveness.* San Francisco, CA: Jossey-Bass.

Cleary, T. (n.d). *Getting ready: A checklist of questions for the teacher.* Victoria, Canada: University of Victoria, Learning & Teaching Centre.

Donald, F. (1997). Private discussion.

Doyle, K. O., & Crichton, L. I. (1978). Student, peer, and self-evaluation of college instruction. *Journal of Educational Psychology, 70,* 815-826.

Doyle, K. O., & Webber, P. L. (1978). *Self-ratings of college instruction.* Minneapolis, MN: University of Minnesota, Measurement Services Center.

Feldman, K. A. (1989). Instructional effectiveness of college teachers as judged by themselves, current and former students, colleagues, administrators, and external (neutral) observers. *Research in Higher Education, 30* (2), 137-194.

Marsh, H. W., Overall, J. U., & Kesler, S. P. (1979). The validity of students' evaluations of instructional effectiveness: A comparison of faculty self-evaluations and evaluations by their students. *Journal of Educational Psychology, 71,* 149-160.

Rehnke, M. A. (1994, October). Teaching and learning. *The Independent.* Washington, DC: Council of Independent Colleges.

Seldin, P. (1976). *Faculty growth contracts.* University of London Institute of Education.

Seldin, P. (1980). *Successful faculty evaluation programs.* Crugers, NY: Coventry Press.

Seldin, P. (1984). *Changing practices in faculty evaluation.* San Francisco, CA: Jossey-Bass.

Seldin, P. (1996, June) *The teaching portfolio.* Paper presented for the American Council on Education, Department Chairs Seminar, Washington, DC.

Seldin, P. (1997). *The teaching portfolios: A practical guide to improved performance and promotion/tenure decisions* (2nd ed.). Bolton, MA: Anker.

Seldin, P. (1998, February). *The teaching portfolio.* Paper presented for the American Council on Education, Department Chairs Seminar, San Diego, CA.

Sorey, K. E. (1968). A study of the distinguishing characteristics of college faculty who are superior in regard to the teaching function. *Dissertation Abstracts, 28* (12-A), 4916.

Wergin, J. E. (1992, September). *Developing and using performance criteria.* Paper presented at the Virginia Commonwealth University conference on faculty rewards.

CHAPTER 6

POST-TENURE REVIEW:
EVALUATING TEACHING

Joseph C. Morreale

There has been much discussion in the literature about maintaining faculty vitality in their later careers. The groundbreaking work of Corcoran and Clark (1985) on faculty vitality has used such words as self-renewal, sense of curiosity, striving to achieve, and continuous improvement to describe faculty vitality. Fundamentally, the vital faculty at an institution are those who demonstrate sustained productivity in their teaching, research, and professional service.

Institutional vitality is equally important. Corcoran and Clark (1985, pp. 62-63) define it as "the creation of an organizational climate or environment that combines individuals and groups in their fulfillment of the institution's mission and supports individuals in their own creative, productive, and energized work life." This should lead to a process of continuous faculty development.

In more recent work, Bland and Bergquist (1997) further link faculty vitality with institutional culture and reward systems. Institutions need to examine their organizational culture, values, and procedures to create a climate that will foster high productivity for senior faculty. In general, several conditions within the academic culture subtly, but effectively, discourage senior faculty from being productive: 1) benign neglect, 2) lack of professional development, and 3) nonrecognition of the stages of productivity. Once tenured, senior faculty are usually left to seek their own professional quality and performance level. Even where annual reviews are present in the evaluation of senior faculty, these are often perfunctory and related to small variations in annual increases. The result is that there is little incentive for senior faculty to continue to perform at high levels. Moreover, if they do seek to gain professional recognition, the reward structure is such that research is the primary mechanism and teaching is considered secondary.

Higher educational institutions spend only a small fraction of their total resources on faculty development. Usually this is a highly competitive process, and the funds are allocated mostly for research and professional association activities. Moreover, the funding often is designed to help junior faculty enhance their careers as they approach tenure. Often, there is little thought to continue and enhance senior faculty development through such prized mechanisms as release time or funding.

There is also a general nonrecognition of the stages of a faculty member's career. Once faculty gain tenure, they have an ability to take a more long-term look at their career and professional interests. This often means more extensive research projects that take longer to develop; text writing gained from a general understanding of their fields; increased emphasis on professional and community service; or, and what we are most interested in here, an increased emphasis on teaching.

BOYER'S FOUR CRITERIA OF SCHOLARSHIP: THE ROLE OF TEACHING

When considering the general role of the faculty member in an institution and, more specifically, the role of teaching, Boyer's four concepts of scholarship (Boyer, 1990) must be considered:

1) Scholarship of discovery: the pursuit of new knowledge in a discipline

2) Scholarship of integration: making connections within and between disciplines

3) Scholarship of application: applying knowledge to contemporary problems

4) Scholarship of teaching: presenting knowledge to students in order to stimulate their understanding and interest in the pursuit of knowledge.

I raise these four categories because teaching is cited as an important and integral part of the academic pursuit and therefore is central to the work of a faculty member.

The American Association for Higher Education's Project on Teaching Initiatives is dedicated to the idea of creating a culture of teaching and learning. In the introduction of its published work, Hutchings (1996) has amplified Boyer's ideas of teaching as scholarship with three additional corollaries:

1) The need to see teaching as a "process of ongoing inquiry and reflection." It is not sufficient to stand and deliver; one must also step back and examine the art of teaching.

2) The need for collegial exchange and publicness. Shulman (1993) has been the foremost advocate of this view of teaching. He contends that assistance and input from colleagues is critical in the development and improvement of teaching.

3) The need for faculty to take professional responsibility for the quality of their work as teachers. In this context, faculty must play a central role in the evaluation of their colleagues' performance and in ensuring and improving its quality. This takes the form of peer review.

The problem on college campuses is the lack of a campus culture in which the quality and improvement of teaching are subjects of ongoing collective faculty attention and responsibility.

It is clear that the degree of emphasis on teaching in faculty work is a function of the mission of the institution. Three general classifications can be made. First are research universities whose main emphasis is on research activities. The emphasis here is typically on the scholarship of discovery and of integration.

A second classification is teaching institutions, which tend to fall into two categories: liberal arts colleges and community colleges. The emphasis here typically is on the scholarship of teaching. Private liberal arts colleges may also stress the scholarship of discovery in order to enhance their reputations and also to develop a professionally oriented faculty, while community colleges may place more emphasis on the scholarship of application.

The third classification is the comprehensive university. In many ways, I find these institutions to be the most complex and most difficult to categorize. The best way to portray them is that they stress teaching, research, and service in some mixture related to their mission. This means that some element of all four types of scholarship is evident and rewarded and that faculty can have varied activities. Oftentimes the scholarship of teaching is placed on an equal par with other modes of scholarship.

Teaching is viewed as an important endeavor at every academic institution, but its weight varies depending on the mission of the institution. At the same time, most faculty do some teaching. Therefore, teaching must be evaluated in some comprehensive and clearly defined manner.

As faculty age and more gain tenure, they become a critical resource for every academic institution. The granting of tenure involves not just the institution's recognition of a long-term commitment to the individual faculty member, but that faculty member's agreement about his or her continued performance as an active member of the faculty.

The need to assess senior faculty centers then on this responsibility to the institution in its granting of a permanent bond between individual and institution. Since the tenured faculty are a fixed and critical resource to the institution (and often the majority of members of the faculty), continued faculty development in terms of institutional and individual needs is essential. Increasingly, the institutional response to this need is the creation of some form of post-tenure review policy.

MODELS OF POST-TENURE REVIEW

There are three prevalent models of post-tenure review: annual review, comprehensive review (periodic/consequential), and triggered review (episodic/consequential). Each is discussed briefly.

Option 1: Annual Review

Annual reviews are common and generally focus on short-term performance (usually to assess one year's performance and distribute merit monies accordingly). In some settings, these reviews are perfunctory at best. In other settings, such reviews simply are not effective in providing direct feedback about long-term career development and overall performance. More often than not, annual reviews are administrative exercises and do not involve significant peer input. Additionally, annual reviews cannot assess achievements requiring a longer period of time, as is frequently the case with multiyear projects, research studies, and many scholarly works.

Post-tenure review policy development usually begins with a careful analysis of the benefits and limitations of existing institutional practices for faculty evaluation and development. At the University of Pittsburgh (1995), analysis led to proposals for modifying and strengthening the longstanding annual performance review process rather than developing a separate periodic post-tenure review process. At the University of Wisconsin, Madison (UWM) (1994), analysis resulted in a separate periodic post-tenure review.

The report of UWM's Planning Committee on Tenured Faculty Review and Development (1994, p. 7) points out that while no system of review is perfect, "the system of annual merit review links an extensive process of yearly evaluation with recommendations on salary, which are frequently market rather than merit driven. The strains in such a system become particularly apparent when compensation is inadequate to meet competition from other educational institutions and other parts of the economy."

Option 2: Comprehensive Review (Periodic/Consequential)

This option involves a periodic comprehensive review of all tenured faculty members, using a prescribed cycle (usually five years). A peer committee, administrators, or both conduct the review. Other characteristics of this approach include the following:

- Results take the form of a performance assessment accompanied by a recommended professional growth and improvement plan.

- Satisfactory performance is used as the baseline.

- The improvement plan establishes goals and timelines and takes into consideration the mission and priorities of the department; a professional development plan is encouraged.

- Institutional support is provided, where available and when appropriate.

- Progress is assessed. If progress is unsatisfactory, another review is mandated in one to two years, and longer-term administrative sanctions may occur.

- An appeals process is usually outlined.

An example of this option is the process at the University of Oregon (1985). A five-year review by an elected peer committee helps identify faculty members who merit special recognition as well as those who need special assistance. Rewards can include a merit increase, reallocation of departmental resources to fund additional research interests or opportunities for curriculum development, additional research or clerical support, or university recognition for achievement. Likewise, actions to improve performance within the university's career support program include consultation with colleagues on problem areas, reallocation of departmental assignments to facilitate improvement in teaching or research, and access to an instructional improvement center or personal counseling. A second post-tenure review follows these formative steps. The policy suggests that if the faculty member is unwilling or unable to perform at acceptable levels, he or she be counseled about alternate career plans or early-retirement options.

Option 3: Triggered Review (Episodic/Consequential)

This comprehensive review of selected tenured faculty members usually is triggered by unsatisfactory performance as identified through another review. Potential consequences are almost always spelled out. Several actions characterize this kind of post-tenure review:

- A peer committee or the administration conducts the review.

- Satisfactory performance is used as the baseline.

- An improvement plan is developed with goals, timelines, expected outcomes, and monitoring.

- Institutional support is provided, where available and as appropriate.

- Progress is assessed.

- If progress is unsatisfactory, sanctions occur.

- An appeals process is outlined.

Such triggered post-tenure evaluations are often deemed more acceptable because they are seen as less time-consuming, with attention focused only on substandard performers. Two institutions in Virginia use these evaluations. At Old Dominion University (1995-97), two consecutive unsatisfactory annual reviews trigger post-tenure review. Longwood College (1995) uses as its trigger either consecutive less-than-satisfactory annual reviews or three less-than-satisfactory annual reviews during a five-year period. The policy at Longwood directs chairs to recommend termination if after two years the faculty member does not make reasonable progress, as judged by the dean, chair, and tenure committee.

How do these models of post-tenure review impact on the evaluation of teaching?

EVALUATING TEACHING IN POST-TENURE REVIEW

Evaluating teaching under post-tenure review is different than evaluating teaching on an annual basis. The purpose of annual reviews is summative in nature. They are designed to determine if the faculty member met his or her teaching obligations for that past year and to measure the effectiveness of teaching. Oftentimes, the evidence is student evaluations and classroom visits by colleagues or the chair of the department. A short-term (one year) view of the faculty member's teaching performance is taken, and rarely is a discussion of teaching philosophy or pedagogy required.

But in post-tenure review, the evaluation is of the performance of a faculty member over a number of years (three to seven). The purpose of the review is primarily developmental, with many more measurements taken of a faculty member's performance. The institution relies on a range of indicators to evaluate the complex activity of teaching and how teaching affects learning.

As McAhren of Washington and Lee University in Virginia (in Galgano, 1990, p. 1) states, "Fostering continued development of teaching skills in post-tenure review of faculty possesses different problems." Most senior faculty are relatively comfortable with their pedagogy and style of teaching after they reach tenure. After all, they have "passed muster" using these teaching techniques and therefore have been confirmed as quality teachers. Yet, they must be both held accountable and encouraged to continue to develop their art of teaching. Placing emphasis on teaching in a comprehensive five-year review is one way to maintain a focus on the importance of this activity in their careers.

At the University of Oregon (1993-94, p.1), a teaching workshop was formed to

"... set forth a policy structure that assists in the systematic and equitable evaluation of teaching and in the encouragement and reward of good teaching at the university. ..." There was great emphasis placed on the systematic, ongoing support, encouragement, and evaluation of teaching after tenure.

The guidelines for tenured faculty assert that:

• Faculty members should continue to update their teaching vitae and teaching portfolios on a yearly basis (see Chapter 9).

- Student evaluations should continue to be conducted routinely (see Chapter 2).

- Within the department, a review and discussion of teaching should be included as a routine component of faculty evaluation and review on a par with the review and discussion of research.

- Every six years (this being the normal period for other academic reviews), the updated record of teaching is submitted to the department for review.

- Any faculty member whose teaching is rated as unacceptable or who wishes to develop teaching abilities further, should establish with the department head new expectations and guidelines for evaluating and improving teaching. This might require further peer review or participation in teaching and improvement activities.

We recognize that post-tenure reviews vary considerably among departments in the seriousness with which they are conducted and taken.

Materials for Evaluation

In a comprehensive system of teaching evaluation for a formative purpose, a variety of materials are suggested. Usually, in a self-evaluation, the faculty member discusses his or her philosophy of teaching and reviews a variety of teaching methods and classes taught. Sometimes this evaluation occurs within the context of the department's course offerings. Typically the evaluation of the professor includes all syllabi for the past five years, classroom visits to at least one class, a statement of self-assessment of teaching, and a teaching portfolio. Moreover, the faculty member is sometimes asked to develop a plan for teaching indicating new pedagogies and new directions in teaching.

A quantitative judgment is made in some of the departments at the University of Hawaii, Manoa (1992). The adopted criteria for post-tenure review in the evaluation of teaching in the department of economics include these performance characteristics:

1) Maintenance of up-to-date knowledge of fields of instruction

2) Planning, organizing, and conducting assigned courses and seminars in a satisfactory fashion

3) Service as chair or member of advanced degree committees

4) Student advising, as assigned, on departmental matters

5) Assistance to students in their professional development outside the classroom

Each of the above areas is rated using a five-point scale.

Multiple Types of Teaching

Two recent examples of institutions applying broader views of the evaluation of teaching follow. This more extensive view of instruction considers different types of teaching modes and pedagogies.

The University of Wisconsin, Green Bay (1996) makes a distinction between classroom teaching and clinical teaching. Classroom teaching is to be evaluated using the following evidence: statement of goals and methods by the faculty member; summary of teaching activities (courses, credits, students, grade distribution); peer review; and student evaluations. Clinical teaching is evaluated like classroom teaching for classroom activities but, in addition, must also include a description of the areas of clinical expertise and activities, evidence of clinical training in professional degree training, postgraduate training, and postgraduate and continuing education courses for the practitioner.

Virginia's Old Dominion University (1995-97) adds three additional categories to those usually applied in the evaluation of teaching:

1) The number of student credit hours produced by the faculty member. The rationale is that the best teachers should be having a major impact on the teaching and educating of a large number of students.

2) Faculty members who teach noncredit courses, workshops, or colloquia in their areas of specialization should also have these evaluated.

3) Faculty members who are assigned to teach credit or noncredit courses, workshops, or colloquia using distance education technologies should have this activity included in their teaching evaluations.

At the same time, teaching performance cannot be viewed in isolation. One of the more subtle problems in promoting teaching effectiveness is creating a departmental climate that encourages and supports faculty development in teaching (see Chapter 10 and Chapter 11). With junior, nontenured faculty, advice from the chair and senior colleagues can often be along the lines of suggested readings of helpful guides on teaching, team teaching a course, or mentoring relationships where senior faculty work with junior faculty to improve their teaching.

At William Paterson College in New Jersey (Gruber, 1990), campus-wide programs focusing on pedagogy are used. Writing Across the Curriculum is perhaps the most visible, but there have been others, such as those on race and gender.

A recent emphasis in the evaluation of teaching is student learning. Some institutions place a great deal of importance on it. This requires a different set of evaluation tools. Some departments at SUNY, Geneseo (Bailey, 1990) participate in external standardized examinations, often sponsored by the Educational Testing Service. Others use the passing of professional standards exams in order to test the learning experiences of students in various programs.

SUMMARY

This examination of the evaluation of teaching in post-tenure review points up several characteristics of such an evaluation:

- It is different from annual review for merit.

- It is much more comprehensive, long-term, and developmental than a merit review.

- It must be consistent with the overall mission of the institution.

- It must be seen in the context of the faculty development plan.

- It uses many more measurements of performance.

- It focuses not just on the faculty member's performance but also on pedagogy, style, and innovation.

- It requires self-assessment by the faculty member.

- It allows for different evaluations for different types of teaching.

- It views the teaching by faculty members in the context of the departmental unit and climate.

- It can be made to emphasize student learning.

WHAT WORKS IN THE EVALUATION OF TEACHING IN POST-TENURE REVIEW?

What are the critical components necessary to be successful in developing a system of evaluating teaching in post-tenure review? I believe that there are nine guiding principles.

1) Setting the Standards in Teaching Performance

Setting the standards for performance in teaching is critical to the process of post-tenure review. These usually define the minimum level of performance. An example of such a standard is taken from the minimal standards for satisfactory faculty performance of the Pamplin College of Business at the Virginia Polytechnic Institute and State University (1995). For teaching, the expectations for faculty include the following:

Effective classroom instruction

- To provide effective instruction to students in the regularly scheduled classes they are assigned by the department head

- To meet all scheduled classes except for absences sanctioned by the department and/or university

- To provide all students with a course syllabus

- To deliver lectures and present material in a well-prepared, professional, and competent manner

Faculty availability

- To be available to meet with their students outside of regularly scheduled class times

Knowledge of discipline

- To remain knowledgeable in their discipline and field of teaching in order that their classroom instruction remains current and reflective of the latest knowledge and academic advancements in the field

Setting standards must take into account the institutional mission, campus norms and values, and departmental expectations as well as the faculty member's career expectations, competencies, and prior levels of achievement.

Sometimes the standards set both the acceptable and superior levels of performance. Standards set to those who are "best in class" help determine superior performance. Comparison of standards to comparable institutions or to those institutions that a particular college or university aspires to be like sets a baseline. Benchmarking becomes an important activity of measuring teaching performance. This also must be viewed within the context of the individual faculty member within a department. Determining criteria and measuring the performance of the faculty member at the onset of a review sets a baseline for determining future improvement.

Criteria and evidence must reflect both institutional and individual goals. And, in most cases, they will be established by faculty peers and administrators (chairs and deans) working together.

2) The Development Plan

In post-tenure review, faculty are required to construct a longer-term professional development plan. Within the plan, they must respond to four important questions:

1) How much emphasis will teaching be given in the development plan?

2) What goals will be achieved in teaching over the next three to five years?

3) Will the faculty member require resources to improve his or her teaching?

4) How will teaching relate to the other activities of the development plan?

3) Determining the Purpose of Teaching

Teaching is no longer viewed as the presentation of knowledge. We have moved on to a concept of teaching as learning. Excellent teachers learn what it takes to make students understand a concept, apply it, and integrate it. What occurs in a faculty development plan involving post-tenure review is the determination of the faculty member's scholarship relative to his or her teaching.

Instructional methods are embedded in the content of the discipline. It is central to the evaluation of teaching to have an understanding of the faculty member's depth of knowledge in a field and his or her ability to impart that knowledge to students. Transmitting knowledge is a necessary but not sufficient condition because the faculty member needs to transform and extend knowledge. The critical purpose of teaching then becomes student learning.

4) Generating Evidence and Providing Feedback

Evidence collected for teaching must be from multiple sources and agreed upon by all of the faculty in a department. The evidence must also be related to work activities involved in teaching. Focusing attention on work activities forces conversation on what "counts" and why. There are two main concerns about this evidence in post-tenure review. One is that the evidence be collected every semester so that a continuous measurement process can be established and progress in improvement can be seen. And two, to make certain that feedback to the faculty member is provided each semester to help improve his or her development. If no progress takes place, additional action and resources must be available to help the faculty member improve.

The trustworthiness of the evidence collected is a critical issue also. Since this evidence will be collected to assess the faculty member's development over a continuous period of time, it must be trustworthy. In assessment terms, this means that it must be reliable, valid, fair, and must achieve the intended consequences.

5) Interpreting the Evidence

Interpreting evidence on teaching for post-tenure review purposes must be handled carefully and within the appropriate context on the part of peers and chairs. Faculty appear to be better at reviewing and rating written documentation. Braskamp and Ory (1994) report significant differences in the consistency of faculty members' abilities to evaluate research and written work than teaching style and observation. Faculty views of teaching evaluation data are uneven and may be influenced by "who as well as what is being evaluated" (p. 234).

Evaluation of faculty teaching effectiveness and performance is best achieved when the faculty member 1) has the opportunity to offer some self-reflection in the review, and 2) has the opportunity to discuss with colleagues the various evidence gathered to reflect his or her teaching performance.

6) Evaluation of the Collective Contribution of Faculty

A faculty member and his or her teaching performance should not be seen in isolation but rather in the context of an entire unit, often a department. This accomplishes at least three things:

1) It better integrates faculty interests and performance with institutional needs.

2) It encourages the evaluation of teaching to be more public and collegial rather than private and individualized.

3) It allows greater department and peer influence on each member of the unit.

In fact, post-tenure review of specific faculty members might be placed within the context of departmental or program review. This would allow each department or program to maximize the best talents of each of its members. Doing so requires that the faculty member see his or her contribution over the next five years in the context of the whole department. This is where the important elements of peer and chair review of the plan are essential. Peers have a direct stake in the progress of each of the department's members, and the chair must relate each member's ideas to the university mission and goals as well as to those of the department and college.

Embedded in the idea of a departmental review is flexible contracts. If a department is judged on the basis of achieving college or university standards in teaching, research, and service, then each faculty member's contribution can be modified to emphasize the area in which they are strongest. Moreover, once the decision has been set at the beginning of the year for a faculty workload vis-à-vis the department's needs, then the evaluations of the faculty member can be related to the relative emphasis previously determined. For example, if a faculty member is an outstanding teacher and is assigned greater teaching responsibilities, he or she is then evaluated accordingly at the end of that year. This can be further expanded to multiple years in faculty development plans. The critical factor here is to see each faculty member's contribution as part of the whole unit and equally valuable.

7) Rewards and Recognition

If quality teaching performance and continued development in teaching is emphasized, such efforts should be placed in high esteem and rewarded accordingly.

Most studies suggest that financial rewards for teaching excellence (e.g., merit raises) be supplemented with nonfinancial ones (e.g., released time) for course development or retraining. Ball State University in Indiana (Edmonds, 1990) established a broad-based committee to investigate the role of teaching at the university and to make recommendations on the improvement of teaching performance. Three recommendations were made to the provost:

1) Individual colleges and departments were urged to reexamine both the level of commitment to and procedures for recognizing excellent teaching.

2) The provost was urged to provide additional support for teaching excellence in both financial and nonmonetary awards.

3) Creation of a recommended institution-wide University Teaching Professorship Program was urged to recognize excellence in undergraduate teaching.

These recommendations led to the reexamination of the role of teaching in various colleges and schools; increased funding by the provost for travel to support faculty participation in conferences and workshops dealing specifically with pedagogical issues; and the implementation of the University Teaching Professorship Program.

8) The Need for Resources

Research and practice strongly suggest that post-tenure reviews of teaching should be tied to faculty development and necessary supporting resources. These resources often include funds for travel, research assistance, extended study, special projects, equipment, and released time. In teaching, improvements can come in style, pedagogy, and greater focus on student learning. In addition, with the increasing use of technology in the classroom and in teaching in general, funding for faculty adoption of and improvement in the use of technology in teaching becomes very important.

The resource issue has raised concerns in the minds of some college administrators about 1) what constitutes reasonable support for professional development when the onus is on the individual to improve, and 2) whether preference should be given to support development plans of poor performers if it means fewer development resources available for strong performers.

Several reports have highlighted the importance of this tie between institutional support for development and improvement plans. The lack of resources for funding faculty development is a commonly expressed problem with post-tenure review at comprehensive institutions. A University of Colorado survey (Wesson & Johnson, 1989) of 526 faculty who had undergone post-tenure review concluded that the overwhelming majority viewed the procedures as having little or no outcome because the resulting development plans lacked needed resources. As a result of this report, a central resource base was later made available for faculty development.

The level of institutional support given to help in the remediation and the development phase is best decided in the context of the overall university budget needs and in relationship to an overall strategic plan. Some institutions do separate development monies targeted for improvement from funds allocated to assist or reward long-term professional development. For most, though, a standard of reasonableness usually prevails in terms of whether the institution can abide both the content of the improvement plan and the financial resources required.

9) Consequences of Continuing Poor Performance

The most formidable question asked by many is what actions are institutions prepared to take when teaching remediation is judged to be unsuccessful or when willful neglect of duty is present? Historically, institutions have avoided dismissal-for-cause actions because of the financial cost to the institution and the emotional burden on those involved in the process. Instead, campuses opt for other less onerous approaches, including buyouts, reassignments, or early retirement transition options. Post-tenure review serves a good purpose insofar as it can create an environment that allows administrative sanctions to occur, even if they never are invoked because other less difficult negotiations are initiated that produce the same desired outcome.

A few private institutions (e.g., Colby-Sawyer College in New Hampshire and Ithaca College in New York) have expanded their dismissal-for-cause provisions to include teaching effectiveness as a permissible example of adequate cause (Trower, 1996). There is a noticeable trend in public institutions and systems to attempt to build sanctions into newly formulated post-tenure review programs. For example, the New Mexico legislature outlines these substantive consequences for unfavorable evaluations in teaching: "1) a two-year probation and reevaluation period; and 2) loss of tenure if, during the subsequent probation and reevaluation period, the faculty member fails to demonstrate improvement in the area of teaching." (State of New Mexico Senate Bill 1131, 1995).

An alternative approach is career counseling. At the University of California, Davis (1993), post-tenure review practices include encouraging faculty who are poor performers to pursue other career options. The department chair is encouraged to discuss with faculty members a change in title and/or duties more reflective of their individual strengths and interests; other career options that fit their strengths; or discussion of early retirement, if it is warranted.

CONCLUSION

This chapter has focused on methods used to sustain and encourage tenured faculty to maintain, develop, and improve quality teaching, including the following points:

- How the vitality of senior faculty is intertwined with the vitality of their institution and how they have a joint responsibility for the continued development of high quality teaching performance.

- The important role of teaching in faculty work, the scholarship of teaching as part of the four key criteria of scholarship put forth by Boyer, and the importance of expanding and enhancing the role of teaching as scholarship.

- The need to position the importance of teaching in the context of the mission of various types of academic institutions and within specific programs and departments.

Much of the discussion focused on post-tenure review models and the importance in them of the evaluation of teaching.

- Three such models were presented: annual review, comprehensive review, and triggered review.

- How the evaluation of teaching is different for tenured faculty than nontenured faculty, as well as methods of evaluation, measures of teaching performance, variations for different types of teaching, and placing teaching in the proper context of mission and culture.

- Critical components for a successful post-tenure review system of the evaluation of teaching including setting standards, creating professional development plans, integrating teaching and learning, generating evidence, providing feedback, interpreting evidence and review by peers, encouraging collective contribution, creating rewards and recognition, the need for resources, and the importance of consequences.

Maintaining excellence in an academic institution requires continuous development of its most critical resource: its permanent tenured faculty. This necessitates a constructive developmental program of post-tenure review. A central focus of this development is enhancing the relationship between faculty and students in teaching and learning and between the faculty member, his or her department, and the institution. Only in the continuous fostering of growth and development in the area of the scholarship of teaching will an institution sustain its vitality, maintain the interest of its diverse students, and assure the survival of both in an ever-changing world.

REFERENCES

Resources

Bailey, C. (1990). In M. J. Galgano (Ed.), *Council of Chairs Newsletter, 2* (1). Bloomington, IN: Organization of American Historians. (http://www.indiana.educ/oah/chairsnl/v2n1.htm).

Bland, C. J., & Bergquist, W. H. (1997). *The vitality of senior faculty members: Snow on the roof—fire in the furnace.* ASHE-ERIC Higher Education Report, 25 (7). Washington, DC: The George Washington University.

Boyer, E. L. (1990). *Scholarship reconsidered: Priorities of the professoriate.* Princeton, NJ: Carnegie Foundation for the Advancement of Teaching.

Braskamp, L. A., & Ory, J. (1994). *Assessing faculty work: Enhancing individual and institutional performance.* San Francisco, CA: Jossey-Bass.

Chan, S. S., & Burton, J. (1995). Faculty vitality in the comprehensive university: Changing context and concerns. *Research in Higher Education, 36* (2): 219-234.

Corcoran, M., & Clark, S. M. (1985). The stuck professor: Insights into an aspect of the faculty vitality issue. In C. Watson (Ed.), *The professoriate: Occupation in crisis.* Toronto, Canada: Ontario Institute for Studies on Education.

Edmonds, A. (1990). The evaluation and reward of teaching: Confessions of a department head who agreed to chair a blue-ribbon committee on evaluating teaching. In M. J. Galgano (Ed.), *Council of Chairs Newsletter, 2* (1). Bloomington, IN: Organization of American Historians. (http://www. indiana.educ/oah/chairsnl/v2n1.htm).

Galgano, M. J. (Ed.). (1990). Evaluating teaching. *Council of Chairs Newsletter, 2* (1). Bloomington, IN: Organization of American Historians. (http://www. indiana.educ/oah/chairsnl/v2n1.htm).

Glassick, C. E., et al. (1997). *Scholarship assessed: Evaluation of the professoriate.* San Francisco, CA: Jossey-Bass.

Gruber, C. (1990). Evaluating teaching at William Paterson College. In M. J. Galgano (Ed.), *Council of Chairs Newsletter, 2* (1). Bloomington, IN: Organization of American Historians. (http://www.indiana.educ/oah/chairsnl/v2n1.htm).

Hutchings, P. (1996). *Making teaching community property: A menu for peer collaboration and peer review.* Washington, DC: American Association for Higher Education.

Licata, C. M., & Morreale, J. C. (1997). *Post-tenure review: Practice, policies, precautions.* New Pathways Working Paper Series, No. 12. Washington, DC: American Association for Higher Education.

Shulman, L. S. (1993, November/December). Teaching as a community property: Putting an end to pedagogical solitude. *Change, 25* (6), 6-7.

Trower, C. A. (1996). *Tenure snapshots.* New Pathways Working Paper Series, No. 2. Washington, DC: American Association for Higher Education.

Wesson, M., & Johnson, S. (1989). *Study of post-tenure review at the University of Colorado.* Report to the Board of Regents. Boulder, CO: University of Colorado.

Institutional Policies Cited

Colby-Sawyer College. (1995, May & October). *Faculty tenure proposal committee report.* New London, NH: Colby-Sawyer College.

Ithaca College. (1993, August). *Faculty handbook,* Section 7.3: Evaluation of Faculty. Ithaca, NY: Ithaca College.

Longwood College. (1995, April). *Policy on post-tenure review.* Farmville, VA: Longwood College.

Old Dominion University. (1995-97). *Faculty handbook.* Section II: Policy and Procedures on Evaluation of Faculty and Post-Tenure Faculty Evaluation Policy: A Summary (1998). Norfolk, VA: Old Dominion University.

State of New Mexico. (1995, March 18). *Legislative Senate Bill 1131, Chapter 150: Requiring a post-tenure review process.*

University of California, Davis. (1993, August 19). Office of the Provost memo: *Implementing of five-year reviews.* Davis, CA: University of California.

University of Hawaii, Manoa. (1992). *Criteria for periodic faculty review, Department of Economics, April 29, 1992 and post-tenure review, Department of Special Education, 1992.* Manoa, HI: University of Hawaii.

University of Oregon. (1985 & 1993-94). Post-Tenure Review, Faculty Legislation, April 6, 1977, as amended April 10, 1985 and 1993-94. *Teaching work group report: Guidelines for evaluating and rewarding teaching at the University of Oregon.* Eugene, OR: University of Oregon.

University of Pittsburgh. (1995, September). *Faculty handbook,* Article III: General Policies of Appointment and Tenure. Pittsburgh, PA: University of Pittsburgh.

University of Wisconsin, Green Bay. (1996). *Faculty governance handbook.* 69-70. Green Bay, WI: University of Wisconsin.

University of Wisconsin, Madison. (1994). *Faculty policies and procedures,* 11-106. Policy on Review of Tenured Faculty (1994) and Report of the Planning Committee on Tenured Faculty Review and Development, February 1993. Madison, WI: University of Wisconsin.

Virginia Polytechnic Institute and State University. (1995, December). *Faculty handbook,* Section 2, 10.4; Post-Tenure Review. Blacksburg, VA: Virginia Polytechnic Institute and State University.

CHAPTER 7

EVALUATING TEACHING THROUGH ELECTRONIC CLASSROOM ASSESSMENT

Devorah A. Lieberman

A general principle of management says, "You cannot manage what you cannot measure." A function as important as teaching must be managed and thus measured well. Here, 'management' means both evaluating an instructor's teaching accurately and giving instructors useful feedback to help them improve their teaching (Pritchard, Watson, Kelly, & Paquin, 1998, xviii).

The evolution of instructor evaluation research has paralleled the movement in student learning assessment research. Both areas of study in higher education examine the importance of and differences between student learning assessment and instructor evaluation. Though the two are not mutually defined, "student learning assessment" has focused primarily on the measurement of student learning, whereas teacher evaluation has focused more on measurement of the quality of teaching (Knapper, 1995). Since we are interested in measuring both student learning and the quality of teaching, this chapter will identify tools that will address the intersection of both.

EVALUATION AND ASSESSMENT

Figure 7.1 (Box E & Box F) identifies the elements of teacher evaluation and addresses the different evaluation aspects that occur within any course. Nearly all courses begin with course objectives (Box A). These objectives guide the overall course and inform both the course design and course activities (Pregent, 1994). The student learning objectives (Box B) are those outcomes that are identified by the instructor (content, knowledge, or attitudes) that should be achieved by the students upon completion of the course. The teaching strategies (Box C) are those media or modes selected by the instructor to convey the information that is to be learned by the students. Examples of teaching strategies are traditional lecture, group activities, pair-shares, or distance learning.

Regardless of the teaching strategy, the instructor believes (based on assumptions) that the mode(s) of information delivery selected are those most likely to guide the students to the identified student learning outcomes. Rarely do instructors ask themselves why they chose a particular mode of teaching or information delivery or why they assume this strategy is the best route to achieving a particular student learning outcome.

Figure 7.1 depicts three tracks (Box D, Box E, and Box F) in terms of instructor evaluation and assessment of student learning. Box D depicts CATs or Techno-CATs, which are feedback tools that assess how much or how well students have learned. This feedback allows for midcourse correction or modification (Box D1). The second form of assessment of student learning in relation to teacher evaluation is formative and is designed by the instructor (within the course) to obtain information about student learning as well as feedback about teacher strategies (Cyrs, 1997). The primary intent of this assessment and teacher evaluation is to perform midcourse modifications and design future course structure. Box E depicts instructor evaluation of student learning (usually through exams, term papers, projects, and presentations). The instructor uses this information for purposes of student grading. Box F depicts student evaluation of instructor teaching. Such data are usually externally driven and are kept in the instructor's files to be used for administrative purposes and personnel decisions (Box F1). We believe that variations of Techno-CATs and other electronic tools may be more valid than traditional paper-and-pencil, end-of-term teacher evaluation forms.

FIGURE 7.1

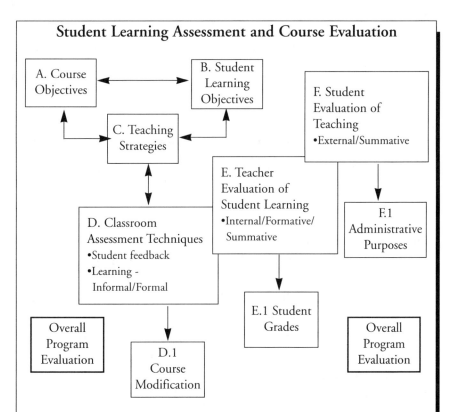

A. Course Objectives. The goals of the course. What the instructor intends to cover and do in a particular course.

B. Student Learning Objectives. What the instructor expects the students to be able to know, to do, or to believe by the end of a module or an entire course. Rubrics are included in this. Rubrics are the yardstick for measuring each of these stated learning objectives.

C. Teaching Strategies. Instructors make assumptions that a particular strategy will be the best path for a student to achieve the designated learning objectives. A few examples of teaching strategies may be traditional lecture, group work, think-pair-share, journaling, community-based learning, Internet searches.

D. Classroom Assessment Techniques. Instructors use CATs to gain information about student learning and to give students immediate feedback about their own learning. The CAT process itself should be a learning tool for the student. CATs usually lead to midcourse modification.

E. Teacher Evaluation of Student Learning. The evaluation form usually results in assigning student grades. Traditionally these are exams, term papers, group projects, reports.

F. Student Evaluation of Teaching. This evaluation process gives the instructor and the administration feedback on student perceptions of quality of instruction. Traditionally, these have been paper and pencil at the end of the course. There are electronic means to collect these data during or at the end of the course which may be more effective than the traditional paper-pencil, end-of-course evaluation forms.

© Lieberman, D., 1999, Portland State University

CLASSROOM ASSESSMENT TECHNIQUES (CATS) AND TECHNO-CATS

Student learning assessment research has taken on a life of its own and is most frequently referred to in terms of Classroom Assessment Techniques (CATS) (Angelo & Cross, 1993). They do not focus solely on teacher evaluation, or even student evaluation, but are used instead primarily to collect data about student learning. These data are meant to inform the instructor as to which teaching strategies are effective as well as what students have learned. Instructors are encouraged to use these data for midcourse modification with the intention of tweaking teaching strategies to meet student learning needs. The final goal is to more effectively achieve desired student learning outcomes and course objectives (see Figure 7.1, Boxes A, B, C and D).

TECHNO-CATS, STUDENT LEARNING ASSESSMENT, AND TEACHING STRATEGIES

For purposes of documenting the quality of teaching, the author believes that student learning (whether it is self-reported or not) is a significant variable in any teaching evaluation context (Lieberman, 1998). Techno-CATs are a means to electronically collect formative information about student learning and can be easily translated to instructor evaluation.

When instructors employ paper-and-pencil CATs, they are confined to real-time, face-to-face student feedback. Techno-CATs give the instructor greater options and freedom to collect data about student learning in relation to their student learning objectives. This process may take place in-class or out-of-class depending on the intention of the instructor. Two particularly important advantages of using Techno-CATs are 1) they allow more in-class time to cover course content and 2) they allow incubation time for students to reflect on their responses in the convenience of their own homes or in a computer lab. Techno-CATs are ways for instructors to gather the information about student learning in relation to a specific teaching strategy from students at any point during the term.

Two modes of evaluation will be addressed in this chapter: synchronous and asynchronous evaluations. Neither mode is inherently better than the other. The context of the course and the purpose for which the evaluation is obtained determine which is more appropriate in a particular situation. The late Professor Tom Creed from St. John's University (http://www.users.csbsju.edu/~tcreed) used Techno-CATs throughout his courses. These are described on his web site as email, threaded discussion, think-pair-share, and quizzes.

ASYNCHRONOUS ELECTRONIC TOOLS FOR INSTRUCTOR EVALUATION

Asynchronous evaluation tools are those for which the student and professor do not have to both be present in the same space or at the same time. These tools may best be used for classes that are conducted via the Internet or another form of distance education. The asynchronous evaluation medium may also be best for classes where the students cannot all be in the same place at the same time. Ideally, this would be appropriate for where the teacher is located in one site, but satellite classes are held elsewhere.

Synchronous Electronic Tools for Teacher Evaluation

Synchronous evaluation tools are those where the students are either located at the same site as the professor or they are communicating in real time with the evaluator (whether it is the professor or an external evaluator). Historically, paper-and-pencil evaluation tools were conducted at one site with the professor in or out of the room (depending on the evaluation protocol), but the continuous variable was that the tool and the students were present and face-to-face. Synchronous evaluation may be conducted with the students at a distance or in real time. This means that the technology is used in a way that permits all the students to complete the evaluation and return it (electronically) at the same time. If a student had a question or if the evaluation had open-ended questions, simultaneous communication with the individual administering the evaluation tool would still be possible.

Why Use Electronic Tools for Evaluating Instruction?

It would be very easy to fall into the trap of promoting the use of electronic evaluation because it seems trendy. Because it may seem cutting-edge to students, they may be more inclined to rate the instructor positively (or not). I propose that the use of technology to either enhance or replace traditional paper-and-pencil evaluation tools follows the principle that new is not always better, but that electronic evaluation methods should be considered where they are either more efficient or perhaps more reliable than traditional paper-and-pencil tools.

A question that could guide the decision-making about spending the time, effort, and university resources needed to design and implement electronic evaluation would be: "Is this the best method for addressing that which I intend to evaluate?" The soundest practice would be to actually triangulate the evaluation process in which the students who are evaluating a particular instructor complete different assessment tools, and scientific inquiry is used to measure differences between the groups and ascertain the validity of the various methods employed.

TECHNO-CATS: FEEDBACK TO THE INSTRUCTOR

Certain Techno-CATs provide feedback to the instructor about student learning and for course modification (Figure 7.1, Boxes D and D1). Such tools, if used for evaluative purposes, might weaken an instructor's desire to ascertain student learning in relation to particular teaching strategies and might also discourage midcourse modification. But when used as ungraded feedback to instructors, they serve as continuous information about student learning and course design.

The Electronic Small Group Instructional Diagnosis (SGID)

The traditional Small Group Instructional Diagnosis (Redmond & Clark, 1982) can be conducted electronically. Rather than involving student class time in completing a 30-minute SGID addressing strengths and weaknesses of the class, students can complete the SGID synchronously from a distance. If the small groups are assigned in class and are using a software supported by their institution that allows online, real-time interaction, the group SGID is easily completed. One group member is the facilitator, and the other group members answer the three questions:

1) What is "working" in this course?

2) What needs improvement in this course?

3) How might the instructor make these improvements in the course?

The threaded discussion can be saved and electronically sent (email or Internet) to the professor.

The benefit of this electronic approach to midterm teacher evaluation is that it does not have to fit in any specific time parameters. The negative aspect is that students have to coordinate their out-of-class time to complete this evaluation in real-time or chat-room mode. Another potential problem is that the students would not be anonymous when their online group SGID is sent to the instructor.

Traditionally, the SGID group participants are anonymous. Current electronic software identifies and saves each electronic participant.

Techno-CATs Teaching Evaluation Matrix

Similarly, teachers can receive formative student feedback on their teaching strategies by having students complete tables about the degree to which they perceive that particular modes of teaching successfully impart information in relation to student learning outcomes.

Classroom assessment matrix. The instructors fill in the list of student assignments and student learning objectives in Table 7.1. The students complete the matrix by rating how a particular assignment helped them to achieve a particular learning objective. Their ratings are on a scale of 1 to 5 (1 is low, and 5 is high). When the instructors construct the skeleton matrix, they are reminded of their intentions in making a particular assignment with certain student learning outcomes in mind.

Teaching evaluation matrix. The teaching evaluation matrix follows a similar format. Using the same 1-5 rating systems as in Table 7.1, students complete their perceptions of how a teaching strategy helped them to achieve particular learning outcomes. Instructors will then be able to ascertain 1) which teaching strategies are perceived as the most related to student learning objectives, and 2) if students perceive that assignments or modes of delivering information related to course learning.

These also can easily be completed asynchronously. If the matrix (see Table 7.1 and Table 7.2) is posted on the course web site, each student can easily complete the boxes of the matrices and electronically send them back to the instructor. If the matrices are posted in an electronic environment (such as WebCT), then the software has the capability of immediately recording all data sent back and computing the average for each student learning objective by course assignment as well as the average student learning objective by teaching mode. This has the potential to be a very successful way of combining Techno-CAT information with teaching evaluation information for midcourse correction or teacher evaluation for administrative purposes.

TABLE 7.1

CLASSROOM ASSESSMENT TECHNIQUE MATRIX

Student Learning Objectives	Course Assignment 1	Course Assignment 2	Course Assignment 3	Course Assignment 4	Course Assignment 5
Objective 1					
Objective 2					
Objective 3					

TABLE 7.2

TEACHING EVALUATION MATRIX

Student Learning Objectives	Teaching Strategy 1 (lecture)	Teaching Strategy 2 (group work)	Teaching Strategy 3 (Internet search)	Teaching Strategy 4 (class discussion)	Teaching Strategy 5 (think-pair-share)
Objective 1					
Objective 2					
Objective 3					

Networked classrooms or labs allow instructors to monitor students online and share the information with the whole class. Thus, teacher evaluation and student assessment tools that are introduced as asynchronous tools can easily be adapted to a synchronous mode in these classes.

Handheld Feedback Devices. Networked and wireless handheld devices are an ideal electronic tool for giving immediate feedback to the instructor, either on student learning or on student perceptions of instructor effectiveness. A successful tool for offering such feedback is the Perception Analyzer (http://www.cinfo.com) created and marketed by Columbia Information Systems of Portland, Oregon. The Perception Analyzer is made up of individual handheld devices, which allow students to give immediate feedback, on a scale of 1–100.

The summative student feedback can be saved and printed out at a later time or viewed on a monitor while the instructor is teaching. The monitor can either be a computer monitor, in which the perception analyzer software is loaded, or it can be a large Infocus-type screen visible to all the students. The instructor can design the method of data collection, analysis, and viewing depending on the intent of the exercise.

Students can view questions (which were previously typed into the computer connected to the projection device) simultaneously as they are projected on the screen. They can be traditional Likert-type questions, rated from "strongly agree" to "strongly disagree," with responses (multiple-choice or true/false) that correspond to numbers on the handheld devices. The questions can even be degree of agreement or disagreement with a range that corresponds to the numbers on the handheld device. Another use of the perception analyzer in teacher evaluation moves away from static evaluation by the students about how much they learned to responses to questions or statements about the course instruction or instructor style.

The perception analyzer has the capability of dynamic continuous formative feedback. If an instructor is teaching a module and all students have a perception analyzer, they can individually turn their dial to higher numbers when understanding the content of the presentation and lower numbers when confused about the content of the presentation. The instructor can either view an ongoing graph of student responses (as a class) during the presentation or on a printout after the presentation has ended. This feedback can be used to either modify or correct upcoming presentations within a particular class or can be placed in a file for personnel purposes. Instructors at Portland State

University have used the perception analyzer as a classroom assessment technique to obtain static information on how students think they are learning specific concepts within a particular class session.

This allows the students to see in histogram form how many students (anonymously) are choosing each response choice. It also gives instructors immediate feedback on how successfully they are teaching the information intended to be learned in a particular session. Students are attracted to the electronic handheld device and take the response process seriously. When the histogram with student responses is projected for all to see, much discussion follows about why students chose certain responses, especially those that were not correct answers. The discussions provide in-depth learning opportunities for the instructor as well as the students.

Current Student Inventory

The Current Student Inventory (CSI) is an evaluation tool designed by Steven Ehrmann and the Flashlight Project (Teaching and Learning with Technology Group; http://www.tltgroup.org). It is a toolkit for evaluation of either teaching strategies and/or students' use of technologies. If an instructor assumes that using a particular technology is the most effective teaching strategy for students to achieve a particular student learning outcome, the tool kit helps collect data to verify or reject that assumption. The tool kit is an inventory of over 500 questions that address student learning, instructor presentation of materials, and student use of technologies.

These questions can be combined with questions created by an institution, a department, or a particular instructor and can be housed in an Internet environment and programmed to be accessed by students any time during or at the end of a course. It is important to ensure that the environment which houses the CSI has the capabilities of automatically providing information on student data. This will decrease scoring time and efforts by the instructor and/or the institution. The CSI is an example of a classroom assessment technique, as shown in Figure 7.1 (Box D), providing student-reported information about a particular teaching strategy.

Several classes at Portland State University are offered either 100% online or in a hybrid fashion. The university wants to know how the students believe they are learning in the online courses or modules compared to their beliefs about learning in traditional face-to-face courses. Rather than linking student responses directly to their learning (e.g., grades, exams, and written work), the Portland State University researchers are interested in the student perceptions of how they are responding to the electronic/virtual learning environment and whether they feel they are learning as much as in traditional courses. The student responses provide midterm feedback to the course instructors as well as to those on campus who are providing pedagogical and technical support to other instructors who plan on launching online courses.

TABLE 7.3

EXAMPLES OF CURRENT STUDENT INVENTORY QUESTIONS

1) How is WebCT being used in your class? (mark all that apply)
a. The entire class is offered via WebCT
b. To supplement the material covered in lectures
c. To provide additional information not received in lectures
d. To permit electronic communication among students
e. To allow students to submit assignments electronically
f. To allow students to take online quizzes
g. Other

2) Think about a similar course you have taken that relied entirely on face-to-face class meetings. Compared to that course, because of the way this course uses WebCT, how likely were you to . . . a) much less likely, b) somewhat less likely, c) about the same, d) somewhat more likely, e) much more likely
 . . . get individualized attention from the instructor
 . . . receive comments from the instructor on assignments quickly
 . . . spend more time studying
 . . . interact with fellow students on course-related work outside of scheduled lecture periods
 . . . keep up with the required work and readings
 . . . learn at your own pace
 . . . feel isolated from the instructor

Table 7.3 includes examples of questions used in this classroom research project. For a complete list of the questions, see the web site http://www.oaa.pdx.edu/cae.

CONCLUSION

The greatest concern faculty express about incorporating formative or summative evaluation tools into their teaching is that the results may negatively affect their professional progress (usually in terms of promotion and tenure). But faculty find the tools critical to course development once they realize that electronic tools can be used for midcourse assessment of student learning and the information gained used to strengthen the rest of the course. In addition, electronic course assessment used for personnel purposes has advantages to faculty over the traditional end-of-term, paper-and-pencil course evaluations. As the professoriate becomes more familiar with technology in the learning environment, electronic tools will become an essential ingredient for evaluating student learning, course design, and presentation of information. The more thoughtful and welcoming we are about the design of Techno-CATs and electronic evaluation tools, the greater strides we will make in advancing teaching and learning.

ACKNOWLEDGMENTS

I would like to thank Amy Driscoll, EdD, California State University, San Marcos, for sharing her Course Alignment Grid (CAG) with me for this publication. Nancy Bowers, PhD, Faculty-in-Residence for Technology, Center for Academic Excellence, Portland State University (PSU), designed the Current Student Inventory questionnaire and analyzed the data for each of the classes surveyed. She is the lead researcher in the CSI research at PSU.

References

Angelo, T., & Cross, P. (1993). *Classroom assessment techniques: A handbook for college teachers* (2nd ed.). San Francisco, CA: Jossey-Bass.

Columbia Information Systems. Perception Analyzer. (http://www.cinfo.com).

Creed, T. (1998). Extending the classroom walls electronically. (http://www.users.csbsju.edu/~tcreed).

Cyrs, T., & Conway, E. (1997). *Teaching at a distance with emerging technologies: An instructional systems approach.* Las Cruces, NM: New Mexico State University, Center for Educational Development.

Ehrmann, S. The Current Student Inventory: The Flashlight Project. (http://www.tltgroup.org).

Knapper, C. (1995). Understanding student learning: Implications for instructional practice. In W. A. Wright (Ed.), *Teaching improvement practices: Successful strategies for higher education* (pp. 58-76). Bolton, MA: Anker.

Lieberman, D. (1998, October). Using technology wisely. *The Advocate.* Washington, DC: National Education Association.

Pregent, R. (1994). *Charting your course: How to prepare to teach more effectively.* Madison, WI: Magna.

Pritchard, R., Watson, M., Kelly, K., & Paquin, A. (1998). *Helping teachers teach well: A new system for measuring and improving teaching effectiveness in higher education.* San Francisco, CA: The New Lexington Press.

Redmond, M. V., & Clark, D. J. (1982). A practical approach to improving teaching. *AAHE Bulletin, 1,* 9-10.

CHAPTER 8

USING THE WORLD WIDE WEB TO IMPROVE TEACHING EVALUATION

Clement A. Seldin

By virtually all measures, the growth of the World Wide Web is colossal. Each day, hundreds of new web sites appear on every conceivable subject. They add to the network of millions of web sites that currently exist. Text, charts, tables, pictures, audio, and video clips on every subject are literally at our fingertips.

For many researchers, the mammoth size and scope of the web provides an invaluable resource that could not have been imagined just a few years ago. As computers and communication increase in power and speed, the web has become the primary research tool for many academics. But for others, the web has become too massive and unwieldy. For them, navigating through a sea of search engines, links, and animations is cumbersome and time consuming.

A colleague recently claimed that searching on the web is the ultimate challenge. She argued that either you find the needle in the haystack within a few minutes (a rare occurrence) or spend hours and hours sifting though multitudes of colorful screens while reviewing semirelated sites, discarding almost all, and bookmarking just a few of potential value. My colleague went on to claim that a walk to the university library is a better idea. The walk is aerobically beneficial, and the card catalog system directs you to the precise shelf on which the books you seek are waiting.

My colleague's concern about the web may be justified. Select any search engine. Embark on a search for sites designed to improve the evaluation of college teaching. Plan to spend days clicking on innumerable links, waiting, and reviewing by clicking numerous times to gain access to various levels of the web site. In most cases, data appear within a few seconds. However, sometimes, the following message appears on the computer screen:

The requested object does not exist on this server. The link you followed is either outdated, inaccurate, or the server has been instructed not to let you have it. Please inform the site administrator of the referring page.

Despite the explosion of new web sites, many sites are dead ends—outdated, inaccurate, or no longer in existence. Some web sites even announce that their information is outdated. For example, the following message appeared on the screen of an international organization's web site devoted to the improvement of teaching and learning in higher education: *This web site is now out of date. It is has not been updated since 1996 because of lacking financial support.*

Occasionally, a dead-end web site provides a new URL (web address) or additional links that may be of help. But most do not.

There are also web sites that appear to be dead end even when you don't understand the language:

ATTENZIONE: Hai raggiunto una pagina che non esiste!!!!

Many researchers perceive the web as instrumental, but with defined limitations. These limitations can be lessened if specific URLs and summary information are provided before you begin to work. In other words, if you go directly to quality web sites, your time is better spent. That is the focus of this chapter, which includes a series of helpful web sites, as well as summary descriptions of what each contains.

How were these sites uncovered? I used two basic approaches. First, I practiced the standard method of using several major search engines to identify web sites focused on improving the evaluation of college teaching. I critiqued the sites in terms of the quality and quantity of information, seeking those that provided both a clear and intelligent examination of key issues. Second, I contacted via email the directors of organizations associated with some of the most helpful web sites, including those in the US, Australia, New Zealand, England, and Scandinavia, and asked them to identify the best web sites that focus on improving the evaluation of college teaching.

What follows are selected web sites that provide helpful information. Certainly, this is a sampling. Readers may be familiar with other web sites that offer comprehensive data. I would be most appreciative if you would email the URLs to me (caseldin@educ.umass.edu), because I would like to expand my efforts to compile a listing of the most useful web sites on this topic.

Finally, both my own search and the recommendations of professionals reveal that the best web sites on improving the evaluation of college teaching are found in teaching and learning centers at institutions of higher education. These centers have various names, such as the Center for Learning and Teaching, Teaching Excellence, or Research on Learning and Teaching. What they have in common is an organized, institutional focus. While many of these centers' web sites are useful primarily to faculty at their specific institution, many also offer helpful information to outsiders.

SAMPLE WEB SITE TITLES AND URLS

Online University Teaching Centers, A Worldwide Listing, Department of Communication Studies, University of Kansas (http://ukanaix.cc.ukans.edu/~sypherh/bc/onctr.html)

Contents. This web site is akin to a table of contents in a comprehensive book on institutions focused on improving college teaching. It provides links to centers for teaching and learning at institutions of higher education in many countries. From this site, you may click and review the web sites at colleges and universities that focus on teaching and faculty development. For those who have interest in using new technologies in their teaching, many sites also provide such information.

This web site contains links to online university and community college teaching centers in Asia, Australia/New Zealand, Canada, Europe, the United Kingdom, and the US.

ERIC Clearinghouse on Higher Education (http://www.gwu.edu/~eriche/)

Contents. The Educational Resources Information Center (ERIC) is a national information system that provides access to an extensive body of education-related literature. It is supported by the US Department of Education, Office of Educational Research and Improvement, and the National Library of Education. It describes itself as "the world's largest educational database."

Using this web site, you can direct three major searches:

1) Search this web site to see what resources are offered

2) Search the database to access abstracts of educational literature

3) Search the Cross-Site Index (CSI) with more than 90,000 files from more than 150 education funded web sites, including 32 ERIC web sites

The Special Interest Group in Faculty Evaluation and Development (SIGFED) of the American Educational Research Association (http://www.uis.edu/~ctl/sigfed.html)

Contents. This web site contains three links:

1) Instructional evaluation and faculty development issues

2) Comments from the SIGFED listserv

3) Share your comments

By clicking on the first link, you can read recent research in several editions of *Instructional Evaluation and Faculty Development* (http://www.uis.edu/~ctl/sigfed/backissues.html), which primarily focus on student ratings, student learning, and teacher competence.

Full texts are provided. By joining the SIGFED listserv, you can enter the discussion group.

The Harriet W. Sheridan Center for Teaching and Learning, Brown University (http://Sheridan-Center.stg.brown.edu/index.shtml)

Contents. This university web site contains the Sheridan Center publications with links to several important dimensions of the evaluation of college teaching, including instructional assessment in higher education, and a teaching portfolio handbook.

Center for Learning and Teaching, Cornell University (http://www.clt.cornell.edu/default.html)

Contents. The Center for Learning and Teaching (CLT) at Cornell provides programs aimed at improving student learning and instructional delivery. While some of the site is specific to Cornell, there is a comprehensive resources link that contains a bibliography of recommended publications and a useful teaching evaluation handbook (http://www.clt.cornell.edu/resources/teh/teh.html) with five chapters of text, tables, illustrations, and examples.

The handbook includes the following specific sections:

- The question of defining excellence in teaching
- The teaching portfolio: documenting teaching and its improvement
- Supporting data: collection and presentation
- Use of student evaluation data
- Criteria for evaluating data on teaching
- Evaluating course and teaching materials

Center for Teaching Excellence, Iowa State University (http://www.public.iastate.edu/~teaching_info/home.html)

Contents. Iowa State University's Center for Teaching Excellence offers "advice, resources, and a forum for discussions that will help the university and its faculty provide students with the best education possible." It also offers colleagues at other universities helpful information and links. Sources of Outside Funds for Teaching (http://www.public.iastate.edu/~teaching_info/outside.html) has direct links to funding sources for innovation projects. There is also a helpful page on how to document your teaching (http://www.public.iastate.edu/~teaching_info/port.html). For those interested in teaching portfolios, see the center's link(http://www.cte.iastate.edu/portfolio.html).

Center for Research on Learning and Teaching, University of Michigan (http://www.umich.edu/~crltmich/)

Contents. This center is "dedicated to the support and advancement of learning and teaching at the University of Michigan, with special emphasis on undergraduate education." While some of the web site is specific to Michigan (e.g., guidebook for new TAs, orientation, and calendar of events), there is a section titled Evaluating Teaching (http://www.umich.edu/~crltmich/guidelines.html) that readers will find useful. It includes 1) principles of teaching evaluation, and 2) sources of data for evaluating teaching: students, colleagues, and self-reflection.

There is also a link to frequently asked questions (FAQs) about student ratings (http://www.umich.edu/~crltmich/crlt.faq.html) with a bibliography organized into the following sections: 1) good overviews of the literature, 2) grading leniency, 3) expressivity, 4) student ratings as a measure of effective teaching, and 5) accuracy and consistency of student ratings.

Searle Center for Teaching Excellence, Northwestern University (http://president.scfte.nwu.edu/)

Contents. This web site makes good use of internal links and anchors that facilitate navigation. Teaching and Learning Issues: Evaluation of Teaching (http://president.scfte.nwu.edu/Evaluate.htm) has three highlighted areas:

1) Student Ratings and the Evaluation of Teaching is a white paper that is well-referenced (http://president.scfte.nwu.edu/White. htm). It includes discussion of student ratings for self-improvement as well as the limitations of student ratings.

2) Peer Review of Teaching Project describes a peer review program developed by Northwestern University and 11 other institutions. This national pilot project, sponsored by the American Association for Higher Education, describes the fundamental steps for developing a system of peer review(http://president. scfte.nwu.edu/Scholars.htm#PeerReview).

3) Teaching Portfolios (http://president.scfte.nwu.edu/Ports.htm) provides a concise overview with a link to an article titled "Recasting the Teaching Portfolio."

The Center for Excellence in Teaching and Learning, The Pennsylvania State University (http://www.psu.edu/celt/index.html)

Contents: This web site features two useful sections:

1) Publications (http://www.psu.edu/celt/publications.shtml) with handbooks, articles, guides, and annotated bibliographies

2) Assessment (http://www.psu.edu/celt/assessment.shtml) with links to classroom observation, assessment techniques and practices, and teaching portfolios.

Center for Teaching and Learning, Stanford University (http://www-ctl.stanford.edu/index.html)

Contents. Stanford University's center publishes a web site with a major link to resources for faculty (http://www-ctl.stanford.edu/ faculty.html). It contains the following resources:

1) Handbook on Teaching at Stanford (helpful for teaching elsewhere)

2) *Speaking of Teaching Newsletter* (full text), including two excellent

articles: "Using Student Evaluations to Improve Teaching" (Volume 9, Number 1); and "Promoting a Culture of Teaching: The Teaching Portfolio" (Volume 7, Number 3)

3) Small group evaluation

4) Interpreting course evaluations

Grayson H. Walker Teaching Resource Center, The University of Tennessee, Chattanooga (http://www.utc.edu/Teaching-Resource-Center/)

Contents. This center links to the university's faculty development site (http://www.utc.edu/Teaching-Resource-Center/Fac_Dev.html) with information on faculty peer evaluation strategies and teaching resources. They also have a comprehensive page on teaching portfolios (http://www.utc.edu/TeachingResourceCenter/PORFO1.HTM).

The Center for Effective Teaching and Learning, The University of Texas, El Paso (http://www.utep.edu/cetal/)

Contents. This web site's major feature is a detailed description of the teaching portfolio. It "aims to provide tools for developing and assessing a faculty teaching portfolio—both as a formative tool and as a summative evaluation of scholarly work" (http://www.utep.edu/cetal/portfoli/index.htm).

Deliberations on Teaching and Learning in Higher Education, United Kingdom (http://www.lgu.ac.uk/deliberations/)

Contents. This site is an electronic magazine for academics, librarians, and educational developers. London Guildhall and Kingston Universities in the UK staff it. Material is organized by discipline and by educational issue.

Content includes:

• Preparing university teachers

• Assessment

- Mentoring

- Teaching portfolios

- Book reviews and annotated bibliographies

- Links to related resources and relevant publishers

Center for Instructional Development and Research, University of Washington (http://weber.u.washington.edu/~cidrweb/index.html)

Contents. This web site contains a large number of linked sites developed by the center for its faculty and students. Of special interest is the section on consultative services for faculty (http://weber.u.washington.edu/~cidrweb/ConsultationServices.html) which includes the following topics:

- Analysis of student ratings

- Course assessment

- Curricular assessment

- Colleague/peer review or assessment

- Teaching portfolios

- Integrating technology in instruction

The University of Washington's Office of Educational Assessment has a very useful web site where faculty can choose from nine assessment forms depending on the course and instructional goals (http://www.washington.edu/oea/iasforms.htm).

CONCLUSION

The World Wide Web is a tremendous resource that offers new opportunities and avenues for research. Because it is a relatively new medium and because of its vastness, it can also be challenging to use efficiently. This chapter offers some web sites that provide relevant information to those who are interested in improving the evaluation of college teaching.

CHAPTER 9

EVALUATING TEACHING THROUGH PORTFOLIOS

John Zubizarreta

In higher education today, teaching evaluation has become a sensitive issue because of increased demands on faculty for assessment and accountability. As funding resources have shrunk, market competition increased, and public outcry for educational reform intensified, personnel decisions about hiring, tenure, advancement, salary, grants, reassigned time, endowed chairs, and merit awards are made increasingly not on the basis of seniority, reputation, or quantity of conventional research or grant writing, but on recorded evidence of continued growth and accountability in the many complex dimensions of the professoriate, particularly teaching. As Seldin (1984, p. 44) pointed out more than a decade ago in a study of faculty evaluation policies and practices, "Greater importance is given today to a wider range of factors in an attempt to achieve reliability and scope of assessing overall faculty performance." In the same study, Seldin adds that evaluation of classroom teaching effectiveness is "the most important factor in faculty evaluation." In a more recent survey, Seldin (1998, p. 3) has followed up his analysis of evaluation practices "in light of both the broad-based assessment movement and the growing scrutiny given to faculty productivity" in current institutional settings. The results indicate that while teaching remains paramount, several important changes have occurred, primarily the greater emphasis placed on multiple sources of information including, of course, student evaluations of classroom instruction, collaborative peer review, and reflective self-appraisals with appropriate evidence (see Chapter 5). Much greater focus is also placed on the importance of faculty development in more sophisticated, comprehensive systems of evaluation which aim to strengthen teaching.

In such a context, teaching evaluation activities must help professors meet the imperative of blending clear, rigorous documentation and assessment with a positive desire to improve teaching and learning. Arreola and Aleamoni (1990, pp. 53-54) argue, for instance, that

> "Time and again, experience has shown that an evaluation system implemented without reference or connection to a faculty development program will generate greater amounts of anxiety and resistance among faculty than a system that is part of a larger faculty development and instructional improvement effort. . . . Ideally, a faculty evaluation system should be an integral part of a larger evaluation and development program."

Making the evaluation of teaching both a summative act of reasoned, fair judgment and a formative process of improvement, inspiration, collegiality, and goal setting is the challenge facing professors and those who evaluate teaching performance.

Achieving the twin aims of responsible evaluation and continual improvement is where the teaching portfolio has made an enormous contribution to transforming the culture of higher education, encouraging professors and evaluators to put more value on reflection and collaboration without minimizing the fundamental need for evidence and accountability. The teaching portfolio is a proven mechanism that offers synergistically not only a practical, written instrument for constructive evaluation but also an ongoing, collaborative strategy that promotes continual revision of the teaching enterprise. The portfolio provides a vehicle for recorded evidence of performance and, more importantly, for reflection, analysis, and strategically delineated action, indispensable steps in teaching enhancement. In the act of writing critically about current, actual teaching efforts and in constructing a rhetorical framework that compels the teacher to gather supporting materials, analyze information, draw substantial conclusions, and posit action plans for better practice, the teacher develops a habit of intentional improvement based on regular and timely assessment. One of the most powerful recommendations of the teaching portfolio, therefore, is that it is a relevant, valid, useful component of a teaching evaluation system, but its prerequisites of reflection and collaboration also serve the increasingly prominent goal of improvement (see Chapter 10).

THE TEACHING PORTFOLIO MODEL

Ample information about the theory, content, and format of a teaching portfolio may be found readily in Shore, et al (1986); Edgerton, Hutchings, and Quinlan (1991); and Seldin (1991, 1993, 1997), all good sources for getting started on portfolios. Seldin's is the most cogent, practical model, focusing on a compact narrative with supplementary materials that support and document the compressed information in the written body of the portfolio. An important note is that virtually all the literature on portfolios advocates the collaboration of a mentor who helps guide the development of the process and who keeps the writer focused on how the portfolio improves teaching while simultaneously providing a venue for scrupulous analysis of hard evidence for evaluation.

A sound teaching portfolio may be defined this way in a single statement: It is an evidence-based written document in which a faculty member strategically organizes concise, selective details of current teaching accomplishment and uses such information for documentation of performance but more significantly for reflective analysis and peer collaboration leading to improvement of teaching and student learning. The portfolio narrative consists of eight to ten pages that gather selected data from three major areas. Here are some representative items that by no means exhaust the possibilities of what may be crucial in a particular professor's portfolio:

1) Information from oneself

- Responsibilities, philosophy, methods, goals

- Materials

- Teaching development activities

2) Information from others

- Student and peer assessments and ratings

- Year-end evaluations by chair and dean

- Honors and awards

- Letters from colleagues, students, alumni

3) Products of student learning

- Pre/post tests of learning

- Classroom assessment activities

- Student exams, projects, presentations, publications, essays in drafts with instructor's formative feedback

- Alumni assessments

The information collected from the three broad areas is organized into main headings reflecting the various, selected facets of a teacher's work. For comprehensive review of instruction and a broader profile of how teaching factors into a professor's overall evaluation, the mentee and mentor, after identifying the key purpose of the portfolio, may decide to use it as the vehicle for demonstrating how teaching is connected to other roles. Consequently, the portfolio offers the written structure needed for reflective analysis of performance, for articulating distinct goals, for conversation about how individual plans support departmental and institutional missions, and for collecting and studying evidence in the various dimensions of a professor's work. The teaching portfolio, then, can be integrated into the professor's additionally required materials for evaluation. The main headings of such a portfolio might look like the following sample, which is the actual table of contents of a teaching portfolio submitted to supplement comprehensive review for yearly merit evaluation:

1) Statement of Faculty Role and Responsibilities

2) Philosophy of Teaching

3) Teaching

    A. Strategies and Methods

    B. Collaborative Scholarship with Students

    C. Syllabi, Reading Lists, Assignments, Handouts, Exams

    D. Technology and Teaching

    E. Student Evaluations

    F. Peer, Chair, Dean Evaluations

    G. Statements from Colleagues and Alumni

    H. Teaching Awards

    I. Evidence of Student Learning

    J. Teaching Improvement

4) Scholarship of Teaching

    A. Classroom Assessment

    B. Applications of Scholarship to Teaching and Learning

5) Teaching-Related Service

    A. Teaching Activities in the Community

    B. Institutional and Professional Commitments Related to Teaching

    C. Letters for Students and Colleagues

6) Development Goals

7) Appendices

    A. Collaborative Scholarship

    B. Student Evaluations

C. Letters from Colleagues within and outside the Department and College

D. Teaching Awards

E. Sample Syllabi, Reading Lists, Assignments, Handouts, Exams

F. Classroom Assessment

G. Products of Student Learning

H. Vitae and Evidence of Teaching-Related Service

I. Sample Recommendations for Students, Colleagues, Alumnae Relations

J. College Service Related to Teaching

K. Evidence of Scholarship of Teaching

The table of contents for a portfolio drafted for evaluating teaching would include a narrative or reflective portion meticulously connected to documentation in an appendix, the hard data needed for clear, honest assessment and reasoned goals. Every significant claim about or analysis of teaching achievement in the rhetoric of the portfolio's narrative body is balanced by select, concrete evidence in keyed appendices. As the professor develops a section on methodology, student evaluations, or classroom assessment outcomes, each reflective statement is documented in an appropriately labeled appendix. If, for instance, the instructor notes that a particular assignment has proved significantly and uniquely to strengthen student learning of special disciplinary content, then evidence might include the assignment sheet, auxiliary handouts, case studies, or models in an appendix for materials; additionally, samples of selected student work in developmental stages might be included in an appendix for products of student learning.

Such strong attention to both critical reflection and evidential information sets the stage for substantial improvement based on research-based analysis of selected dimensions of teaching, and the meticulous attention to hard documentation from multiple sources sharpens the portfolio's reliability in evaluation. Noting the currently increasing influence of self-evaluation in a "multi-source evaluation process," Seldin (1998, p. 7) underscores the importance of documentation: "More and more institutions are convinced that value exists in a reflective, candid self-appraisal and explanation of a faculty member's teaching objectives, methodologies, and shortcomings. . . . [H]owever . . . to be useful in personnel decisions the self-evaluation must be accompanied by solid evidence of accomplishment." Seldin adds that in combining reflective self-analysis with hard documentation, portfolios "provide evaluators with hard-to-ignore information on what individual professors do in the classroom and why they do it. The result? Evaluators are less inclined to look at teaching performance as a derivative of student ratings" (see Chapter 5).

The Importance of Collaboration in Evaluating Teaching

The mentoring process is an integral facet of the teaching portfolio; without collaboration, the portfolio is not much more than a privately constructed, elaborate personnel file. Mentoring is what transmutes the uninspiring collection of mere evidence for evaluation into a developmental process leading to improvement. A collaborator also helps keep the mentee focused and on task, and a faculty member can produce a valid and useful document in four or five days of concentrated work with a mentor. Zubizarreta (1994, p. 325) suggests that when the purpose of mentoring is to consult on preparing for evaluation, the mentor "ensures a fresh, critical perspective that encourages cohesion between the portfolio narrative and supporting appendix evidence." Coherence among stated philosophy, methodology, goals, and other parts of the narrative is vital, and similarly, coherence between the narrative and the evidence in the appendix is a paramount concern of an alert mentor. Without such collaboration and relying solely on quantitative ratings without context and collaborative review by a colleague, evaluation is a risky, lonely, and nonformative enterprise.

Faculty often fear that a portfolio is a fatiguing venture, an exhaustive history of teaching which includes every minute detail of a professor's career, but remember that it is, instead, a selective profile of current teaching efforts. Depending upon the faculty member's purpose for writing a portfolio, topics are developed and evidence gathered because they highlight an instructor's range of responsibilities, pedagogical values, strategic successes and disappointments, representative materials, evaluations, opportunities for improvement, and goals. If the purpose is strictly evaluation for personnel decisions, no ethical transgression is committed if one of the criteria for selectivity is the faculty member's motivation to exhibit a portfolio of best practices. It would be rare, if not nonexistent, for instance, for a research scholar to submit for evaluative review a list of all rejected articles and failed projects; instead, when personnel decisions are at stake, professors appropriately want to be judged on their best work. Despite the perception that the selection of best work is tainted and unhelpful, the truth is that, as Braskamp and Ory (1994, p. 111) point out, the most powerful reflective analysis leading to improvement often occurs in exactly the kind of retrospective selection of successful practice represented in a portfolio designed to make a case for teaching: "Making a case implies that faculty select their best work for display, but the selection may represent the best thinking as well as, or instead of, the most highly rated performance. . . . Growth may require reflection and discussion based on the problems and issues identified." The full scope of a professor's credentials should be, in any case, available for open review in an honest, balanced, well-designed, comprehensive evaluation system.

Institutional support and a climate of collaborative trust are also crucial to ensuring successful use of portfolios in personnel decisions (see Chapter 11). Faculty are less resistant to new and different methods of evaluation when they know that such activities are valued and rewarded within a collegial community of teaching scholars and when they are convinced that the genuine aim of review is to improve teaching. Evaluation systems that rely solely on student ratings, for example, foster mistrust because no one flashlight on faculty performance can fully illuminate the complex and ever-evolving role of the professor. If the portfolio is used as a means of nurturing collaboration and a collective sense of purpose centered on individual and program improvement within a context of comprehensive evaluation, then faculty are more willing to engage positively in assessment of their work.

Another level of institutional resolve needed is when department chairs are recruited as collaborators into the process of portfolio writing and into the complex task of understanding and judging portfolios for personnel decisions. With such administrative involvement, the potential for stronger, more complete, and effective evaluation is boosted, and teaching in the department becomes more valued. Deans and other administrators, too, must be informed about the purpose, scope, strengths, and limitations of portfolios.

As an important first step in introducing the portfolio concept on a campus, faculty and evaluators must invest collectively in the importance of teaching in the institutional mission and need to take voluntary ownership of how and why portfolios enhance teaching performance while at the same time providing a valid tool for evaluation. Later, as individual instructors revise their portfolios to reveal growth, colleagues, chairs, and deans witness firsthand the authentic benefits of reflective practice over time in improving evaluations.

LESSONS LEARNED IN USING PORTFOLIOS FOR EVALUATION

The primary purpose of developing a teaching portfolio is improvement. Nevertheless, because of the portfolio's emphasis on concrete evidence from a variety of sources, it can also be an indispensable facet of a comprehensive system of evaluation. We know, for example, that despite the portfolio's strong grounding in narrative self-evaluation as opposed to the perceived integrity of objective data from rating forms, a rigorously constructed portfolio, under the prerequisite guidance and scrutiny of a mentor, cannot hide weak performance because "... the evidence is just not there." Seldin (1997, p. 20) argues, "Fancy covers, computer graphics, and attractive printer fonts cannot disguise weak performance for a professor any more than [they] can for a student. On the other hand, for an excellent teacher, the portfolio offers an unmatched opportunity to document classroom practices that have previously gone unrecognized and unrewarded."

It is not surprising, then, that even as early as 20 years ago, Centra (1979, p. 47) declared that although self-assessment reports were "generally minor factors in tenure and promotion evaluations" at the time, "the use of self-assessment or self-reports . . . is increasing among some colleges." Of course, what is missing from the self-reports described by Centra are the uncompromising focus on reflection necessarily tied to specific evidence and the influence of peer collaboration and review, hallmarks of the teaching portfolio process when engaged properly. Braskamp and Ory's work (1994, pp. 106-107) on faculty assessment reveals the contemporary importance of the portfolio model in providing a rich, reliable "portrayal" of faculty work, a term they prefer because it correlates with the wide understanding of the purpose and value of portfolios. A portrayal, they contend, suggests "a rather proactive stance, that is, it implies that faculty are deliberately constructing something to educate others. It implies communication." Portfolios are especially well-suited, then, for evaluation purposes because as portrayals or acts of communication, they are "a public statement and document," serving as "an instrument of accountability—a means to demonstrate one's contributions to the common good. It becomes a reminder to faculty that they do not determine their value or worth alone but are to be judged in a public way for their contributions to the common good."

However, before portfolios are integrated into teaching evaluation protocols, a number of lessons should be observed:

1) Start with a cadre of volunteers from across disciplines and ranks, a group of faculty willing to develop portfolios that will serve as publicly displayed models for revaluing the importance of reflective practice, of the scholarship of teaching, of critically analyzed evidence, of collaboration in personnel decisions.

2) Clearly define specific criteria for narrative length, substance, amount and types of evidence. One effective model is to require a core of narrative areas and types of evidence that would standardize all portfolios across ranks and disciplines but allow a prescribed number of flexible options each faculty could elect to ensure the signature quality of each portfolio's profile of individual effort and accomplishment.

3) Commit to workshops of four or five days for portfolio development with the collaboration of trained mentors. Faculty development must be an integral part of any successful evaluation system.

4) Involve evaluators and administrative staff not only in becoming educated about the nature and scope of portfolios and how to use them fairly when evaluating faculty work, but also in developing portfolios themselves to experience the value of reflection, analysis of evidence, goal-setting, and collaboration in evaluating and improving administrative roles.

5) Explore strategies unique and appropriate to one's own campus for incorporating portfolios into comprehensive programs of faculty development and evaluation. Using portfolios for evaluation should be tailored to individual campus cultures.

6) Assess the impact and uses of portfolios on a campus after a couple of pilot years, and adjust and refine the process to keep pace with institutional priorities and strategic directions. With systematic, flexible, careful implementation, employing portfolios for personnel decisions, evaluation of teaching, pre- and post-tenure review, and merit decisions can be done constructively to enhance faculty morale and provide an effective and collaborative process for improvement which does not compromise reliability and accountability.

EVALUATING PORTFOLIOS

The following is a list of important questions to ask when portfolios are scrutinized by peer or administrative reviewers, especially for evaluation purposes:

1) Is the portfolio focused on current information?

2) Does the portfolio balance information from self, from others, and from products of student learning?

3) Is there coherence among the various components of the portfolio, revealing demonstrated effectiveness in practice tied to an articulate philosophy?

4) Does the portfolio demonstrate teaching consistent with depart mental and institutional strategic priorities and missions?

5) Is the evidence presented valid documentation as defined by the institutional culture of evaluation?

6) Are multiple, selective sources of information included, offering a diverse and objective assessment of teaching?

7) Does the portfolio adequately supplement narrative description, analysis, and goals with empirical evidence in the appendix?

8) Does the portfolio include a core of agreed-upon seminal state ments with accompanying evidence?

9) Do products of student learning reveal successful teaching?

10) Does the portfolio provide evidence of efforts to improve teach ing? Is there evidence of improvement in methods, materials, evaluations, goals?

11) Is the portfolio the only source of information on teaching effec tiveness? Or is it complemented by additional materials and cor roborative information about a professor's complex and varied roles?

12) How does the portfolio profile individual style and achievements? Is a strong case made in both narrative form and in supporting documentation in the appendix for the complexity and individu ality of a professor's particular teaching effort in a particular discipline with a particular group of students?

13) Does the portfolio meet established length and content require ments?

Seldin (1993, pp. 77-86) provides several models of rating forms that can be used by evaluators in making discriminating decisions about the quality of portfolios submitted for personnel decisions.

FIGURE 9.1

Portions of a Rating Form for Portfolios

FOCUS: INSTRUCTIONAL DELIVERY

SUGGESTED PORTFOLIO MATERIALS:

Student evaluations
Peer reviews
Letters
Other material

SUGGESTED QUESTIONS:

How do the ratings compare with those of other faculty in similar courses?
What are this faculty member's strengths and weaknesses?
What trends are apparent across courses?
What evidence exists of improvement?
Other questions relevant to individual department and discipline

RATING: 0   1   2   3   4   5

FOCUS: COURSE MANAGEMENT

SUGGESTED PORTFOLIO MATERIALS

Syllabi
Student ratings summary
Peer observation
Evidence presented by chair

SUGGESTED QUESTIONS:

Are students informed of course requirements and deadlines?
Is the grading policy clearly articulated and specified?
Are student assignments and examinations returned in a timely fashion?
Does the faculty member provide useful feedback on student performance?
Does the faculty member maintain ample, regular office hours?
Are student records clearly maintained?

RATING: 0   1   2   3   4   5

Adapted from Seldin, P. (1993). Successful use of teaching portfolios.
Bolton, MA: Anker.

One model, for example, identifies four major areas of teaching performance, offers suggested materials that may be included in a portfolio to demonstrate achievement in those areas, and recommends critical focus questions that reviewers may use to frame an evaluation of a portfolio. Figure 9.1 is an abbreviated look at such a structure which may be easily reorganized and developed into an attractive, practical form for institutional use.

A very different approach to evaluating portfolios is also described in Seldin's (1993) book. This method (see Figure 9.2) engages evaluators, too, in substantive reflection to try to understand and judge the scope and quality of the information communicated in a portfolio. Again, fundamental areas of performance are stated, with ample space available under each for comment, and evaluators are asked to respond in narrative, short-answer form with references to specific issues and details.

Clearly, individual institutions use widely different approaches to making reasoned judgments about portfolios. Logging onto the Internet site for Deliberations: Using Portfolios for Educational Development at (http://www.lgu.ac.uk/deliberations/portfolios/urls.html) offers an opportunity to view a myriad of stratagems at US and worldwide institutions, with multiple links to varied information about portfolios. What is most important is that faculty embrace the model and that the system does not duplicate evaluative efforts—that is, the use of portfolios for personnel decisions should be part of a comprehensive approach to faculty evaluation, and the methodologies chosen for developing and judging portfolios should be consistent with institutional goals and priorities. In other words, using portfolios formally for assessment and evaluation should essentially strengthen and develop institutional culture and institutional commitment to teaching excellence.

FIGURE 9.2

Portions of a Form to Evaluate Portfolios

Directions: In evaluating a professor on each item, please do not let timidity prevent you from being explicit about a candidate's assets. Equally important, try to be just as candid about the candidate's shortcomings. This assessment should be based only on information and evidence presented in the professor's teaching portfolio. As a reminder, all of us who teach—even in the same discipline—have varying concentrations of knowledge in the field and varying familiarity with teaching approaches.

I. Broad Teaching Skills: Within the discipline, which area do you regard as this professor's strongest? Which teaching method does he or she use most effectively?

II. Course Organization and Planning: How effectively does this professor use class time? Develop presentations that are well planned and organized?

III. Feedback to Students: How does this professor inform students of their performance? Review tests and assignments with them?

IV. Instructor-Student Rapport: How would you describe the atmosphere in the professor's classroom? How does this professor encourage students to seek help when necessary?

V. Knowledge of Discipline: How would you judge the professor's mastery of content in the courses currently taught? Efforts to stay current in the field?

VI. Personal Beliefs About Teaching: How would you describe this professor's attitude to teaching? Has it changed in recent years? In what ways?

VII. Overall Evaluation of Teaching: Considering the previous items, how would you rate the teaching performance of this professor?

Adapted from Seldin, P. (1993). Successful use of teaching portfolios. Bolton, MA: Anker.

FREQUENTLY ASKED QUESTIONS ABOUT
PORTFOLIOS AND EVALUATION

Seldin, Annis, and Zubizarreta (1995) offer answers to several common questions about the teaching portfolio, but here are a few queries and challenges that seem to recur often when the topic turns specifically to the use of portfolios in personnel decisions:

1) Focusing exclusively on instructional performance and omitting other facets of faculty roles, does a teaching portfolio intensify the perceived notion that teaching and scholarship are disconnected, that a faculty member's teaching and intellectual development are separate and should be evaluated separately, that teaching is evaluated less reliably than scholarship or service?

Boyer (1990) and other educational leaders have recognized the scholarship of teaching and have taken lead positions in revaluing the complexity and variety of faculty roles. Such reexamination of the professoriate has made the portfolio a particularly cogent instrument in articulating, explaining, and assessing a teacher's effectiveness. The sample "Table of Contents" cited earlier in this chapter suggests how the portfolio approach can bring coherence to the faculty role in order to make evaluation more comprehensively appreciative of multiple responsibilities. The portfolio process facilitates intellectual growth through the instrument's component of written reflection tied to critical analysis of research generated by evidence of teaching performance and outcomes. The portfolio's scholarly potential comes from its provision of a vehicle for critical inquiry based on evidence and sound judgment, the kind of analysis that seldom accompanies added lines to a résumé but that does occur during research and writing for professional enhancement and for maintaining a genuine commitment to the active life of the mind. Thus, in a real sense, teaching and scholarship, practice, and discourse, cohere in the portfolio process: Portfolio writing demonstrates how the act of teaching and the evaluation of teaching and other activities of the professoriate are inseparable from intellectual growth and serious scholarship.

2) In short, what is the most important feature of a portfolio developed for evaluation purposes?

Actually, several connected key points are crucial. A portfolio written expressly for evaluation must emphasize different kinds of evidence from a variety of sources, must focus on documentation of student learning, and must reveal coherence between philosophy and practice and between the reflective narrative (the case for teaching) and concrete evidence in the appendix.

3) Is the portfolio written for evaluation different from the portfolio for improvement? Do I have to develop two separate drafts?

The portfolio written for personnel decisions must include scrupulous proof of teaching performance in order to provide empirical evidence for sound evaluation. But improvement, too, demands rigorous and detailed description and analysis before the process of change can begin. The portfolio is a product of scholarship in that it engages faculty in ongoing examination of data regarding teaching accomplishment, in reflective analysis of information, in reasoned conclusions about individual teaching effort, and in written documentation. Research improves disciplinary expertise precisely because it guides a writer to a higher level of knowledge through the agency of close, careful, detailed analysis. Similarly, concrete, lasting improvement of teaching depends upon an instructor's willingness to study evidence of past performance and to formulate specific plans for development. The process of collecting such evidence is instructive in itself, for the teacher gains a new perspective on old data, prompting fresh goals and reaffirming old values and successes. The attention to documentation in a portfolio is just as vital for improvement as it is for evaluation. The portfolio's structure as a narrative document tied to an appendix of hard evidence stimulates the process of formative analysis while simultaneously providing a bank of reliable, useful information for evaluation. Hence, the portfolio ably serves the dual purposes of improvement and evaluation. Written on computer disk as a simple word processing document or uploaded to a web page with multiple links to narrative and graphical sections and multiple forms of evidence, the portfolio is easily adapted to many purposes (see Chapter 7).

4) If documentation in an appendix is crucial, then how much is too much? How big should the appendix be? When does one stop collecting materials?

Just as the information included in the narrative section of the portfolio is selective information, the appendix should consist of judiciously chosen evidence. A good rule to remember is never to discard anything: letters from colleagues; comments from students; announcements of awards; statements of congratulations or thanks; copies of successful assignment sheets, with accompanying student products; records of effective advisement, independent studies, or direction of student projects; student rating forms; departmental evaluations; email records; electronic listserv or web-based discussions in courses; and importantly, copies of strong (and weak) student works, such as essays, with evidence of the teacher's feedback on drafts. But in the appendix, materials should be carefully sorted to support the portfolio definitively but succinctly. As new items are added, old ones are removed. If a particular portfolio requires additional appendix space for supplemental descriptions, crucial hard copy articles, or audio or videotapes, then the instructor may briefly discuss such materials in the narrative, perhaps provide a brief summary of the nature of the evidence in one of the appendices, and make the items available for inspection in a designated location if the portfolio is used for evaluation. Selectivity is equally important for improvement, encouraging the teacher to focus carefully and realistically on particular goals. The portfolio is not an exhaustive document, and it certainly should not be an exhausting one, either.

5) Is the portfolio an excessively subjective document? How can it be used for valid assessment? Doesn't subjectivity interfere with reliability for evaluation?

Faculty who raise the issue of subjectivity have not engaged in one of the most invigorating, rewarding, and crucial activities of writing a portfolio: the collaborative effort between the instructor and a mentor who helps steer the direction of the portfolio to meet the professor's goals. Collaboration—especially if the mentor is an outside consultant or a peer outside the discipline—ensures a fresh, vital, critical perspective that encourages cohesion between the portfolio's narrative and appendices. On the other hand, a mentor in a faculty member's discipline permits an insider's understanding of unique pedagogical issues and can be very helpful in sorting through information about specific courses or teaching practices. Zubizarreta (1995), for example, suggests a useful model for developing a course portfolio that would benefit from the collaboration of a mentor who teaches the same course. An effective mentor does not assist the instructor in producing or, worse, fabricating subjective, effusive, culled information. Instead, a trained mentor flushes out objective information that is already evident or readily discovered in a teacher's work, keeping in mind the primary objective of helping a colleague improve instruction. Collaboration, then, is a pivotal dimension of the portfolio that counters subjectivity and connects the portfolio to objective criteria of excellence.

CONCLUSION

Accountability, assessment, and productivity are no longer mere buzz-words in the margins of the academy. Actually, the imperatives pre-scribed by such pressures are standard operational procedure on most campuses. The model of reflective practice demonstrated by the teaching portfolio emerges as one compelling solution to the need for professors to evaluate rigorously and improve systematically standards for teaching and learning. Varied methods of evaluating teaching and other activities of the professoriate exist and should be implemented just as carefully as portfolio strategies. Reexamining what and how we teach but more importantly why, with the aim of improving the impact of our practice on student learning, is a worthwhile endeavor that pays off in many different ways, including stronger, more reliable evaluation and more accent on the benefits of collaboration and clear communication of the case for teaching.

When the teaching portfolio concept is expanded to include reflective analysis of and goals for research and service, it can serve as a compelling structure for comprehensive review in a well-designed system of evaluation. Indeed, portfolios are in the vanguard of development strategies designed to transform the way teaching is viewed and reward-ed in the context of complex faculty roles. Besides ourselves as faculty, who else stands to benefit more from such reform of evaluation proce-dures and improvement efforts if not students? The positive answer is enough to recommend the teaching portfolio as a cornerstone of any institutional system of evaluation which, if done right, leads to improvement of teaching and learning. Nothing else is more important in our work.

References

Arreola, R. A., & Aleamoni, L. (1990). Practical decisions in develop-ing and operating a faculty evaluation system. In M. Theall & J. Franklin (Eds.), *Student ratings of instruction: Issues for improving practice.* New Directions for Teaching and Learning, No. 43. San Francisco, CA: Jossey-Bass.

Boyer, E. L. (1990). *Scholarship reconsidered: Priorities of the professo-riate.* Princeton, NJ: Carnegie Foundation for the Advancement of Teaching.

Braskamp, L. A., & Ory, J. C. (1994). *Assessing faculty work: Enhancing individual and institutional performance.* San Francisco, CA: Jossey-Bass.

Centra, J. A. (1979). *Determining faculty effectiveness: Assessing teach-ing, research, and service for personnel decisions and improvement.* San Francisco, CA: Jossey-Bass.

Edgerton, R., Hutchings, P., & Quinlan, K. (1991). *The teaching port-folio: Capturing the scholarship of teaching.* Washington, DC: American Association for Higher Education.

Seldin, P. (1984). *Changing practices in faculty evaluation.* San Francisco, CA: Jossey-Bass.

Seldin, P. (1991). *The teaching portfolio: A practical guide to improved performance and promotion/tenure decisions* (1st ed.). Bolton, MA: Anker.

Seldin, P. (1997). *The teaching portfolio: A practical guide to improved performance and promotion/tenure decisions* (2nd ed.). Bolton, MA: Anker.

Seldin, P. (1998, March). How colleges evaluate teaching. *AAHE Bulletin, 50* (7), 3-7.

Seldin, P., Annis, L., & Zubizarreta, J. (1995). Answers to common questions about the teaching portfolio. *Journal on Excellence in College Teaching, 6* (1), 57-64.

Seldin, P., & Associates. (1993). *Successful use of teaching portfolios.* Bolton, MA: Anker.

Shore, B. M., et al. (1986). *The teaching dossier* (Revised ed.). Montreal, PQ: Canadian Association of University Teachers.

Zubizarreta, J. (1994, December). Teaching portfolios and the beginning teacher. *Phi Delta Kappan, 76* (4), 323-26.

Zubizarreta, J. (1995). Using teaching portfolio strategies to improve course instruction. In P. Seldin & Associates, *Improving college teaching* (pp. 167-79). Bolton, MA: Anker.

CHAPTER 10

ADMINISTRATIVE COURAGE TO EVALUATE THE COMPLEXITIES OF TEACHING

Joan DeGuire North

With over 13 years in academic administration, I have become increasingly uncomfortable with the whole context of teaching evaluation, including my own role as dean. We have evaluated teaching largely based on our cherished assumptions and the legacy of past practices in evaluating it. Nowadays, one reads about many challenges to the traditional assumptions about teaching, and, surely, it is time to reexamine the ways we evaluate it.

HISTORIC VIEW

In the historic view of teaching, a tweedy professor talks to students who soak up the professor's knowledge and enthusiasm for the field. Students who fail to absorb the intellectual juices flowing around them are considered lazy little sponges. Reference works and teaching conferences provide all of the techniques needed for teaching well. With this approach, most faculty members pick up fairly effective teaching techniques from various cookbooks within the six-year window for tenure. In fact, most professors come to relative comfort within a short time, freeing them to divert their attention to other (more important?) matters (North, 1995).

Teaching as a Simple Activity

According to this paradigm, the fairly simple teaching evaluation exercise focuses on the professor's knowledge, actions, and characteristics. Does the professor know more than the textbook, speak clearly, organize the materials well, appear enthusiastic, ask good questions, pace through the material efficiently, and have good eye contact? Is he or she likable? The spotlight is entirely on the professor, and students are the photographers. Student evaluations dominate the evidence for effective teaching. Literature on evaluation of teaching grows heavy with empirical research on statistical fine points related to validity and reliability of student evaluations (see Chapter 2).

The typical administrator's role in the evaluation of teaching is also simple: Calculate the student evaluations, and compare the results of one faculty member against the evaluations of other faculty members. This simplistic view of teaching and its evaluation fits well into the administrators' responsibility to treat people uniformly and fairly across campus. We use small common denominators and standard, simple ways of measuring quality to provide the comfort of comparability and the appearance of fairness. Who can argue that a 2.5 isn't comparable to another 2.5? The naiveté of this attempt at simplicity and fairness across the board reminds me of a cartoon which was circulating in 1982 when Congress was (again) trying to simplify the federal tax process. The form asks one question and requires only one action. It asks: "How much money did you make this year?" And then it directs: "Send it all in."

Weeding in the Dark

Another assumption within this traditional approach to evaluating teaching is that the administrator (usually the dean, but sometimes the vice president, if the dean is shirking his or her duty) serves as the weeding agent, probing personnel files and departmental recommendations for any hints of weakness. There is an unspoken understanding that the departments will not point the way to any uncertainties they might have. At my end of the food chain, the dean has to play a hide-and-seek game with departmental recommendations and glowing peer evaluations, never certain if the department wants or doesn't want a culprit found.

With this uncertainty about the department's true professional judgment, administrators cling tightly to quantitative student evaluations and pray that negative personnel decisions do not turn sour or if they do, that there is enough of the right kind of documentation to substantiate negative action and a very good university attorney. This kind of thinking led me to lament the 1998 retirement of senior attorney John Tallman, University of Wisconsin System, as follows:

SAY IT ISN'T TRUE

How can you leave us,
stuck as we are in
all the messes, muddy trenches,
unresolved places, mid-crises,
about to be sued, wanting to sue,
thinking "bite me,"
in a stew, without a clue,
under incomplete personnel rules,
wandering aimlessly,
tripping over dead bodies and partially-true rumors,
hearing scandal, repeating the line,
running amok, causing a scene,
dropping the ball, losing the war,
hitting a snag, twisting in the wind,
hanging on paradox, afraid of the puzzle,
too young to retire, and alone, all alone?

This little ditty captures, I hope humorously, the dread that many administrators harbor when contemplating evaluation decisions: fear and loathing over possible legal ramifications. The university attorneys coach us on "doing things right," as notions of "doing the right thing" fade. For instance, legal advisors counsel deans to carefully curtail their verbosity when informing faculty members of personnel recommendations; they claim that less is better. But doing the right thing might actually call for including more detailed feedback. If fear clutches administrators in this process, it absolutely paralyzes candidates and gives peers indigestion. The administrators want to make sure that they weed out the right people for the right reasons, using "objective" data. The peers want to make sure that they are not blamed for any negative decisions and worry that any association with bad news will boomerang and hit them when their turn arrives. The candidates, twisting, twisting in the wind, beg for clues about what is going to happen to them under the shroud of evaluation. But they are not likely to get much enlightenment from departments busy "washing their hands" or from administrators cautiously weighing each word.

Faculty members have always known that there is something wrong with the simple view of teaching. But attacks on that view took the form of resentment toward student evaluations instead of demands to reconsider the assumptions about teaching which undergird this approach. Now, at long last, new assumptions are clamoring for attention, forcing us to acknowledge the need for more complexity and shifting roles in the evaluation of teaching.

New Assumptions

Teaching as Learning

First, we are slowly coming to grips with the notion that teaching cannot exist without learning, a simple concept that changes everything (Barr & Tagg, 1995). Peter Seldin tells a wonderful story about a "Stripe" cartoon in which Stripe boasts that he has taught his dog to whistle. Skeptical friends convene in the fellow's backyard to witness this miracle. After waiting for over an hour and hearing nothing but "Arf, arf, arf," the group confronts the braggart, saying, "We don't hear your dog whistling!" Stripe says, "I said I taught him. I didn't say he learned it." Teaching and learning are clearly different.

If one's expanded view of teaching includes evidence of influencing student learning, how does one document success at this new challenge? Learning over what period of time? What kind of learning: intellectual, social, attitudinal? Do all students have to learn the same content or can variations occur? Do we need to measure the strength of the faculty influence itself or just the outcome, however it was achieved (cause and effect)? Do we take into account that some learners are more ready than others, so that teaching is easier for some of us than others? Where would we look for evidence of effective learning?

Those who have resented the near monopoly of student evaluations as the measure of effective teaching may view this attention to student learning as the last straw in the fight for peer control over teaching evaluation. Actually, peers can play a more vital role than ever. Peers are ideally suited to assess the appropriateness of course goals, to help define types of evidence for student learning, to evaluate the evidence, and to come to judgment (see Chapter 4).

Students can—and should—continue to describe and evaluate their experiences in classes. They are often accurate and reliable observers, but conflicts between the instructor's goals and their own expectations can too easily influence them, especially as we make the transition from teacher-centered pedagogy to more active student learning. We must listen to students in our classes because they have the front seat in observing the drama play out and because we need to know how they feel about the interaction. But students cannot be the sole source of information on which we base opinions about teaching effectiveness (see Chapter 2).

The Teacher as Person

We come face to face with greater complexity inherent in teaching when we begin to acknowledge the connection between teaching and the inner life of the teacher. In recent years, we have heard more about the personal, passionate core of teaching, which moves our thinking about teaching from mere outward behaviors to what one author calls "the humanity of teaching" (Schmier, 1995). Authors such as Jane Tompkins and Parker Palmer (Tompkins, 1996; Palmer, 1998) shed light on how the inner landscape influences a teacher's relationship to the content, to the students, and to the teaching process itself. Palmer explains, "Teaching, like any truly human activity, emerges from one's inwardness, for better or worse. As I teach, I project the condition of my soul onto my students, my subject, and our way of being together" (p. 2). These authors remind us that teaching is essentially a fully human activity, not just a manifestation of a talking head coming solely from one's intellect. Schmier (1995, p. 24) elaborates, ". . . the most effective teaching technique that I have at my disposal is me, the teacher, and human being. . . . The essence of my teaching is to recognize myself and to understand myself in my teaching. My power to teach, then, flows not just from my mastery of the subject, or from my use of technology, or from the power I have over the students, but from my own self-mastery."

We are poorly equipped to act as evaluators for this inner area, certainly with our traditionally simple, quantitative approaches to evaluation. We seldom even discuss this aspect of teaching, possibly because "the very term 'professional' connotes the impersonal, as if our profession were a mask designed to conceal our individual identities" (Banner & Cannon, 1997, p. 42). And yet it is hard to argue that the personal dimension does not influence the effectiveness of teaching. How does one measure the faculty member's humanity and add this dimension into an evaluation formula? Perhaps a shift from a quantitative to a qualitative approach will provide some answers.

ASSUMPTIONS INTO ACTION

Complexity of Teaching Requires Colleague Assessment

If we are going to use complex qualitative data to assess teaching effectiveness, faculty colleagues must take the spotlight in evaluation. Delving into content issues, the interplay of content/student learning/faculty orchestration, and the heart of the teacher requires mature professional judgment from colleagues who know the context. Only colleagues can detect the scent of staleness, and only colleagues can provide the spark that can lead to revitalization.

If departments take a more active role in assessing teaching effectiveness, we need not continue the guessing game between departments and the dean or between the department and the faculty member. When people viewed teaching as simple and able to be gauged mostly by student evaluations, deans could accept token evaluation from departments. But no more. With the sure knowledge of the full complexity of teaching, the role of peers in evaluating the gestalt of a person's teaching is inescapable. We administrators must then stop overrelying on student evaluations, guessing what the department hopes the administrator will do, and being preoccupied with fairness across the campus. Instead, we must insist on complex information in personnel files to support recommendations, rely on more honest and deep department review and recommendations, and commit ourselves to view each person individually within his or her own context.

Rich Information about and from Students

We need to collect much more information about and from students. We should find ways to use student achievements to document the effectiveness of the faculty member's strategies. Did the students learn what we hoped? Is what we hoped sufficient? Did the instructional techniques match the course goals? Is there evidence of classroom research, that is, testing various ways to attain student success?

What students say about their connections with a faculty member, how he or she helped them grow as scholars and as individuals, can also be an ultrasound view to the inner person of the faculty member. Even as faculty members, we can remember our teachers: "They drew us to them because they possessed a certain gravitas, or they exemplified the great pleasure of knowing, or because their enthusiasm for their subjects filled their classrooms, or because of their modesty" (Banner & Cannon, 1997, p. 42).

We should encourage the use of student comments as well as numerical ratings because comments create a clearer context than the numbers do. The most that the score 2.7, for example, suggests is that the students were mildly displeased. About what? Being belittled or being challenged beyond their expectations? One author (McKnight, 1990, p. 57) points out, "We know that much is lost and distorted in the process of transforming complex concepts into numerical values. . . . This is one reason why most evaluation materials include a section for comments" (see Chapter 3).

Faculty Reflections

We should encourage faculty members to include in their personnel files brief reflections about their teaching. Here, professors can set out the context of the course and the students, as well as their hopes, experiments, and results. Reflections are not self-evaluations but are thoughtful comments on teaching as a "human endeavor complicated by the fact that it involves heterogeneous groups of humans under constantly changing sets of conditions" (Theall, 1998).

For me, the professor's personal reflections have been the most eye-opening new information in personnel files. I have to admit that I never fully grasped the heroic undertaking of many faculty members, especially new ones, pushing to influence student learning until I began to read their reflections in personnel files. Laments one faculty member:

> This makes the third time that I have taught this class, and each semester students comment that I rush the class, and I do. This semester I didn't rush the course, but I could not cover all the course content I had planned. I feel like I have let the students down; they will really need that material in the next course. Why can't this be a three-hour course?

How can we judge such a person's success or failure in the classroom without knowing this core piece of information provided by the personal reflection? Reflections have revealed struggles with students unwilling to engage in active learning, with attempts to concentrate on classes after the death of a spouse, and with heart-wrenching disappointments over cultural differences. When the agony of defeat comes through, the reader-evaluator rightly relates more to the agony than to the defeat. We see the heart coming through, and we note that this person cares, tries, and tries again—surely factors associated with effective teaching. Also, faculty members seem to appreciate the opportunity to "speak" to the evaluators, to direct them to one or another aspect of teaching performance, to provide interpretation, to share thoughts, and to add their person to the evidence (see Chapter 9).

Reflections are especially useful in post-tenure review, when the focus is more on the faculty member's future directions than on narrow comparisons (North, 1999) (see Chapter 6).

Depth, Not Comparisons

If those of us who evaluate teaching understand the complexity of teaching, we have to study each personnel case, deeply, on its own merits and resist the pull of treating everyone exactly the same. Like it or not, we administrators and faculty colleagues are forced to rely more on our own professional and personal judgments of effectiveness, unscientific as they might be, using numbers as guides not conclusions. I struggled with more than one faculty member whose low student evaluations masked almost Herculean efforts to create more effective classes.

By truly thinking about student learning and about the human elements of a faculty member under review, we open a vast field of questions and possibilities, a space so daunting that old ways of evaluating teaching fail.

Immersion into Emerging Literature

Faculty on personnel committees, department heads, deans, and other academic administrators can expect to find themselves adrift in irrelevant eddies of information if they do not continue to read about teaching. The debates of yore about what constitutes good teaching have given way to miles of print about student learning, about the soul of teaching, about how to create learning communities in distance classrooms simultaneously—in sum—about the basic principles of good teaching/learning. Asking what constitutes good teaching is no longer a rhetorical question (see Chickering, Gamson, & Barsi, 1989; Angelo, 1993). There are serious and genuine debates and significant scholarship about teaching and anyone involved in its evaluation or its practice would be remiss to miss the emerging news. When the academy decided that teaching was a worthy topic in itself, the experts created a rich pasture for study.

We academic administrators—and faculty colleagues—need to change our judgments about teaching effectiveness in fundamental ways to embrace expanded assumptions and purposes of teaching. We are at the threshold of major shifts in our understanding of the teaching-learning process, and few in academe hold much affection for the current shortcuts, which we mistakenly call teaching evaluation. Let's not be like the characters in the television program, *MASH,* who, when asked how they get used to the war, responded, "We get used to not getting used to it."

REFERENCES

Angelo, T. A. (1993). A "teacher's dozen": Fourteen general, research-based principles for improving higher learning in our classrooms. *AAHE Bulletin, 45* (8).

Banner, J. M., & Cannon, H. C. (1997). The personal qualities of teaching: What teachers do cannot be distinguished from who they are. *Change, 29* (6).

Barr, R. B., & Tagg, J. (1995). From teaching to learning: A new paradigm for undergraduate education. *Change, 27* (6).

Chickering, A. W., Gamson, Z. F., & Barsi, L. M. (1989). Faculty inventory: *Seven principles for good practice in undergraduate education.* Racine, WI: The Johnson Foundation.

McKnight, P. (1990). The evaluation of postsecondary classroom teaching: A wicked problem? In M. Theall & J. Franklin (Eds.), *Student ratings of instruction: Issues for improving practice.* New Directions for Teaching and Learning No. 43. San Francisco, CA: Jossey-Bass.

North, J. (1995, October). Read my lips: The academic administrator's role in the campus focus on teaching. *AAHE Bulletin, 48* (2).

North, J. (1999, April). Post-tenure review: Rehabilitation or enrichment? *AAHE Bulletin, 51* (8).

Palmer, P. (1998). *The courage to teach: Exploring the inner landscape of a teacher's life.* San Francisco, CA: Jossey-Bass.

Schmier, L. (1995). Random thoughts: *The humanity of teaching.* Madison, WI: Magna.

Theall, M. (1998, October 9). Email communication to the Professional and Organizational Development Network (POD) listserv.

Tompkins, J. (1996). *A life in school: What the teacher learned.* Reading, MA: Addison-Wesley.

CHAPTER 11

BUILDING A CLIMATE CONDUCIVE TO EFFECTIVE TEACHING EVALUATION

Mary Lou Higgerson

Some time ago there was a cartoon in *The Chronicle of Higher Education* that pictured a faculty member speaking to the department chair and the caption read, "I love teaching. It's being evaluated that I don't like." This theme is echoed by chairs and deans who participate in leadership seminars or campus workshops when they disclose that they don't mind evaluating faculty who are doing a great job in the classroom, but often dread teaching evaluations when faculty are not meeting performance expectations.

Despite the fact that most institutions have policies that require the evaluation of teaching, many faculty (and some academic administrators) remain guarded about the teaching evaluation task and process. In some instances, faculty fear how the results of teaching evaluation will be used, or they find the administrator's role in teaching evaluations intrusive. Some administrators believe that the evaluation of teaching places them in the uncomfortable role of critic or judge. It is important to remember that these reactions are indicative of individual perceptions about teaching evaluation and not inherent in the evaluation of teaching. Academic administrators can enhance the effectiveness of teaching evaluation by creating a climate within the department that is conducive to a positive perception of the teaching evaluation process.

Climate refers to the personality of the department (Higgerson, 1996). Psychologically based, the department climate influences how individual faculty interpret and respond to information. An evaluative comment about teaching made by a chair in a department whose climate is characterized by collegiality and mutual respect among colleagues is likely to be perceived and accepted as constructive. The exact same comment, however, will produce a different reaction if uttered in a department that is perceived by faculty as competitive and punitive. Take for example the evaluative statement, "Student ratings suggest that students find the course content difficult to understand." This single statement can prompt a wide range of reactions depending on the department climate for teaching evaluation. If the climate is conducive to the effective evaluation of teaching, the subsequent discussion between chair and faculty is likely to focus on how the course content might be made more clear to students. If, however, the statement is made in a climate that is not conducive to the effective evaluation of teaching, the chair is likely to find that the faculty member becomes defensive and even resistant to suggestions for improvement.

The advantage of having a department climate that is conducive to the effective evaluation of teaching is immense. Evaluative comments will be more favorably received and the formative benefits of teaching evaluation will more likely be realized in a healthy department climate. Furthermore, both administrators and faculty will be more comfortable with the teaching evaluation process. Consequently, building a healthy climate is an essential precondition to the development of an ongoing teaching evaluation program. A review of the characteristics of a healthy department climate will help to illustrate the tremendous influence that department climate has on the effective evaluation of teaching.

CHARACTERISTICS OF A HEALTHY DEPARTMENT CLIMATE

Although the terms "culture" and "climate" are sometimes used inter-changeably, they refer to two different things. Whereas culture derives from shared values, climate accrues from shared perceptions. The department culture is more resilient to sudden changes because it derives from strongly held values. The department climate, however, can change with variations in individual or group perceptions. For example, should faculty become persuaded that the chair is not genuinely interested in the improvement of teaching, this perception will adversely influence the department climate for the evaluation of teaching. Whether accurate or inaccurate, faculty perception shapes faculty performance and the department climate for evaluating teaching.

A department climate is considered healthy if faculty perceptions evidence the existence of certain specific characteristics (Higgerson, 1996). First, faculty must understand and accept the department mission. It is not enough for faculty to have a printed copy of the department mission. Rather, faculty must have a working understanding of the mission that enables them to articulate and carry out the goals of the unit. The mission helps individual faculty know what activities are valued. If quality instruction is a key component of the department mission, then faculty will recognize the evaluation of teaching as important to the department mission and not merely a check on individual performance.

Second, a healthy department climate exists only when there is mutual trust and respect among department members. The presence of mutual trust and respect signifies a confidence in the individual and collective competencies of department members. There are no hidden agendas and everyone can be counted upon to carry out the goals of the department. Further, there is a collective understanding of, and appreciation for, the contribution of each individual faculty member to the department mission. Evaluative comments about teaching are more likely to be accepted as constructive because individual faculty sense an underlying appreciation for their work and trust the motives of colleagues who offer them.

Third, faculty can air differences of opinion constructively without fear of retaliation. The administration does not impose a single viewpoint, but encourages faculty to express individual perspectives. It is important that faculty perceive that all views will be heard and considered. When faculty are able to communicate openly about department issues, they are generally less defensive and more accepting of policy and procedures that are likely to incite resistance in a department with a poor climate. This makes change possible. For example, a proposed policy that calls for the evaluation of tenured faculty is less likely to be resisted when the faculty can openly discuss their concerns about the policy without their motives being suspect. The professional airing of different views enables all to help shape policy and practice in a manner that is likely to increase faculty commitment to the change.

Fourth, a healthy department climate is characterized by the presence of well-meaning cooperation among faculty. Cooperation implies a productive working relationship in which there is mutual investment of time and expertise in order to reap mutual benefit. Cooperation among department members must transcend individual agendas which may relate to particular subspecialties of the discipline or curricular turf. Cooperation also means working together to advance the department mission and not merely complying with any one person's wishes. In other words, a department will have a more effective teaching evaluation program when faculty are motivated to design a teaching evaluation process because it facilitates their professional development, benefits students, and enhances the quality of the curriculum and not merely because it complies with a directive from the dean.

Fifth, in a healthy department climate there is effective communication among all department members. All faculty must be (and feel) included in department communication. If part-time faculty are not included in department discussions about curricular issues, it is likely that they will perceive as unimportant their role in carrying out the teaching mission of the department. Effective communication implies that all faculty receive relevant information that enables them to work productively. It means that faculty are able to discuss difficult or potentially sensitive issues in a professional manner.

A healthy department climate facilitates effective department management by setting the tone for how faculty work with one another to conduct department business. Department members are generally more accepting of new ideas and less resistant to change. A healthy department climate is central to an effective program of teaching evaluation because it makes possible an exchange of professional views and constructive evaluative comments. It also answers, or at least minimizes, the concerns of those faculty who might otherwise resist constructive suggestions designed to improve teaching.

Building the Department Climate

The department climate does not automatically mirror the campus climate. In other words, it is possible to have a department with a healthy climate on a campus characterized by generally low morale. It is also possible to have a department with a very destructive climate on a campus which enjoys a positive climate. The department climate develops from the perceptions of department members. While campus conditions may influence faculty perceptions, it is the internal department conditions and practices that ultimately shape faculty perceptions.

Department climates can change for the better or worse as faculty form and revise perceptions about the department and the campus. It is the administration's communication with faculty about department issues and procedures that fuel faculty perceptions. If a chair, for example, presents the new assessment initiative as a waste of time, then faculty are likely to draw a similar conclusion. This chair should not be surprised if faculty fail to accept responsibility for the assessment activity and resist investing their time and effort to help the department comply with the guidelines for the new initiative. Similarly, if academic administrators make clear that quality instruction is valued, faculty are more likely to invest personal time and talent in teaching. Moreover, faculty will be more receptive to teaching evaluation processes that improve their performance in the classroom. When faculty perceive teaching evaluation as a constructive process with tangible benefits they will welcome rather than resist the activity.

Faculty rely on the department chair and other academic administrators to interpret campus policy and practice. Consequently, administrators can help shape faculty perceptions of teaching evaluation as a constructive process that is essential to teaching improvement and quality instruction. There are several ways in which administrators can help to shape faculty perceptions of teaching evaluation.

Set the Tone during the Hiring Process

Starting with the position advertisement, academic administrators set the tone for effective teaching evaluation when searching for new faculty. At a minimum, the position advertisement must make clear the value placed on teaching and the department's ongoing commitment to teaching improvement. This will signal all applicants that quality teaching is expected and valued in the department. This expectation should be reinforced during the interview process. Faculty candidates may be asked to teach a sample class and visit classes conducted by master teachers in the department. The interview should include discussion about teaching methods and student needs so applicants learn that quality teaching and the effective evaluation of teaching is an integral part of the department culture. All administrators interviewing the candidates should review department and campus procedures for evaluating teaching.

Academic administrators are the primary interpreters of campus and department policy for faculty. If effective teaching is essential to building a case for tenure and promotion, the hiring administrators need to make this clear to candidates who interview for faculty positions. Effort spent during the interview and hiring process will make subsequent discussion and evaluations easier to conduct. Similarly, chairs and deans need to reinforce the teaching priority when conducting performance evaluation sessions with faculty, reviewing faculty goals statements, leading department or college discussions on mission or curriculum, or handling more routine matters such as the course schedule.

Academic administrators can also assign mentors for new faculty hires who will provide one-on-one assistance regarding teaching. A department or campus program that asks senior faculty to serve as mentors for new faculty on teaching reminds all faculty that teaching is a priority for the department. It also provides a vehicle for ongoing discussion about teaching and makes teaching improvement a department and campus goal. One additional benefit of such a program is that all new faculty become connected with the department sooner.

HELP FACULTY CONNECT INDIVIDUAL AND DEPARTMENT GOALS

The role of faculty carries a high degree of autonomy in that, for the most part, faculty structure their own day and decide how to invest their time. Unless the chair helps faculty understand and accept department goals, the unit will be a collection of individuals with their own agendas. Chairs can help build within faculty an operational understanding of department goals by making clear the expectations for individual faculty performance (Higgerson, 1996). Similarly, deans need to help faculty understand college expectations for teaching. This requires that chairs and deans interpret campus and department policy for faculty. The campus tenure policy, for example, may stipulate the need to document teaching effectiveness. The chair must help faculty translate that more general standard into meaningful activities. How is teaching judged to be effective? Is it determined by student ratings on a standardized evaluation instrument, colleague visitation and report, or other indicators? Academic administrators can reduce individual frustration and help keep faculty working toward department and campus priorities by making performance expectations clear.

Making performance expectations clear and helping faculty understand how individual goals relate to department and college goals is an ongoing task that cannot be limited to an annual performance evaluation session. Rather, administrators need to reinforce formal evaluation with informal evaluative comments. As educators we know that evaluative comments have more meaning if they are uttered in the context of the activity being observed. Constructive suggestions for improved performance will have more impact if they are timed with ongoing activities to which they refer. By using informal evaluative comments to reinforce the formal evaluation process, administrators help to sustain continuous performance evaluation that enhances faculty development.

Informal evaluative comments made by an administrator will have an impact on others whenever or wherever they are made. Academic administrators are never off duty (Higgerson, 1996). This fact was painfully learned by one chair who, during a discussion of department mission, suggested that the unit narrow the breadth of its offerings because it did not have the talent to cover certain courses which the chair identified by name. You can imagine the reaction of the faculty who taught these particular courses. While the faculty teaching these courses would quickly confess that the course content was not within their most comfortable range of teaching expertise, it was still upsetting to hear the chair's comment. The evaluative comment made in the context of shaping the department mission had a negative connotation for the teaching abilities of a few faculty members. When administrators understand that they are never off duty, they can begin to use informal evaluative comments to systematically reinforce faculty performance in relation to department and campus goals.

Engage Faculty in the Development of Evaluation Procedures

If teaching evaluation is new in the department, chairs need to involve faculty in the design of the evaluation procedures. Similarly, if the college or campus wishes to revise its procedure for evaluating teaching, the administration needs to engage faculty in the revision process. The effective administrator will want to solicit faculty ideas for every aspect of the evaluation procedure (Higgerson, 1996). This will shift the focus from will we evaluate teaching to how will we evaluate teaching. It also allows faculty to take ownership for the process, which will ensure smoother implementation. Faculty commitment to teaching evaluation can be sustained by allowing faculty to take an active part in reviewing and revising procedures for teaching evaluation. On a regular basis, academic administrators should encourage faculty to discuss the usefulness of the current teaching evaluation process in terms of the outcomes desired by faculty and the department or campus.

During the evaluation process, administrators should engage faculty in personal goal setting and self-evaluation. Only when faculty members participate in setting their own goals are they likely to be committed to achieving them. It also empowers faculty to assume more control of their own professional development. In addition, a goal statement serves to let the administrator know whether the faculty member understands job performance expectations. Further, a faculty member's self-assessment of performance will reveal whether the faculty member can assess his or her own behavior relative to the standard for promotion and tenure. Typically, it will also reveal whether the faculty member has strategies for improvement. Most administrators find it easier to offer evaluative comments on items initially raised by the faculty member.

REDUCE DEFENSIVENESS ABOUT TEACHING EVALUATIONS

When the evaluation of teaching is confined to a formal annual evaluation session, faculty are more likely to be anxious about teaching evaluations. Administrators can reduce the anxiety that may be associated with the evaluation of teaching by making teaching evaluation a year-round (not yearly) activity (Higgerson, 1996). The more often faculty hear and offer constructive comments about teaching, the less anxious they will be about teaching evaluation. Ideally, administrators want to keep teaching evaluation in a coaching mode rather than assuming the role of judge or critic. This is easier to do if the evaluation of teaching is ongoing.

With the expectation for the ongoing evaluation of teaching established, administrators can further reduce individual defensiveness to evaluative comments by making faculty performance (and not personality) the focus for evaluative comments. There is a significant difference between the following two statements made by a department chair during a faculty evaluation:

A) "You need a fair system for grading students' work."

B) "Students want to know how they are doing in a course throughout the term."

The first statement is likely to be interpreted as a personal comment that questions the faculty member's motives. It is more likely to increase defensiveness because it implies that the faculty member does not use a fair grading system. It also fails to advise the recipient about how to remedy performance that is unacceptable. In contrast, the second statement is focused on performance that is expected and not personality. It implies that the evaluator believes that the individual has the motive and ability to improve performance and it is, therefore, less likely to cause the faculty member to become defensive. Administrators can keep evaluative comments constructive by resisting any temptation to label an individual or attribute substandard performance to some inherent aspect of a person's personality or motives.

MAKE TEACHING IMPROVEMENT POSSIBLE

For teaching improvement to be possible, administrators need to make performance goals specific and manageable (Higgerson, 1996). Consider the following statements:

A) Faculty are expected to provide students with a course syllabus that details the grading criteria.

B) You need to work harder at teaching.

The first statement is constructive because it makes clear a specific goal that is manageable. The second statement, however, is so general that, as a goal, it is meaningless. It implies that one's teaching performance is in need of improvement, but does not offer any advice on what one might do to improve teaching. Administrators need to help faculty think in terms of specific goals that are easily defined and manageable. If a faculty member promises to "work harder" at teaching, the administrator should pursue the discussion until the faculty member has a specific set of goals and actions steps. Until general statements like "work harder" are linked to specific goals and behavior, they represent only one's intent.

Administrators should also link evaluative comments to specific examples and offer specific suggestions for improvement. This will help to provide faculty with a clear operational understanding of criteria (see Chapter 3). Suppose a faculty member receives low student ratings on the following two items: "makes assignments clear" and "responds to questions." Those data might prompt the following evaluative comments from the department chair:

A) "Students have a hard time understanding you."

B) "Do you allow ample time for discussion when passing out an assignment?" Depending on the faculty member's reply, the chair might add: "How might you build more opportunity for student questions about assignments and course content into each class?"

Comment A is less specific and, as a result, more personal. The statement is likely to produce a defensive response from the faculty member. Worse yet, the statement offers no hint of remedy for low student ratings on these particular survey items. Comment B gives the faculty member the benefit of the doubt. It assumes that the faculty member does attempt to explain assignments and answer questions, but focuses on what else might be done to have student ratings improve.

Finally, establish a time frame for achieving goals (Higgerson, 1996). Especially with faculty who may need more coaching, set a date for reviewing progress. This establishes an expectation for continued performance evaluation, which helps to keep evaluation in a coaching, formative mode. Make certain that the time frame is realistic in light of the remedy being tried. Above all, remember that campus policy establishes the minimum expectation. Hence, if the campus policy requires one formal evaluation session each year, there is nothing to prevent a chair from meeting more often with individual faculty for the purpose of evaluating teaching.

RECOGNIZE AND REWARD IMPROVEMENT IN TEACHING

When the effort invested to improve teaching is recognized and rewarded, faculty will remain committed to the improvement of teaching (Higgerson, 1996). Often recognition carries as much weight, if not more, than monetary reward. Rewards need not be limited to salary increases or other monetary awards. Instead, rewards might include being nominated for a campus teaching award, being recognized in the department or college newsletter, or being held up as a model example for less experienced colleagues. Only academic administrators who faithfully recognize and reward improvement in teaching will be able to sustain an ongoing program of evaluation that results in teaching improvement.

The academic administrator's role in building a climate conducive to effective teaching evaluation can be further illustrated through an analysis of hypothetical situations. What follows are two different department scenarios in which the chair's approach to teaching evaluation alters the outcome of the process. In reading each scenario, consider whether the department exhibits the characteristics of a healthy department climate and whether the chair uses the suggested strategies for building a constructive department climate.

TWO SCENARIOS

Department A

Sam got to the office early because he wanted to organize the newest information regarding his teaching before his annual performance evaluation meeting with the chair. As he shuffled through the files on his desk, he tried to remember what he might have that his chair had not yet seen. His chair had talked with him about the student ratings for the previous term. They had discussed the letters that his colleagues wrote to describe his teaching following visits to his class. Over the past break, the chair reviewed the syllabi he designed for the current semester. It seemed to Sam that he and his chair talked so often about his teaching that the annual performance evaluation session required by campus policy was perhaps unnecessary. Nevertheless, Sam looked forward to the meeting because conversations with his chair about teaching were always helpful and motivating. At the last moment, Sam decided to take copies of the class assignments he was using in a new course that he was teaching this term for the first time.

The chair had his office door open, ready for Sam's arrival. After a few pleasantries, Sam and his chair were ready to discuss the purpose for the meeting.

Chair: It looks like you brought some papers for me. I imagine that this is evidence documenting your teaching effectiveness.

Sam: I brought copies of the assignments I'm using in the new class that I'm teaching.

Chair: That's great. Let me take a look at them. I remember that we agreed there was a need to improve the student ratings on two particular survey items: "makes criteria for grading clear" and "grades fairly." Let me read one of these and see if I would know what to do.

Sam: I had Susan read through the assignment before I passed it out to my students. You were right. It is helpful to use my faculty mentor to check the clarity of assignments I use in class. She had some good suggestions that I incorporated in the final copy.

Chair: These seem much clearer than the batch you showed me when we reviewed the student ratings of your teaching from last term. I especially like how you stipulate the grading criteria for each assignment as part of the handout. How did the students react?

Sam: Okay, I think. I had fewer students asking questions after class and only one call from a student the night before the assignment was due.

Chair: Did the student call because the assignment wasn't clear?

Sam: Actually, the student was concerned that the assignment was impossible to complete in one night, but this didn't surprise me since I gave the class a full week to do the work.

Chair: In general, how did the students do on these assignments?

Sam: Overall, the grades are good. In fact, most students have averages that are at least one letter grade higher than the grade they earned in the prerequisite course that I taught last term. I hope I don't get a reputation as an easy teacher.

Chair: There's a big difference between being clear and being easy. Make the grading criteria clear for students and be consistent in applying the criteria to student work. Then, assuming students study the material, there is no reason why you should not see students do their best work in your class. We will want to check these particular survey items again at the close of the term to learn how students perceive your efforts.

Department B

Alex could hardly focus on the stack of papers he was grading. This was the day he had dreaded for weeks. Soon he would meet with his chair for his annual performance evaluation meeting. Alex had vivid memories of the performance evaluation meeting held one year ago. The chair's message was very clear and to the point. Alex would need to improve his teaching if he hopes to earn tenure at this institution. Alex remembers how nervous he was as the chair sifted through the various survey items on the student evaluation form, painstakingly reading every item that had a mean score which was substandard. There seemed to be so many that Alex had difficulty noting them all. He did remember two that seemed to be of greatest concern to the chair: "makes criteria for grading clear" and "grades fairly." Since last year, Alex worked very hard at his teaching in hope that the student evaluations would improve, and they did, slightly. He hopes that his chair will notice the improvement and prays that it will somehow be enough. Soon Alex finds himself seated in the chair's office and the performance evaluation is underway.

Chair: It looks like you brought some papers for me. I imagine that this is evidence documenting your teaching effectiveness.

Alex: I brought copies of my syllabi and student ratings collected since the evaluation one year ago.

Chair: That's great. Let me take a look at them. I remember that we agreed there was a need to improve the student ratings.

Alex: Yes, and I worked very hard to do that. I believe you'll notice some improvement.

Chair: These don't seem much better. What did you do to improve your student ratings?

Alex: Everything. It seems that I am prepping for class constantly.

Chair: Have you thought about seeking help from some of our senior faculty? We have some terrific teachers in this department. I believe that they could help you.

Alex: Everyone is so busy that I hate to ask them to spend time on my work. I hope you believe that I have been working to improve the student ratings.

Chair: Unfortunately, when it is time to compile the documentation for your tenure application, results will count more than effort. I do appreciate that you are willing to work hard to improve your teaching. It is absolutely essential to earning tenure at this institution.

Alex: I recognize that, and you can count on me to give it 150% over the next year.

Chair: I guess that is all we can ask. Let me know if I can help you.

LET'S ANALYZE THE SCENARIOS

Sam and Alex teach in departments that are very different.

- Sam benefits from ongoing discussion about teaching with his chair and colleagues whereas Alex does not.

- Sam has an assigned mentor while Alex is left on his own to devise strategies that will improve his teaching.

- Sam is on a first-name basis with the colleague who is his mentor whereas Alex expresses his reluctance to ask senior faculty for help with his teaching.

- In Department A, the chair makes specific suggestions on what the faculty member might do to improve whereas the chair in Department B assigns full ownership for designing teaching improvement strategies to the faculty member when he says, "Let me know if I can help you." Yet Alex believes that he is "prepping for class constantly" with little to show for it in terms of improved student ratings. Although Alex has full responsibility for devising a teaching improvement strategy, he is not likely to know what to do next to realize higher student evaluations of his teaching.

The climate for the evaluation of teaching is markedly different in the two departments. Sam can be relaxed about the upcoming annual performance evaluation meeting with his chair because he can anticipate what will be discussed and knows that he has been making acceptable progress in improving his teaching. Indeed, Sam looks forward to the meeting because it is an opportunity to get more help from his chair on how best to further improve his teaching. Alex, on the other hand, is very anxious about the upcoming performance evaluation meeting. His recollection from last year's evaluation is that he had better work hard to improve. He is not even clear on the specifics of what needs improvement, only that it is essential to improve if he hopes to earn tenure. Alex has no idea if the modest improvement in the student ratings of his teaching will meet the department standard.

The chair's comments in each department begin in the same way, but the conversation rapidly moves in different directions because Sam and Alex are in departments that have different climates for teaching evaluation. Sam is able to have a very precise conversation about specific teaching strategies and how each strategy may improve the students' assessment of his teaching. Sam's chair makes very specific suggestions and makes connections between what Sam is doing and the student evaluation survey items. Sam is not defensive because the chair demonstrates his belief that Sam can improve his teaching by suggesting specific action steps for Sam to implement. Alex becomes more defensive because his chair is only specific about the need for him to improve his teaching in order to earn tenure. Clearly Alex does not have the sense that his chair believes he can meet performance expectations in teaching.

ADDITIONAL BENEFITS FOR ACADEMIC ADMINISTRATORS

Academic administrators can accrue several important benefits from building a climate conducive to the effective evaluation of teaching (Hecht, Higgerson, Gmelch, & Tucker, 1999). First, administrators improve their own credibility with faculty. Through effective evaluation of teaching, administrators can demonstrate their genuine desire to help faculty succeed. They can evidence their understanding of campus policy regarding faculty performance as it relates to criteria for promotion and tenure or merit pay. It is more difficult, for example, for faculty to resent or resist a chair who offers constructive evaluative comments with the express purpose of helping the individual faculty member improve and succeed. It is difficult to imagine any other administrative responsibility that provides a better opportunity for administrators to demonstrate their sincere interest in the professional development of faculty. Consequently, effective teaching evaluation does much to enhance the administrator's credibility with faculty.

Second, administrators can increase faculty commitment to improving instruction. When academic administrators treat teaching as a key ingredient of faculty success, faculty will be more committed to improving their teaching. Faculty, however, are likely to be less committed to improving teaching if the administration communicates that research (or some other activity) is the primary ingredient for success. In this regard the administration's practice is more persuasive than the policy. If, for example, the policy stipulates that effective teaching is essential to earning tenure and promotion when the practice demonstrates that one's publications carry more weight than one's teaching evaluations, faculty will invest more energy on research. The faculty are likely to conclude that the standard for effective teaching is not terribly high if the record of publication is strong.

Third, administrators who build a climate conducive to effective teaching evaluation will have fewer grievances resulting from promotion and tenure review. When the expectations for performance are clear, faculty are better able to assess whether their achievements in the classroom satisfy the department and campus standard for teaching success. Decisions about tenure and promotion or merit pay become predictable in that faculty can more accurately assess their own achievements relative to department and campus standards. Typically personnel decisions lead to grievances and court cases when faculty are surprised by the outcome. Even when a faculty member did not make satisfactory progress toward tenure, a grievance is not likely if the faculty member understands and expects the negative tenure decision.

LET'S RECAP

Take a moment to consider whether the climate on your campus or in your department is conducive to the effective evaluation of teaching. First, determine whether the climate is healthy by asking

- Do faculty understand and accept the department mission?

- Is there mutual trust and respect among department members?

- Can faculty air differences of opinion constructively without fear of retaliation?

- Is there a spirit of well-meaning cooperation among faculty?

- Do department members communicate effectively?

Second, assess your input as an academic administrator:

- Have I set the tone for teaching evaluation during the hiring process?

- Have I helped faculty connect individual and department goals?

- Have I engaged faculty in the development of evaluation procedures?

- Have I reduced defensiveness about teaching evaluation?

- Have I made teaching improvement possible?

- Have I recognized and rewarded improvement in teaching?

Your answer to these questions will help you identify what you can do to build a climate that is conducive to the effective evaluation of teaching. The tangible benefits to students, faculty, department, and the campus make the strategic effort essential.

References

Hecht, I. D., Higgerson, M. L., Gmelch, W., & Tucker, A. (1999). *The department chair as academic leader.* Phoenix, AZ: American Council on Education/Oryx.

Higgerson, M. L. (1996). *Communication skills for department chairs.* Bolton, MA: Anker.

CHAPTER 12

BUILDING SUCCESSFUL TEACHING EVALUATION PROGRAMS

Peter Seldin

M any colleges and universities attempt to improve their programs to evaluate teaching. They try to downgrade gossip, hearsay, and bias as evidence, and they restructure the evaluative process along more objective lines. Their efforts to separate the teaching wheat from the chaff are admirable. Unfortunately, they are not always successful. Why? The reasons are varied.

Some institutions embrace a quick-fix approach. Others adopt seriously flawed evaluation methods. Still others leave faculty in the dark about how their teaching performance will be evaluated. The inevitable result is an unfortunate mixture of faculty confusion, disillusion, even friction.

CAUSES OF FAILURE

Teaching evaluation programs often fail on two counts: First, they fail to motivate faculty members to improve their performance; second, they fail to distinguish between poor, adequate, and good teaching. Why do these evaluation programs fail? Experience suggests the following explanations.

1) The Evaluation Program Itself May Start out Flawed

It may be so loose and vague that faculty members and administrators do not know how it works. Or it may be so comprehensive and detailed—complete with assigned weights to various aspects of teaching and sources of evaluative information—that it self-destructs.

2) The Data Are Improperly Used

The evaluation program is constructed to serve two distinct purposes: to improve teaching performance and to provide data for salary, contract renewal, promotion, and tenure decisions. Too often administrators gather data designed to improve teaching performance but quietly use these data also for personnel decisions. Ethics and morality aside, these administrators are ripping apart the evaluation program. A program designed to improve teaching is quite different from one designed for personnel decisions.

3) The Evaluation Program Lacks the Safety Valve of Built-in Feedback to Monitor the Program

A regular review of the program is vital to its success. The kind of review—formal or informal—depends on campus needs, traditions, and politics. But if needed, the review must trigger reforms of the program.

4) One Faculty Member or a Group of Faculty Members Wants the Program to Fail

How do they work to defeat it? Through shrugs, platitudinous attitudes, buck-passing, and know-nothing responses like, "We can't do anything because we don't have enough data." Administrators possess the same power to defeat. A warm smile and a pleasantry can quietly sabotage a fledgling program. As educational reformers know, changes won on paper can be lost in performance. By lack of ability or interest, or by covert opposition, some faculty members and administrators are able to destroy efforts to restructure the evaluative process.

5) Improper Administration

Among the most common mistakes are a) inconsistent standards, b) unclear instructions on forms, and c) irregular rating schedules. Any one of these mistakes contributes to faculty confusion and distrust. And that inevitably leads to overt or covert faculty opposition. Unfortunately, such opposition is often compounded by administrative efforts to silence the faculty opposition which, in turn, convinces faculty that the administration stands in an adversary relationship. In truth, how the program is administered can be almost as important to its success as program content.

REVISING A FAILING SYSTEM

Assume that there is general agreement on the part of faculty members and administrators that a college or university's teaching evaluation program is failing. Assume further that there is genuine desire to locate and correct the program's errors. In specific terms, what should the institution do?

One proven approach begins with the appointment of a well-structured study group. The group's members should be selected carefully. They must be highly regarded on campus for their integrity. The group is charged with preparing a written plan that answers the following questions:

1) What goals are appropriate for our teaching evaluation program?

2) What parts of the present program hinder achievement of these goals and should be discarded?

3) What parts contribute to achievement of these goals and should be retained?

4) What can and should we do to improve the program and better achieve our institutional evaluation goals?

5) On our campus, do we possess appropriate resources—financial and human—to bring about these improvements?

6) Would the addition of outside experts help us achieve our goals?

7) What is a realistic time frame to revise the program?

At the outset, most study groups seek to widen their base of campus support. Some expand their membership to represent all academic divisions. Others appoint an advisory committee in order to bring in outside guidance and advice.

Virtually every successful study group does three things:

1) They seek out influential faculty because they know that if the heavyweights believe in the program's worth, other faculty are likely to follow their lead.

2) They use appropriate communication channels. They hold open faculty forums so that group members can answer questions and consider comments and suggestions. They obtain wide faculty feedback about attitudes and perceptions concerning teaching evaluation through surveys and interviews. They report periodically on their activities and progress through newsletters and general faculty meetings.

3) They resist the impulse to develop new forms right away. Far better is to begin by seeking consensus about purpose. Then, broaden the base of the study group by expanding membership. Next, conduct a campus-wide survey of faculty to get reactions to the current program, obtain feedback on what is needed to improve it, and tap faculty attitudes about specific evaluation techniques such as peer observation. Finally, after open hearings have been held to discuss the survey findings, forms and procedures are developed and a trial run scheduled.

CHARACTERISTICS OF A SUCCESSFUL
TEACHING EVALUATION PROGRAM

What steps must an institution take to develop a teaching evaluation program that is flexible, comprehensive, and fair? What common characteristics appear routinely in successful evaluation programs? The following guidelines may act as therapy for ailing teaching evaluation programs.

Decide the System's Purpose

It is crucial to decide at the outset which purpose the evaluation program is to serve: To provide appropriate data upon which to base personnel decisions for tenure, promotion in rank, or contract renewal, or to improve faculty teaching performance. The types of information gathered as well as the evaluation procedures depend directly on the system's purpose. Many institutions have developed separate programs for each of these two different purposes.

Seek Administrative Backing

No program designed to evaluate teaching can survive without unremitting public, top-level, administrative support. They have the power and influence to break logjams, offer compromises, and to lend the force of their administrative office to publicize the program and wrap it in good will.

Secure Faculty Involvement

If the teaching evaluation program is to be acceptable to the faculty, they must have a strong hand in developing and running that program. Faculty members must feel, with justification, that they control their own destiny. If they do, they will "own" the program they helped develop. They will more readily accept implementation and be more likely to consider the results fair and meaningful.

Overcome Faculty Resistance

Professors, like most human beings, tend to react to evaluation as an implicit threat. No one likes to be threatened. How can this natural resistance be overcome? Experience suggests that it is best met with sympathetic understanding and a trade-off approach emphasizing positive advantages to faculty in more objective administrative approaches to personnel decisions and in improved teaching performance.

Using administrative muscle-power to end faculty resistance will achieve neither objective. More effective approaches include:

1) Protecting each faculty member's privacy by prohibiting public dissemination of his or her evaluation without prior written approval

2) Viewing the teaching evaluation program as experimental and conducting dry runs to gain experience and to uncover and correct program weaknesses

3) Allowing one or even two years for acceptance and implementation

Use Open Communication

No teaching evaluation program stands much chance of success unless it is candidly and fully explained to the faculty and administration, and is understood and accepted by both. Any sugarcoating or obfuscation in the explanation or implementation dooms the program to failure.

Every step of the program must be openly arrived at, fully discussed, and widely publicized. Every doubt must be resolved; every question answered satisfactorily. Faculty forums or open hearings are particularly useful in analyzing and discussing draft documents and in distributing progress reports as the evaluation program develops.

Rely on Campus Influentials

Every college and university has faculty influentials whose support is mandatory if the teaching evaluation program is to succeed. The support of this handful of influential faculty is essential to the program's acceptance by the rest of the faculty. For that reason it is important to seek their advice, to court their support.

Collect Multisource Information

A common mistake is to accept student ratings as the only needed source of information on teaching effectiveness (see Chapter 2). In truth, if a three-dimensional and reasonably accurate picture of a faculty member's teaching effectiveness is to be obtained, a number of relevant sources of information must be consulted.

Each source of information—student, peer, administrator, self-assessment—offers important but limited insights. No single source is enough for tenure, promotion, or retention decisions. What information can be expected from each source?

From students. Students provide assessment of teaching skills, content and structure of the course, organization of course materials, teacher-student interaction, clarity of presentation, work load, and student advising.

From faculty peers. Faculty peers provide a review of teaching materials (assignments, handouts, tests, papers), mastery and currency of subject matter, and interest and concern for teaching.

From administrators. Administrators provide an appraisal of the workload and other teaching responsibilities, student course enrollment, and teaching improvement.

From the professor. The professor provides self-appraisal as a teacher, illustrative course material, evidence of student learning and student advising.

Select the Teaching Evaluation Instruments

Avoid reinventing the wheel. Don't start from scratch by developing original teaching evaluation instruments. Instead, look over the programs and forms that are already in successful use at other comparable institutions. One caution: adapt, don't adopt. Modify whatever procedures, policy, or forms are necessary to tailor them to local needs, politics, and traditions.

Use Campus Expertise

Many colleges and universities can tap their own faculty for experts trained in test construction, research design, and statistics. Such experts can shape the questionnaires and forms and can structure appropriate methods of collecting data. If needed, specialists from other institutions, more experienced in handling the sometimes tricky adaptation of an evaluation program, can augment the on-campus expertise.

Discuss Expectations

Each faculty member must know what is expected of him or her. An annual meeting with the department chair is a good opportunity to discuss what constitutes satisfactory and exemplary performance. That meeting should also yield 1) agreement on the criteria, and their weights, for the faculty member's teaching evaluation; and 2) the yard-sticks which will show how the faculty member fared in meeting the agreed-upon performance standards.

Should the faculty member fail in serious respect to meet the standards, that failure should be discussed with him or her far in advance of a possible termination decision. The faculty member should be given every opportunity to improve his or her performance. Doing so may require lessening of committee work for a period of time. Or it may require the assistance of instructional developers (see Chapter 3).

Train the Evaluators

When asked to appraise their colleagues' performance, many faculty members find themselves in alien territory. For this task, they need training, or at the least, some orientation sessions. It is axiomatic that the better the training, the better the evaluators (see Chapter 4).

What should evaluators be taught? In brief, they must learn

1) What to look for

2) How to use the evaluation instruments

3) How to work effectively with other evaluators

4) How results will be used

5) How teaching evaluation leads to teaching improvement

6) The function and responsibilities of the evaluators

7) Recent research findings on teaching evaluation

8) The mechanics of the program

Who should do the training? It is best done by faculty colleagues highly respected for their solid knowledge of the campus teaching evaluation program. Sometimes, those colleagues are aided by outside experts well-known for their general knowledge of teaching evaluation.

Administer the Rating Forms

No matter how good the forms and how effective the training, faulty administration can wreck the evaluation program. The most common defects include an irregular rating schedule, bias resulting from flawed instructions, inadequate or inconsistent standards, or poorly constructed rating forms.

Dry runs can discover and eliminate bugs in the system. They provide needed experience in the construction and administration of ratings forms. And they stimulate faculty thinking about the content of the forms and desirable modifications.

For example, dry runs can help an institution decide whether a single rating form or multiple rating forms should be used by students at the college or university. (A single form offers the enticing possibility of comparing faculty members throughout the department or institution. But the single form can be treacherous in small or laboratory classes and may not be appropriate given certain policies or practices.)

When should the rating forms be administered? It depends on the purpose. Experience suggests that if the purpose of the teaching evaluation is for personnel decisions, the forms should be completed within the last two weeks of the semester. Caution: Avoid placing excessive importance on one classroom observation or one class's student ratings. They may do gross injustice to the faculty member's performance. Far better are evaluation data from several sources over several semesters. Under no circumstances should a single appraisal from a single source justify a retention, promotion, or tenure decision.

When ratings are used for teaching improvement, it is best to issue the rating forms to students, faculty observers, and to the to-be-appraised faculty member early in the semester, not later than five or six weeks into the term. By doing so, the faculty member's performance can be monitored and deficiencies corrected. Caution: Improvement in performance depends on frank, sympathetic discussion of ratings with the faculty member by a respected peer who can point out deficiencies and suggest specific remedies.

Evaluate the Program

Every workable teaching evaluation program must contain a built-in feedback mechanism to monitor the evaluation process. Faculty knowledge of—and participation in—the feedback mechanism adds to the program's viability. When faculty know that they can reshape an evaluation program, it adds stability and strength to that program.

Maintain the Program

The operation of a teaching evaluation program means coping with constant problems. Some problems involve students. For example, evaluation fatigue may set in if they are asked too frequently for ratings. The result? Diminished student eagerness for the program. Other problems involve faculty. Some faculty members may dislike the task of reviewing a colleague's teaching materials. Others may balk at the huge expenditure of time and energy required by a classroom observation program. Still others may find self-evaluation the equivalent of self-torture.

Solving these and other problems requires continuity of the faculty and the active public support of the administration. Sympathetic and understanding students, faculty, and administration, working together in a cooperative venture, works best.

Follow Civil Rights Guidelines

The evaluation policies and practices must be in accordance with established civil rights guidelines. In recent years, few institutions have been lucky enough to escape lawsuits triggered by aggrieved faculty who believe they have been denied contract renewal, promotion, or tenure for discriminatory reasons.

Evaluation programs in increasing numbers are being challenged in court as biased or inadequate. And a mounting number of institutions have been judged in violation of law and have been ordered by the courts to reverse personnel decisions. It is critically important, therefore, for colleges and universities to shore up inadequacies and erase inequities before the courts order it done. Following are some suggested guidelines:

1) Evaluation forms must be written in clear and concise language.

2) Evaluators must be adequately trained in how to use the evaluation instruments and how to interpret results.

3) Classroom observation by colleagues must follow a list of teaching behaviors previously discussed with the faculty members being observed.

4) The criteria and procedures used must be fully understood by both the faculty and the academic administration.

5) The components of the teaching evaluation program must be job-related and subject to empirical validation.

6) Multiple sources of evaluation are required, and each source's appraisal must be pursued independently.

7) The administration and scoring of the evaluations must be standardized.

8) Student evaluations containing comments about faculty members must not be summarized. Either all or none of the comments should be made public.

9) If an institution's written guidelines state that a particular source of information will be used in evaluating teaching performance, that source must be used.

10) A careful appraisal of teaching performance must contribute to every personnel decision.

11) Self-evaluation should not be the primary source of information in appraising teaching performance for retention, promotion, or tenure decisions.

12) The evaluation program must not contain any bias or give any appearance of containing bias.

Include Grievance Procedures

A grievance mechanism must be included in every evaluation program whose results apply to personnel decisions. The grievance procedures must be detailed in advance, and an appeals procedure should be available. Since group decisions are generally more acceptable, personnel decisions should be appealed to the faculty senate or another such august body rather than to the president or academic vice president.

A FINAL WORD

It is always easier to raise questions about teaching evaluation than to offer answers. Nevertheless, equipped with hindsight and the benefit of research, we know many more things than we knew a decade ago, even a year or two ago. We know the following:

1) There is no perfect teaching evaluation program, nor can there be. Such a system will probably always remain beyond reach. But with enough time, effort, and goodwill, we can come reasonably close.

2) Teaching evaluation is both a process and a result: a way to determine goals, to appraise the processes for reaching them, and to assess the extent to which they have been met.

3) Faculty evaluation is a complex process, and no single source of data is adequate. The combined appraisals of students, colleagues, administrators, and the faculty member's self-assessment are required for reasonably reliable and valid judgments.

4) The evaluation program must be administratively manageable and both cost- and time-efficient.

5) Teaching evaluation is an evolving process and that any component (e.g., student ratings) may be fashionable this year and obsolete the next.

6) Many faculty members have legitimate fears that evaluation data will be misused or abused in tenure, promotion, and contract renewal decisions.

7) The cornerstone of any evaluation program is its acceptance by the faculty, which rests on faculty confidence in the program's integrity, which, in turn, rests on the faculty's active participation in the program's development.

8) Solidly constructed evaluation programs provide each faculty member with factual information on his or her strengths and weaknesses and encourages consultations with teaching improvement specialists (or colleagues with appropriate expertise) to improve performance.

9) It is almost always necessary to separate the two functions of teaching evaluation—improvement and personnel decision-making—into distinct evaluation processes.

10) Sizable differences in culture and tradition among colleges and universities mean that a successful teaching evaluation program in one institution may be less successful in another.

11) Faculty resistance to evaluation programs can be emotional and deep-rooted and can assume the form of apathy or covert or overt resistance.

12) Many faculty members and academic administrators find it awkward and disturbing to appraise teaching performance, and they require training for the task.

13) Active support and involvement of top-level administrators is key to publicizing the program and keeping it moving forward.

14) The evaluation program must be designed to include reviews so that biased or inappropriate items can be eliminated during the evaluative process.

15) Teaching evaluation programs used for tenure, promotion, or contract renewal must include an appeals procedure to assure a fair result.

16) Teaching evaluation is only a means to an end—the improvement of teaching in order to improve student learning.

APPENDIX: SELECTED FORMS
TO EVALUATE TEACHING

Instead of creating original teaching evaluation forms, most colleges and universities can benefit from the models already developed elsewhere.

Obviously, the rating forms must be congenial in nature and content with the goals of a particular college or university. And the selection of the questionnaire items will depend on local conditions as well as institutional and department objectives. In general, therefore, it is sounder to adapt—not adopt—an already existing model and reshape it to meet local conditions and needs.

Eight field-tested models for evaluating teaching are presented in the appendix to this chapter. They should not be considered as the definitive word, but rather as a starting point for campus discussion intended to mold and reshape the model for a better fit with institutional or department needs.

APPENDIX 12.1

STUDENT PERCEPTIONS OF TEACHING

Instructor's Name _____

Course Number _____Today's Date _____

Please respond to the following statements concerning your participation in this class, the course itself, and the instructor. Your responses will be used to improve instruction. To indicate whether you disagree or agree with the statements, use the scale of 1 to 5.

STRONGLY DISAGREE 1 2 3 4 5 STRONGLY AGREE

PERSONAL:

1. I am prepared for this class.	1	2	3	4	5
2. I seek help when I need it.	1	2	3	4	5
3. I have learned the material of this course.	1	2	3	4	5
4. *	1	2	3	4	5
5. *	1	2	3	4	5

COURSE:

6. The course is well organized.	1	2	3	4	5
7. The course requirements are clearly stated.	1	2	3	4	5
8. Assignments are pertinent to the course objectives.	1	2	3	4	5
9. Contrasting theories are presented.	1	2	3	4	5

10. Current developments are presented.	1	2	3	4	5
11. The stated objectives of the course are met.	1	2	3	4	5
12. My overall rating of this course: (1-poor, 2-fair, 3-moderate, 4-good, 5-excellent)	1	2	3	4	5
13. *	1	2	3	4	5
14. *	1	2	3	4	5

INSTRUCTOR:

15. The instructor is prepared for class.	1	2	3	4	5
16. The instructor provides a classroom environment that is conducive to learning.	1	2	3	4	5
17. The instructor effectively communicates ideas and information.	1	2	3	4	5
18. The instructor is enthusiastic about the course.	1	2	3	4	5
19. The instructor encourages student participation.	1	2	3	4	5
20. The instructor is available to give help.	1	2	3	4	5
21. The instructor uses appropriate methods to evaluate student performance.	1	2	3	4	5
22. The instructor treats students with courtesy and respect.	1	2	3	4	5

23. My overall rating
of this instructor:
(1-poor, 2-fair, 3-moderate,
4-good, 5-excellent)   1   2   3   4   5

24. *   1   2   3   4   5

25. *   1   2   3   4   5

*Spaces for optional questions supplied by the instructor

OPEN-ENDED COMMENTS:

The instructor's strengths are:

The instructor's weaknesses are:

The following is most valuable in this course:

The following would improve this course:

Additional comments:

APPENDIX 12.2

STUDENT PERCEPTION REPORT

Course Title _____Course Number _____

Instructor(s) _____

MARKING DIRECTIONS:

Use a number two pencil to fill out the form. Please answer each question by darkening the one circle that best represents your view. Make solid marks that fill the circle completely.

Strongly Agree	=	SA
Agree	=	A
Uncertain	=	U
Disagree	=	D
Disagree Strongly	=	DS
Not Applicable	=	NA

PLEASE RATE THE FOLLOWING:

1. This course challenged
my abilities.   SA   A   U   D   SD   NA

2. The instructor effectively
communicated the content
of the course.   SA   A   U   D   SD   NA

3. The instructor communicated
his/her expectations of
the students.   SA   A   U   D   SD   NA

4. The instructor was
prepared for class.   SA   A   U   D   SD   NA

5. The instructor provided a
clear syllabus at the beginning
of the course.   SA   A   U   D   SD   NA

6. The expression of differing
viewpoints was encouraged.   SA   A   U   D   SD   NA

7. The instructor used audiovisual
aids or other teaching tools which
improved my understanding of
the course content.   SA   A   U   D   SD   NA

8. The instructor was available
for advice and assistance.   SA   A   U   D   SD   NA

9. The textbook for this course
was current and informative.
(if applicable)   SA   A   U   D   SD   NA

10. The readings for the course
were relevant to the subject.
(if applicable)   SA   A   U   D   SD   NA

11. The quizzes/tests were fair.
(if applicable)   SA   A   U   D   SD   NA

12. I would recommend this
course to a friend.   SA   A   U   D   SD   NA

13. The instructor was an
effective classroom teacher.   SA   A   U   D   SD   NA

ART STUDIO EVALUATION ONLY

14. Critiques were effective.   SA   A   U   D   SD   NA

15. The course helped me to
develop my creative potential.   SA   A   U   D   SD   NA

16. The course helped me to
develop my artistic judgment.   SA   A   U   D   SD   NA

17. The instructor was responsive
to the specific needs of the class.   SA   A   U   D   SD   NA

18. The instructor allowed
experimentation within
the medium.   SA   A   U   D   SD   NA

19. The instructor encouraged
creative and experimental applications
to principles taught.   SA   A   U   D   SD   NA

20. The instructor worked with
individual students to promote
personal potential.   SA   A   U   D   SD   NA

21. The instructor was enthusiastic
about the subject taught.   SA   A   U   D   SD   NA

22. The instructor was
responsive to student questions.   SA   A   U   D   SD   NA

23. The instructor allowed
students to risk new ideas.   SA   A   U   D   SD   NA

SCIENCE LABORATORY EVALUATION ONLY

24. The laboratory exercises were
well coordinated with the
lecture topics.   SA   A   U   D   SD   NA

25. There was enough discussion
of results after experimental labs.   SA   A   U   D   SD   NA

26. Materials were readily
available during the lab period.   SA   A   U   D   SD   NA

27. The lab instructor was
available during the lab period.   SA   A   U   D   SD   NA

28. The lab instructor explained lab
procedures and safety precautions
pertinent to the exercises.   SA   A   U   D   SD   NA

WRITTEN COMMENT SECTION

a. What were the strengths of this course?

b. What were the weaknesses of this course?

c. What is your opinion about the teaching you received in this course?

d. What is your overall opinion about this course?

APPENDIX 12.3

STUDENT EVALUATION FORM

TO THE STUDENT. Please give your careful responses to the questions below. Keep in mind that class structures vary widely and that not all of these questions, or every part of them, apply equally to every class.

Please write legibly in answering the questions. Your thoughtful and responsible comments will be of great help in our efforts to improve teaching.

1. COURSE CHOICE. Why did you take this course? Was it an elective or a requirement?

2. YOUR PARTICIPATION. How would you assess your own performance in the course? Estimate the percent of classes that you attended.

3. COURSE CONTENT. Please comment on how assigned work outside of class contributed to the learning process. What books, labs, drills, etc. were most useful to you? Which were least useful and why?

4. EVALUATION. Please comment on the process by which you were evaluated in this course. Were tests, paper assignments, and/or projects a fair measure of your knowledge of the material covered in the course? Was the degree of difficulty and the workload appropriate to the level of the course?

5. EFFECTIVENESS OF INSTRUCTION. Please discuss the effectiveness of the instructor in communicating and explaining new knowledge and concepts, facilitating the development and refinement of skills, and/or raising issues for discussion?

Considering your responses to the questions above, please provide your overall assessment of the quality of the course and the effectiveness of the instruction in the context of all of the courses you have taken. (Fill in the appropriate circle):

POOR	FAIR	GOOD	VERY GOOD	EXCELLENT
Quality of the Course: O	O	O	O	
Effectiveness of the Instruction: O	O	O	O	

APPENDIX **12.4**

CLASSROOM OBSERVATION REPORT

Instructor evaluated _____

Course _____Number of students present _____

Date _____

Evaluator(s) _____

Purpose. The purpose of this classroom observation is (1) to provide a database for more accurate and equitable decisions on tenure, promotion, and merit increase and (2) to improve faculty performance.

Instructions. Please consider each item carefully and assign the highest scores only for unusually effective performance. Questions 12 and 13 have been deliberately left blank. You and the instructor being evaluated are encouraged to add your own items. Each instructor should be observed on two occasions, and the observer(s) should remain in the classroom for the full class period. It is suggested that the observer(s) arrange both pre- and post-visit meetings with the instructor.

Highest		Satisfactory		Lowest	Not Applicable
5	4	3	2	1	NA

_____ 1. Defines objectives for the class presentation.

_____ 2. Effectively organizes learning situations to meet the objectives of the class presentation.

_____ 3. Uses instructional methods encouraging relevant student participation in the learning process.

_____ 4. Uses class time effectively.

_____ 5. Demonstrates enthusiasm for the subject matter.

_____ 6. Communicates clearly and effectively to the level of the students.

_____ 7. Explains important ideas simply and clearly.

_____ 8. Demonstrates command of subject matter.

_____ 9. Responds appropriately to student questions and comments.

_____ 10. Encourages critical thinking and analysis.

_____ 11. Considering the previous items, how would you rate this instructor in comparison to others in the department?

_____ 12.

_____ 13.

_____ 14. Overall rating

Would you recommend this instructor to students you are advising? (Please explain.)

What specific suggestions would you make concerning how this particular class could have been improved?

Did you have a pre-visit conference? _____

A post-visit conference? _____

APPENDIX 12.5

CLASSROOM OBSERVATION REPORT

Instructor evaluated _____

Observer(s)_____

Number of students present _____Course _____

Date _____

Instructions. Several days prior to the classroom visit, the instructor should provide the observer(s) with a copy of the course syllabus containing course objectives, content, and organization.

Procedure. The observer(s) should meet with the instructor several days **in advance** of the visit to learn the instructor's classroom objectives as well as the teaching methods to be used. Within several days **after** the visit, the observer(s) should meet with the instructor to discuss observations and conclusions.

1. Describe the instructor's content mastery, breadth, and depth.

2. Describe the method(s) of instruction.

3. How clear and well-organized is the presentation?

4. Describe the form and extent of student participation.

5. What specific suggestions would you make to improve this instructor's teaching?

Please feel free to use the reverse side of this page to elaborate on your comments.

APPENDIX 12.6

FACULTY SELF-EVALUATION OF TEACHING

Name: _____Date:_____

Department: _____

1. In which area of your teaching discipline do you consider yourself strongest?

2. What is your greatest strength as a teacher? Your greatest weakness?

3. What was your most important accomplishment as a teacher in the past year?

4. Compared to others in your department, how do you assess that accomplishment?

5. How would you describe the atmosphere in your classroom?

6. What has been your greatest shortcoming as a teacher over the past three years?

7. Compared to others in your department, how do you assess your overall teaching performance? On what do you base your assessment?

APPENDIX 12.7

FACULTY SELF-EVALUATION OF TEACHING

Name: _____ Date: _____

Department: _____

Highest				Lowest	Not Applicable
5	4	3	2	1	NA

_____ 1. Were the major objectives of your course made clear to your students?

_____ 2. Were class presentations well-planned and executed?

_____ 3. Were classroom examinations appropriate to course objectives?

_____ 4. Were suitable instructional materials used?

_____ 5. Did your classroom presentations arouse student interest and enthusiasm?

_____ 6. Did you encourage your students to ask for your help without hesitation?

_____ 7. Did you use class time well?

_____ 8. Were difficult topics explained clearly?

_____ 9. How do you judge your mastery of the course content?

_____10. Considering your answers to the previous questions, how do you rate your overall teaching performance?

APPENDIX 12.8

ANNUAL ACTIVITY LIST: TEACHING

Name:_____

Department: _____

Rank: _____

TEACHING

SEMESTER	COURSE NUMBERS	RELEASED TIME CREDIT

Teaching strengths and weaknesses:

1. Teaching philosophy:

2. Instructional practices:

3. How do students react to my teaching?

4. Evidence of efforts to improve teaching:

5. Evidence of teaching enhancement efforts:

6. Integration of global, ethical, diversity issues, etc.:

7. Contributions to new course or curriculum development:

8. Plans to improve student learning:

9. How my current research enhances my teaching:

10. How my consulting/professional activities enhance my teaching:

11. Other teaching-related matters, new this year:

(Source: Lubin School of Business, Pace University. Reproduced by permission.)

CHAPTER 13

SUMMARY AND RECOMMENDATIONS FOR EVALUATING TEACHING

Peter Seldin

This book offers a broad range of strategies for evaluating teaching in colleges and universities. These chapter-by-chapter key points and recommendations show how administrators and faculty members can effect needed changes for improving the evaluation of teaching throughout the institution. An advisory note: The full meaning of each of these points can best be understood and appreciated by reading the chapters themselves.

CHAPTER 1. CURRENT PRACTICES—GOOD AND BAD— NATIONALLY

Peter Seldin

1) How do colleges evaluate teaching today? How has it changed over the past decade or two? This chapter provides the answers to the survey response of nearly 600 academic deans.

2) Student ratings have become the most widely used source of information on teaching effectiveness.

3) Self-evaluation, classroom visits, and course syllabi and exams have gained currency in the evaluation of classroom teaching.

4) The department chair and academic dean are still major sources of information, but with sharply diluted power. Also maintaining major roles are committee evaluation and colleagues' opinions.

5) Alumni opinions, grade distribution, long-term follow-up of students, student examination performance, and enrollment in elective courses continue to carry little weight.

6) In altering their teaching evaluation practices, colleges are gathering information from more sources, and doing so more systematically.

CHAPTER 2. STUDENT RATINGS OF TEACHING: USES AND MISUSES

William E. Cashin

1) The primary misuse of student ratings of teaching is the overreliance on them. On many college and university campuses, student ratings are the primary—if not the only—systematic data that are collected to evaluate teaching. Most student rating forms focus on what goes on in the classroom and so ignore important aspects of teaching that the students do not see or know about. There is almost universal agreement that effective evaluation of teaching requires using more than just student rating data.

2) There is a vast literature on student ratings, over 2,000 studies. Almost all of the objections about student ratings, for example, that they are biased by variables not related to effective teaching, have not been supported by the research. There are ways to control those few variables that may be sources of bias, such as student motivation to take the course, differences among academic fields, and possibly level of the course—freshman versus graduate student.

3) There is general agreement about how to use student rating data appropriately, especially about the more technical aspects. Past and present reviewers continue to conclude that student ratings tend to be statistically reliable, valid for most uses, relatively free

from bias or the need for control, and useful both to improve instruction and to make personnel decisions.

4) There are two areas about the use of student ratings that have been rather neglected. The first is how the forms are actually administered on most campuses. The second, and most important, is how the data are interpreted. Experience suggests that even data from well-developed forms are misunderstood or simply ignored. Despite years of research, faculty and administrators tend to put more credence in their limited personal experience, or to select one or two atypical studies to support their negative beliefs about student ratings (Cohen, 1990), than to be guided by the bulk of the research.

5) If we know how to use student rating data appropriately, why don't we? Cashin speculates that US higher education still pursues the wrong priorities: research and specialization. Graduate programs still socialize their students to aspire to behave like PhDs in some bygone German university, ignoring if not eschewing teaching, especially undergraduate teaching. Specialization has successfully replaced liberal education. Cashin suggests that Arrowsmith's (1967) 32-year-old conclusion is still accurate: that as far as teaching is concerned, US higher education is still a desert:

> At present the universities are as ungenial to teaching as the Mojave Desert to a clutch of Druid priests. If you want to restore a Druid priesthood, you cannot do it by offering prizes for Druid-of-the-year. If you want Druids, you must grow trees (pp. 58-59).

CHAPTER 3. USING STUDENT FEEDBACK TO IMPROVE TEACHING

Michele Marincovich

1) Given the evidence that consultation about student evaluations significantly increases the likelihood of teaching improvement, probably the single most important step that institutions can take

to make their teaching evaluation systems more effective is to provide a peer and/or professional teaching consultation service.

2) To increase both their faculty's confidence in the teaching evaluation system and the faculty's ability to make use of their evaluation data, administrators need to set the teaching evaluation system within a scholarly/academic context by disseminating the results of research from the teaching evaluation field and by making resources available to aid in the interpretation of evaluation data.

3) The implementation of a teaching evaluation system should strive for quick processing, a student body aware of its responsibility to provide thoughtful comments, and a grace period for teachers new to the profession or new to the particular institution.

4) For too many faculty, attention to teaching evaluations comes not when they are satisfactory or even outstanding but when they are troublesome. Administrators should take advantage of both annual reviews and informal meetings to give the positive reinforcement that teaching accomplishment deserves and the constructive support that less-than-satisfactory evaluations should receive.

5) Any official teaching evaluation system should make sure that faculty know about the availability and desirability of midterm evaluation procedures. Faculty should realize that professors who do midterm evaluations can achieve higher end-of-term evaluations.

6) Faculty who employ and follow up on their own methods of obtaining student feedback should be careful not to operate in a vacuum. Their sincere efforts to strengthen their classes can backfire if they respond haphazardly to what they think they are hearing from their students.

CHAPTER 4. EVALUATING TEACHING THROUGH PEER CLASSROOM OBSERVATION

Deborah DeZure

1) Peer observation of teaching offers critical insights that are needed to provide a fuller and more accurate picture of instructional effectiveness than allowed by student evaluations alone, but as it is currently practiced, it is not a very reliable or valid tool, particularly for high-stakes decisions such as tenure and promotion.

2) The sources of bias and unreliability of peer observation of teaching are known and can be reduced by establishing a process to plan and implement a systematic approach that can be used for all instructors.

3) Reliability and equity can be increased through training of observers, basing conclusions on more than one observation by more than one observer, basing the process on consensus about what constitutes good teaching in the discipline with shared criteria for teaching effectiveness, establishing and monitoring a process that is used consistently for all instructors and observers, assuring that all participants know the processes that will be used, providing opportunities for input by the instructor at several points in the process, and using a validated observation instrument.

4) Key decisions in establishing a process for peer observation include clarifying the following:

- Who will plan and supervise the process once it is established

- The purpose (summative, formative, or a combination)

- The selection process for observers, the possible pool of observers, number and consistency of observers, how often and which courses they observe

- Expectations for observer training

- Whether visits will be announced or unannounced

- Expectations for pre- and post-observation meetings, the classroom observation, and the written report(s)

- Shared criteria for teaching effectiveness in the discipline

- Methods used to document observations, including the use of forms, checklists or narrative approaches

- How to accommodate individual differences in instructional style (e.g., problem-based learning, simulations) and special cases (e.g., team-teaching, teaching online).

5) The process should be flexible enough to adapt to innovation and change in instructional approaches used in the future.

6) There is no single best model, but it should reflect institutional culture, disciplinary paradigms, departmental policies, and available resources. The process will inevitably reflect compromises among competing needs and possibilities because best practices may not be viable given limited time and resources of departments and faculty. Nevertheless, through careful deliberations, units can establish their priorities, make informed choices, and develop a process that is implemented consistently. In doing so, they will establish the basis for equitable treatment and improved if not optimal effectiveness.

CHAPTER 5. SELF-EVALUATION: WHAT WORKS? WHAT DOESN'T?

Peter Seldin

1) Self-evaluation is widely popular today as a component in the assessment of teaching performance. There is considerable recognition that faculty members can and do produce not only insights into their own course and instructional objectives, but also solid clues to their classroom teaching competency.

2) To be useful for personnel decisions, a self-evaluation needs to address a faculty member's objectives, activities, accomplishments,

and failures. It must be structured to uncover teaching specifics, and illustrative material and hard evidence of accomplishment are needed.

3) At many colleges, self-evaluation is found to be more useful to improve teaching than to aid personnel decisions. The reason may be that asking the instructor for a searching self-reflection, with no fear of retribution, opens the instructor to more self-recognition and provides a fresh basis for the improvement of teaching skills.

4) Faculty growth contracts are centered on self-evaluation. The contract is prepared by the faculty member and spells out the instructor's academic goals for the year, the plan to achieve each goal, and the budget required. The growth contract offers a systematic approach to charting the direction of professional growth and self-assessing the year's performance.

5) Teaching portfolios are anchored by self-evaluation. The process of developing a portfolio is as important as its content. During the process of deciding how to most effectively document their teaching, instructors are forced to review their strengths and weaknesses and rethink their philosophy of teaching and classroom objectives.

CHAPTER 6. POST-TENURE REVIEW: EVALUATING TEACHING

Joseph C. Morreale

1) The evaluation of teaching in post-tenure review is different from annual merit evaluations. It must be much more comprehensive, long-term and developmental; be seen in the context of a faculty development plan; be consistent with the overall mission of the institution; be viewed in the collective context of the departmental unit and climate; and use many more measures of performance.

2) Setting the standards for performance in teaching is critical to the process of post-tenure review. These usually involve setting the minimum or acceptable level of performance, but also superior

levels of performance. These performance standards should be benchmarked against other comparable institutions.

3) Evidence collected for teaching must be from multiple sources and agreed upon by all members in the department. Evidence must be continuous and collected every semester, and feedback to the faculty member must be provided to ensure faculty development in teaching. Interpreting evidence is best achieved when the faculty member has the opportunity to offer some self-reflection in the review and to discuss with colleagues the various evidence gathered.

4) Teaching evaluation of an individual faculty member must be placed within the context of the department or program. In this way, each faculty member can view his or her own development over the next five years in relationship to other members of the department. This can lead to connecting post-tenure review with program review.

5) Quality teaching performance and continued development in teaching must be valued highly by the institution and rewarded accordingly. Financial rewards for teaching excellence are important but so are nonfinancial ones, such as release time for course development or retraining. Moreover, faculty development plans in teaching must be supported with resources for travel, research assistance, extended study, special projects, equipment.

6) Under post-tenure review and the evaluation of teaching, there must exist consequences for continuing poor performance. Quality teaching and learning is too vital to any institution to allow continuous poor performance by any tenured faculty member. Such required actions range from reassignments, alternative career development, buyouts, and early retirement transition to dismissal-for-cause.

CHAPTER 7. EVALUATING TEACHING THROUGH ELECTRONIC CLASSROOM ASSESSMENT

Devorah A. Lieberman

1) The key to using electronic assessment tools in the classroom is to approach the process with the attitude that trying new strategies is worthwhile and can provide much more information than traditional paper-and-pencil approaches.

2) Check out home pages of others who are using Techno-CATs or other electronic evaluation tools. Three that are full of ideas are:

http://www.users.csbsju.edu/~tcreed

http://www.tltgroup.com

http://www.oaa.pdx.edu/cae

3) Thoughtful design and implementation of electronic assessment tools can easily result in publishable data that can be documented in promotion and tenure materials as "Scholarship of Teaching."

4) National organizations are interested in presentations that address electronic assessment of teaching and learning. A few of these organizations are the Professional and Organizational Development (POD) Network, the AAHE Assessment Conference, and the Lilly Conferences.

5) Faculty are generally willing to put forth effort in learning about electronic assessment tools if the university will provide the support to teach them the tools and to help them overcome unexpected electronic obstacles in the process of implementation.

CHAPTER 8. USING THE WORLD WIDE WEB TO IMPROVE TEACHING EVALUATION

Clement A. Seldin

1) As computers and communication increase in power and speed, the web has become the primary research tool for many academics.

But for others, navigating the web has become cumbersome and time-consuming.

2) Despite the explosion of new web sites, some are "dead ends"—outdated, inaccurate, or no longer in existence.

3) Through the use of several search engines and the email responses of teaching evaluation specialists around the world, a number of current and especially helpful web sites are identified.

4) Many of the best web sites on improving the evaluation of teaching are found in teaching and learning centers based in colleges and universities. Examples:

> a) The Sheridan Center for Teaching and Learning, Brown University
>
> b) Center for Teaching Excellence, Iowa State University
>
> c) Center for Teaching and Learning, University of Michigan
>
> d) Center for Teaching and Learning, Stanford University
>
> e) Center for Instructional Development and Research, University of Washington

5) For each site identified in the chapter, the URLs are provided as well as a summary description of the site's contents.

Chapter 9. Evaluating Teaching Through Portfolios

John Zubizarreta

1) The teaching portfolio—as a continual, scholarly process of reflective practice, rigorous assessment of selective evidence, and peer collaboration—provides a structure for both constructive evaluation and ongoing improvement of teaching. In the act of writing critically about current, actual teaching efforts and in constructing a rhetorical framework that compels the teacher to gather supporting materials, analyze information, draw substantial conclusions, and posit action plans for better practice, the teacher develops a habit of intentional improvement based on regular and

timely assessment. The portfolio is a relevant, valid, useful component of a teaching evaluation system, but its prerequisites of reflection and collaboration also serve the goal of improvement.

2) For evaluation purposes, the teaching portfolio must be grounded firmly in ample but selected documentation collected in an appendix that supports the reflective narrative in which the faculty member articulates and analyzes crucial dimensions of teaching such as philosophy, methodology, materials, evaluation data, outcomes of learning, and goals. Every substantive claim or report of teaching accomplishment must be keyed to different kinds of evidence from a variety of sources.

3) Collaboration is an essential component of portfolio development. The value of such peer review and mentoring is that collaboration helps to stem subjectivity, encourage reflection tied to evidence, uncover strengths and challenges in teaching performance, and stimulate specific goals for improvement. Collaboration also helps make teaching a more publicly assessed and scholarly endeavor, ultimately strengthening the reliability of evaluations.

4) The teaching portfolio should not be the only means of assessing and evaluating faculty performance. Portfolios should be integrated into comprehensive systems of faculty evaluation and rewards. Portfolios, like any system of evaluation, should also be integrally connected to effective faculty development programs.

5) Successful use of portfolios for personnel decisions and fair, consistent evaluation of portfolios are tricky issues that require careful, slow implementation. Faculty need to own the process from the beginning. Portfolios should not be mandated at first. A core of agreed-upon, required items should be included in all portfolios, while also respecting and allowing for the individual nature of each portfolio's profile of a unique teaching effort. A cache of good models should be available for faculty, and administrative faculty and staff need to be clearly informed and involved in introducing portfolios to a comprehensive system of evaluation on a campus.

Chapter 10. Administrative Courage to Evaluate the Complexities of Teaching

Joan DeGuire North

1) Earlier beliefs about teaching evaluation focused somewhat simplistically on the faculty member's behaviors in the classroom and did not include an examination of student behaviors and student learning. A companion practice was administrators' and faculty members' overreliance on student evaluations of teacher behavior for personnel decisions, especially within the context of a pointedly legalistic approach to evaluation.

2) New assumptions about teaching are emerging which suggest a new look at evaluating teaching. Two of those assumptions involve a) looking at student learning to measure teaching effectiveness and b) considering the inner person of the faculty member as a valid aspect of the teaching-learning formula.

3) These assumptions suggest that teaching is far more complex than we assumed previously. This complexity requires that the evaluation of teaching be a process in which a) the professional judgment of colleagues takes a central role, b) additional information from students is needed, c) reflections of faculty members reveal the inner planning leading to the teaching act.

4) While it may have been possible in the past to compare teachers with each other to identify which are doing well and which are not, the complexity of teaching makes surface comparisons less meaningful than deep analysis of each individual.

5) Teaching and its evaluation are not immutable concepts whose mysteries have long since been discovered, so it behooves faculty and administrators involved in evaluation to keep tuned to the emerging literature.

CHAPTER 11. BUILDING A CLIMATE CONDUCIVE TO EFFECTIVE TEACHING EVALUATION

Mary Lou Higgerson

1) Building a healthy climate is an essential precondition to the development of an ongoing teaching evaluation program.

2) The same evaluative comment can provoke different reactions from faculty depending on the department climate.

3) A healthy climate is characterized by acceptance of the mission, mutual trust and respect, constructive airing of differences, well-meaning cooperation, and effective communication.

4) Academic administrators shape faculty perceptions of teaching evaluation by setting a positive tone for evaluation during the hiring process, helping faculty connect individual and department goals, engaging faculty in the development of evaluation procedures, reducing defensiveness about teaching evaluation, making teaching improvement possible, and recognizing and rewarding improvement.

5) Building a climate conducive to effective teaching evaluation will also improve administrator credibility, increase faculty commitment to improving instruction, and minimize grievances resulting from promotion and tenure review.

CHAPTER 12. BUILDING SUCCESSFUL TEACHING EVALUATION PROGRAMS

Peter Seldin

1) Teaching evaluation programs often fail on two counts: They fail to motivate faculty members to improve their performance, and they fail to distinguish between poor, adequate, and good teaching.

2) One proven approach to revising a failing evaluation system begins with the appointment of a well-structured study group charged

with preparing a written plan. The most effective groups solicit the support of influential faculty, use a variety of communication channels to tap faculty reactions and attitudes about specific evaluation techniques, and resist the impulse to develop new forms right away.

3) Characteristics of successful teaching evaluation programs include deciding the system's purpose; seeking administrative backing, securing faculty involvement, successfully overcoming faculty resistance, using open communication, collecting multisource information, training evaluators, and properly administering the rating forms.

4) It is almost always necessary to separate the two functions of evaluating teaching—improvement and personnel decision-making—into distinct evaluation processes.

5) There is no perfect teaching evaluation program, nor can there be. Such a system will probably always remain beyond reach. But with enough time, effort, and good will, we can come reasonably close.

6) Field-tested teaching evaluation forms are included in the appendix to Chapter 12.

REFERENCES

Arrowsmith, W. (1967). The future of teaching. In C. B. T. Lee (Ed.), *Improving college teaching* (pp. 57-71). Washington, DC: American Council on Education.

Cohen, P. A. (1990). Bring research into practice. In M. Theall, & J. Franklin (Eds.), *Student ratings of instruction: Issues for improving practice.* New Directions for Teaching and Learning, No. 43 (pp. 123-132). San Francisco, CA: Jossey-Bass.

REFERENCES

Aleamoni, L. M. (1976). Typical faculty concerns about student evaluation of instruction. *National Association of Colleges and Teachers of Agriculture Journal, 20,* 16-21.

Aleamoni, L. M. (1987). Student rating myths versus research facts. *Journal of Personnel Evaluation in Education, 1,* 111-119.

Aleamoni, L. M. (1987). Techniques for evaluating and improving instruction. *New Directions for Teaching and Learning, No. 31.* San Francisco, CA: Jossey-Bass.

American Association of University Professors. (1974). Committee C. Statement on teaching evaluation. *AAUP Bulletin, 60* (2), 166-170.

Angelo, T. A. (1993). A "teacher's dozen": Fourteen general, research-based principles for improving higher learning in our classrooms. *AAHE Bulletin, 45* (8).

Angelo, T., & Cross, P. (1993). *Classroom assessment techniques: A handbook for college teachers* (2nd ed.). San Francisco, CA: Jossey-Bass.

Arreola, R. A. (1995). *Developing a comprehensive faculty evaluation system: A handbook for college faculty and administrators on designing and operating a comprehensive faculty evaluation system.* Bolton, MA: Anker.

Arreola, R. A., & Aleamoni, L. (1990). Practical decisions in developing and operating a faculty evaluation system. In M. Theall & J. Franklin (Eds.), *Student ratings of instruction: Issues for improving practice.* New Directions for Teaching and Learning, No. 43. San Francisco, CA: Jossey-Bass.

Arrowsmith, W. (1967). The future of teaching. In C. B. T. Lee (Ed.), *Improving college teaching* (pp. 57-71). Washington, DC: American Council on Education.

Baez, B., & Centra, J. A. (1995). *Tenure, promotion, and reappointment: Legal and administrative implications.* ASHE-ERIC Higher Education Report, No. 1. Washington, DC: George Washington University.

Bailey, C. (1990). In M. J. Galgano (Ed.), *Council of Chairs Newsletter, 2* (1). Bloomington, IN: Organization of American Historians. (http://www.indiana.educ/oah/chairsnl/v2n1.htm).

Baiocco, S. A., & DeWaters, J. N. (1998). *Successful college teaching: Problem-solving strategies of distinguished professors.* Boston, MA: Allyn & Bacon.

Banner, J. M., & Cannon, H. C. (1997). The personal qualities of teaching: What teachers do cannot be distinguished from who they are. *Change, 29* (6).

Barber, L. W. (1990) Self-assessment. In J. Millman & L. Darling-Hammond (Eds.), *The new handbook of teacher evaluation.* Newbury Park, CA: Sage.

Barr, R. B., & Tagg, J. (1995). From teaching to learning: A new paradigm for undergraduate education. *Change, 27* (6).

Beidler, P. G. (1997). What makes a good teacher? In J. K. Roth (Ed.), *Inspiring teaching: Carnegie professors of the year speak.* Bolton, MA: Anker.

Berk, R. A. (1979). The construction of rating instruments for faculty evaluation. *Journal of Higher Education, 50,* 650-669.

Bland, C. J., & Bergquist, W. H. (1997). *The vitality of senior faculty members: Snow on the roof—fire in the furnace.* ASHE-ERIC Higher Education Report, 25 (7). Washington, DC: The George Washington University.

Boice, R. (1991). Quick starters: New faculty who succeed. In M. Theall & J. Franklin (Eds.), *Effective practices for improving teaching.* New Directions in Teaching and Learning, No. 48. San Francisco, CA: Jossey-Bass.

Boyer, E. L. (1990). *Scholarship reconsidered: Priorities of the professoriate.* Princeton, NJ: Carnegie Foundation for the Advancement of Teaching.

Braskamp, L. A., & Ory, J. C. (1994). *Assessing faculty work: Enhancing individual and institutional performance.* San Francisco, CA: Jossey-Bass.

Braxton, J. M., Bayer, A. E., & Finkelstein, M. J. (1992). Teaching performance norms in academia. *Research in Higher Education, 33* (5), 533-569.

Brinko, K. T. (1991). The interactions of teaching improvement. In M. Theall & J. Franklin (Eds.), *Effective practices for improving teaching.* New Directions for Teaching and Learning, No. 48. San Francisco, CA: Jossey-Bass.

Brinko, K. T., & Menges, R. J. (Eds.). (1997). *Practically speaking: A sourcebook for instructional consultants in higher education.* Stillwater, OK: New Forums Press.

Carnegie Foundation for the Advancement of Teaching (1994). *National survey on the reexamination of faculty roles and rewards.* Princeton, NJ: Carnegie Foundation for the Advancement of Teaching.

Cashin, W. E. (1989). *Defining and evaluating college teaching.* IDEA Paper No. 21. Manhattan, KS: Center for Faculty Evaluation and Development, Kansas State University, (This paper is now available on the Internet: www.idea.ksu.edu.)

Cashin, W. E. (1990, January). *Student ratings of teaching: Recommendations for use.* IDEA Paper No. 22. Manhattan, KS: Center for Faculty Evaluation and Development, Kansas State University.

Cashin, W. E. (1990a). *Student ratings of teaching: Recommendations for use.* IDEA Paper No. 22. Manhattan, KS: Center for Faculty Evaluation and Development, Kansas State University. (This paper is now available on the Internet: www.idea.ksu.edu.)

Cashin, W. E. (1990b). Students do rate different academic fields differently. In M. Theall & J. Franklin (Eds.), *Student ratings of instruction: Issues for improving practice.* New Directions for Teaching and Learning, No. 43 (pp. 113-121). San Francisco, CA: Jossey- Bass.

Cashin, W. E. (1994). Student ratings of teaching: A summary of the research. In K. A. Feldman & M. B. Paulsen (Eds.), *Teaching and learning in the college classroom* (pp. 531-542). Needham Heights, MA: Ginn.

Center for Teaching Effectiveness. (1996). *Preparing for peer observation: A guidebook.* Austin, TX: The Center for Teaching Effectiveness, University of Texas, Austin.

Centra, J. A. (1973). Self-ratings of college teachers: A comparison with student ratings. *Journal of Educational Measurement, 10* (4), 287-295.

Centra, J. A. (1979). *Determining faculty effectiveness: Assessing teaching, research, and service for personnel decisions and improvement.* San Francisco, CA: Jossey-Bass.

Centra, J. A. (1993). *Reflective faculty evaluation: Enhancing teaching and determining faculty effectiveness.* San Francisco, CA: Jossey-Bass.

Centra, J. A. (1996). Identifying exemplary teachers: Evidence from colleagues, administrators, and alumni. In R. J. Menges & M. D. Svinicki (Eds.), *Honoring exemplary teaching.* New Directions for Teaching and Learning, No. 65, (pp. 51-56). San Francisco, CA: Jossey-Bass.

Chan, S. S., & Burton, J. (1995). Faculty vitality in the comprehensive university: Changing context and concerns. *Research in Higher Education, 36* (2): 219-234.

Chickering, A. W., & Gamson, Z. F. (1994). Seven principles for good practice in undergraduate education. In K. A. Feldman & M. B. Paulsen (Eds.), *Teaching and learning in the college classroom* (pp. 255-263). Needham Heights, MA: Ginn.

Chickering, A. W., Gamson, Z. F., & Barsi, L. M. (1989). *Faculty inventory: Seven principles for good practice in undergraduate education.* Racine, WI: The Johnson Foundation.

Chism, N. V. N. (1999). *Peer review of teaching: A sourcebook.* Bolton, MA: Anker.

Clark, D. J., & Bekey, J. (1979). Use of small groups in instructional evaluation. *POD Quarterly, 1,* 87-95.

Cleary, T. (n.d). *Getting ready: A checklist of questions for the teacher.* Victoria, Canada: University of Victoria, Learning & Teaching Centre.

Cohen, P. A. (1980). Effectiveness of student rating feedback for improving college instruction: A meta-analysis of findings. *Research in Higher Education, 13* (4), 321-341.

Cohen, P. A. (1981). Student ratings of instruction and student achievement: A meta-analysis of multisection validity studies. *Review of Educational Research, 51,* 281-309.

Cohen, P. A. (1990). Bring research into practice. In M. Theall & J. Franklin (Eds.), *Student ratings of instruction: Issues for improving practice.* New Directions for Teaching and Learning, No. 43 (pp. 123-132). San Francisco, CA: Jossey-Bass.

Cohen, P. A., & McKeachie, W. J. (1980). The role of colleagues in the evaluation of teaching. *Improving College and University Teaching, 28,* 147-154.

Colby-Sawyer College. (1995, May & October). *Faculty Tenure Proposal Committee Report.* New London, NH: Colby-Sawyer College.

Columbia Information Systems. Perception Analyzer. (http://www.cinfo.com).

Corcoran, M., & Clark, S. M. (1985). The stuck professor: Insights into an aspect of the faculty vitality issue. In C. Watson (Ed.), *The professoriate: Occupation in crisis.* Toronto, Canada: Ontario Institute for Studies on Education.

Creed, T. (1998). Extending the classroom walls electronically. (http://www.users.csbsju.edu/~tcreed).

Cyrs, T., & Conway, E. (1997). *Teaching at a distance with emerging technologies: An instructional systems approach.* Las Cruces, NM: New Mexico State University, Center for Educational Development.

Davis, B. G. (1993). *Tools for teaching.* San Francisco, CA: Jossey-Bass.

Dilts, D. A., Bialik, D., & Haber, L. J. (1994). *Assessing what professors do: An introduction to academic performance appraisal in higher education.* Westport, CT: Greenwood.

Donald, F. (1997). Private discussion.

Doyle, K. O. (1983). *Evaluating teaching.* Lexington, MA: DC Heath.

Doyle, K. O., & Crichton, L. I. (1978). Student, peer, and self-evaluation of college instruction. *Journal of Educational Psychology, 70,* 815-826.

Doyle, K. O., & Webber, P. L. (1978). *Self-ratings of college instruction.* Minneapolis, MN: University of Minnesota, Measurement Services Center.

Eble, K. E. (1988). *The craft of teaching,* (2nd ed.). San Francisco, CA: Jossey-Bass.

Edgerton, R., Hutchings, P., & Quinlan, K. (1991). *The teaching portfolio: Capturing the scholarship of teaching.* Washington, DC: American Association for Higher Education.

Edmonds, A. (1990). The evaluation and reward of teaching: Confessions of a department head who agreed to chair a blue-ribbon committee on evaluating teaching. In M. J. Galgano (Ed.), *Council of Chairs Newsletter, 2* (1). Bloomington, IN: Organization of American Historians (http://www.indiana.educ/oah/chairsnl/v2n1.htm).

Ehrmann, S. The current student inventory: The Flashlight Project. (http://www.tltgroup.org).

Eisenberg, R. (1996). Personal correspondence.

Elbow, P. (1992). Making better use of student evaluations of teachers. *Profession, 92,* 42-27.

Feldman, K. A. (1976). Grades and college students' evaluations of their courses and teachers. *Research in Higher Education, 4,* 69-111.

Feldman, K. A. (1977). Consistency and variability among college students in rating their teachers and courses: A review and analysis. *Research in Higher Education, 6,* 233-274.

Feldman, K. A. (1987). Research productivity and scholarly accomplishment of college teachers as related to their instructional effectiveness: A review and exploration. *Research in Higher Education, 26,* 277-298.

Feldman, K. A. (1989). The association between student ratings of specific instructional dimensions and student achievement: Refining and extending the synthesis of data from multisection validity studies. *Research in Higher Education, 30,* 583-645.

Feldman, K. A. (1989). Instructional effectiveness of college teachers as judged by themselves, current and former students, colleagues, administrators, and external (neutral) observers. *Research in Higher Education, 30* (2), 137-194.

Feldman, K. A. (1992). College students' views of male and female college teachers, Part I: Evidence from the social laboratory and experiments. *Research in Higher Education, 33,* 317-375.

Feldman, K. A. (1993). College students' views of male and female college teachers, Part II: Evidence from students' evaluations of their classroom teachers. *Research in Higher Education, 34,* 151-211.

Feldman, K. A. (1994a). The association between student ratings of specific instructional dimensions and student achievement: Refining and extending the synthesis of data from multisection validity studies. In K. A Feldman & M. B. Paulsen (Eds.), *Teaching and learning in the college classroom* (pp. 543-576). Needham Heights, MA: Ginn.

Feldman, K. A. (1994b). Effective college teaching from the students' and faculty's view: Matched or mismatched priorities? In K. A Feldman & M. B. Paulsen (Eds.), *Teaching and learning in the college classroom* (pp. 335-364). Needham Heights, MA: Ginn.

Feldman, K. A. (1996, Spring). Identifying exemplary teaching: Using data from course and teacher evaluations. In R. J. Menges & M. D. Svinicki (Eds.), *Honoring exemplary teaching.* New Directions for Teaching and Learning, No. 65 (pp. 41-49). San Francisco, CA: Jossey-Bass.

Flash, P., Tzenis, C., & Waller, A. (1995). *Using student evaluations to increase classroom effectiveness* (2nd ed.). Minneapolis, MN: The Faculty and TA Enrichment Program, University of Minnesota.

Franklin J., & Theall, M. (1990). Communicating student ratings to decision- makers: Design for good practice. In M. Theall & J. Franklin (Eds.), *Student ratings of instruction: Issues for improving practice,* No. 43 (pp. 75-93). San Francisco, CA: Jossey-Bass.

Galgano, M. J. (Ed.). (1990). Evaluating teaching. *Council of Chairs Newsletter, 2* (1). Bloomington, IN: Organization of American Historians (http://www. indiana.educ/oah/chairsnl/v2n1.htm).

Geis, G. L. (1991). The moment of truth: Feeding back information about teaching. In M. Theall & J. Franklin (Eds.), *Effective practices for improving teaching.* New Directions for Teaching and Learning, No. 48. San Francisco, CA: Jossey-Bass.

Glassick, C. E., et al. (1997). *Scholarship assessed: Evaluation of the professoriate.* San Francisco, CA: Jossey-Bass.

Goodwin, L. D., & Stevens, E. A. (1996). The influence of gender on university faculty members perceptions of 'good' teaching. In D. E. Finnegan, D. Webster, & Z. F. Gamson (Eds.), *Faculty and faculty issues in colleges and universities* (pp. 272-286). Needham Heights, MA: Allyn & Bacon.

Graf, D. L., & Wheeler, D. (1996). *Defining the field: The POD membership survey.* Valdosta, GA: POD Network.

Gruber, C. (1990). Evaluating teaching at William Paterson College. In M. J. Galgano (Ed.), *Council of Chairs Newsletter, 2* (1). Bloomington, IN: Organization of American Historians (http://www.indiana.educ/oah/chairsnl/v2n1.htm).

Guidelines for observing an instructor's case-teaching approach and behavior. (1995, May 5). Cambridge, MA: Harvard Business School Press.

Hativa, N., & Marincovich, M. (Eds.). (1995). *Disciplinary differences in teaching and learning: Implications for practice.* New Directions for Teaching and Learning, No. 64. San Francisco, CA: Jossey-Bass.

Hecht, I. D., Higgerson, M. L., Gmelch, W., & Tucker, A. (1999). *The department chair as academic leader.* Phoenix, AZ: American Council on Education/Oryx.

Helling, B. B. (1988, Winter). Looking for good teaching: A guide to peer observation. *Journal of Staff, Program, and Organizational Development, 6* (4), 147-158.

HEP. (1997). *Higher Education Directory* (15th ed.). Falls Church, VA: Higher Education Publications.

Higgerson, M. L. (1996). *Communication skills for department chairs.* Bolton, MA: Anker.

Hildebrand, M. (1975). How to recommend promotion for a mediocre teacher without actually lying. In C. S. Scott and G. L. Thorne (Eds.), *Professorial assessment in higher education.* Monmouth, OR: Oregon State System of Higher Education.

Hildebrand, M., Wilson, R. C., & Dienst, E. R. (1971). *Evaluating university teaching.* Berkeley, CA: Center for Research and Development, University of California.

Hoffmann, R., & Coppola, B. P. (1996). Some heretical thoughts on what our students are telling us. *Journal of College Science Teaching, 25,* 390-394.

Hutchings, P. (Ed.). (1995). *From idea to prototype: The peer review of teaching: A project handbook.* Washington, DC: American Association for Higher Education.

Hutchings, P. (1996). *Making teaching community property: A menu for peer collaboration and peer review.* Washington, DC: American Association for Higher Education.

Ithaca College. (1993, August). *Faculty Handbook,* Section 7.3: Evaluation of Faculty. Ithaca, NY: Ithaca College.

Jacoby, K. E. (1976). Behavioral prescriptions for faculty based on student evaluations of teaching. *American Journal of Pharmaceutical Education, 40,* 8-13.

Keig, L., & M. D. Waggoner. (1994). *Collaborative peer review: The role of faculty in improving college teaching.* ASHE-ERIC Higher Education Report, No. 2. Washington, DC: The George Washington University.

Keller, G. (1985, January/February). Trees without fruit: The problem with research about higher education. *Change,* 7-10.

Knapper, C. (1995). Understanding student learning: Implications for instructional practice. In W. A. Wright (Ed.), *Teaching improvement practices: Successful strategies for higher education* (pp. 58-76). Bolton, MA: Anker.

Levinson-Rose, J., & Menges, R. J. (1981). Improving college teaching: A critical review of research. *Review of Educational Research, 51* (3), 403-434.

Lewis, K. G. (1991-92). Making sense (and use) of written student comments. *Teaching Excellence, 3* (8), 1-2.

Licata, C. M., & Morreale, J. C. (1997). *Post-tenure review: Practice, policies, precautions.* New Pathways Working Paper Series, No. 12. Washington, DC: American Association for Higher Education.

Lichtenstein, G., & Deitz, J. (1998). (Survey of 16 research university teaching centers regarding their current services and priorities). Unpublished survey.

Lieberman, D. (1998, October). Using technology wisely. *The Advocate.* Washington, DC: National Education Association.

Longwood College. (1995, April). *Policy on Post-Tenure Review.* Farmville, VA: Longwood College.

Lowman, J. (1995). *Mastering the techniques of teaching* (2nd ed.). San Francisco, CA: Jossey-Bass.

Lowman, J. (1996, Spring). Characteristics of exemplary teachers. In R. J. Menges & M. D. Svinicki (Eds.), *Honoring exemplary teaching.* New Directions for Teaching and Learning, No. 65, (pp. 33-40). San Francisco, CA: Jossey-Bass.

Marincovich, M. (1998). *Ending the disconnect between the student evaluation of teaching and the improvement of teaching: A faculty developer's plea.* National Center for Postsecondary Improvement, Deliverable #4010.

Marsh, H. W., & Dunkin, M. J. (1997). Students' evaluations of university teaching: A multidimensional perspective. In R. P. Perry & J. C. Smart (Eds.), *Effective teaching in higher education: Research and practice* (pp. 241-320). New York, NY: Agathon.

Marsh, H. W., & Dunkin, M. J. (1992). Students' evaluations of university teaching: A multidimensional perspective. In J. C. Smart (Ed.), Higher education: Handbook of theory and research, Vol. 8 (pp. 143-233). New York, NY: Agathon. [Reprinted in R. P. Perry & J. C. Smart (Eds.), (1997). *Effective teaching in higher education: Research and practice* (pp. 241-320). New York, NY: Agathon Press.]

Marsh, H. W., Overall, J. U., & Kesler, S. P. (1979). The validity of students' evaluations of instructional effectiveness: A comparison of faculty self-evaluations and evaluations by their students. *Journal of Educational Psychology, 71,* 149-160.

Marsh, H. W., & Roche, L. (1993). The use of students' evaluations and an individually structured intervention to enhance university teaching effectiveness. *American Educational Research Journal, 30* (1), 217-251.

McKeachie, W. J. (1979, October). Student ratings of faculty: A reprise. *Academe,* 384-397.

McKeachie, W. J. (1997). Good teaching makes a difference—And we know what it is. In R. P. Perry & J. C. Smart (Eds.), *Effective teaching in higher education: Research and practice* (pp. 396-410). New York, NY: Agathon.

McKeachie, W. J. (1999). *Teaching tips: Strategies, research, and theory for college and university teachers* (10th ed.). Boston, MA: Houghton Mifflin.

McKnight, P. (1990). The evaluation of postsecondary classroom teaching: A wicked problem? In M. Theall & J. Franklin (Eds.), *Student ratings of instruction: Issues for improving practice.* New Directions for Teaching and Learning No. 43. San Francisco, CA: Jossey-Bass.

Menges, R. J. (1990). Using evaluative information to improve instruction. In P. Seldin & Associates, *How administrators can improve teaching: Moving from talk to action in higher education.* San Francisco, CA: Jossey-Bass.

Menges, R. J. (1999). Appraising and improving your teaching: Using students, peers, experts, and classroom research. In W. J. McKeachie, *Teaching tips: Strategies, research, and theory for college and university teachers.* (10th ed.). Boston, MA: Houghton Mifflin.

Menges, R. J., & Brinko, K. T. (1986). *Effects of student evaluation feedback: A meta-analysis of higher education research.* Paper presented at the 70th annual meeting of the American Educational Research Association, San Francisco, CA. (ED 270 408).

Miller, R. I. (1992). Personal correspondence.

Millis, B. J. (1994). *Guide to good practices in class visits.* College Park, MD: University of Maryland.

Millis, B. J., & Kaplan, B. B. (1995). Enhancing teaching through peer classroom observations. In P. Seldin & Associates, *Improving college teaching* (pp. 137-152). Bolton, MA: Anker.

Morrison, A. A. (1995). Analyzing qualitative responses on student evaluations: An efficient and effective method. *Higher Education Research and Development Proceedings, Vol. 18,* 559-564.

Murray, H. G. (1984). The impact of formative and summative evaluation of teaching in North American universities. *Assessment and Evaluation in Higher Education, 9* (2), 117-132.

Murray, H. G. (1997). Effective teaching behaviors in the college classroom. In R. P. Perry & J. C. Smart (Eds.), *Effective teaching in higher education: Research and practice* (pp. 171-204). New York, NY: Agathon.

Murray, H. G., & Renaud, R. D. (1995, Winter). Disciplinary differences in classroom teaching behaviors. In N. Hativa & M. Marincovich (Eds.), *Disciplinary differences in teaching and learning: Implications for practice.* New Directions for Teaching and Learning, No. 64 (pp. 17-34). San Francisco, CA: Jossey-Bass.

North, J. (1995, October). Read my lips: The academic administrator's role in the campus focus on teaching. *AAHE Bulletin, 48* (2).

North, J. (1999, April). Post-tenure review: Rehabilitation or enrichment? *AAHE Bulletin, 51* (8).

Old Dominion University. (1995-97). *Faculty Handbook.* Section II: Policy and Procedures on Evaluation of Faculty and Post-Tenure Faculty Evaluation Policy: A Summary (1998). Norfolk, VA: Old Dominion University.

Ory, J. C. (1990). Student ratings of instruction: Ethics and practice. In M. Theall & J. Franklin (Eds.), *Student ratings of instruction: Issues for improving practice.* New Directions for Teaching and Learning, No. 43 (pp. 63-74). San Francisco, CA: Jossey-Bass.

Overall, J. U., IV, & Marsh, H. W. (1979). Midterm feedback from students: Its relationship to instructional improvement and students: Cognitive and affective outcomes. *Journal of Educational Psychology, 71,* 856-865.

Palmer, P. (1998). *The courage to teach: Exploring the inner landscape of a teacher's life.* San Francisco, CA: Jossey-Bass.

Pihakis, J., & Marincovich, M. (In preparation). Making use of students' open-ended comments on teaching evaluation forms.

Rehnke, M. A. (1994, October). Teaching and learning. *The Independent.* Washington, DC: Council of Independent Colleges.

Pregent, R. (1994). *Charting your course: How to prepare to teach more effectively.* Madison, WI: Magna.

Pritchard, R., Watson, M., Kelly, K., & Paquin, A. (1998). *Helping teachers teach well: A new system for measuring and improving teaching effectiveness in higher education.* San Francisco, CA: The New Lexington Press.

Redmond, M. V., & Clark, D. J. (1982). A practical approach to improving teaching. *AAHE Bulletin, 1,* 9-10.

Richlin, L. & Manning, B. (1995). *Improving a college/university teaching evaluation system: A comprehensive two-year curriculum for faculty and administrators.* Pittsburgh, PA: Alliance.

Rodabaugh, R. C. (1994). College students' perceptions of unfairness in the classroom. In E. C. Wadsworth & Associates (Eds.), *To Improve the Academy,* Vol. 13 (pp. 269-281). Stillwater, OK: New Forums Press and the Professional and Organizational Development Network in Higher Education.

Schmier, L. (1995). *Random thoughts: The humanity of teaching.* Madison, WI: Magna.

Seldin, P. (1976). *Faculty growth contracts.* University of London Institute of Education.

Seldin, P. (1980). *Successful faculty evaluation programs.* Crugers, NY: Coventry.

Seldin, P. (1984). *Changing practices in faculty evaluation.* San Francisco, CA: Jossey-Bass.

Seldin, P. (1989). How colleges evaluate faculty. *AAHE Bulletin, 41* (7): 3-7.

Seldin, P. (1991). *The teaching portfolio: A practical guide to improved performance and promotion/tenure decisions* (1st ed.). Bolton, MA: Anker.

Seldin, P. (1995). *Improving college teaching.* Bolton, MA: Anker.

Seldin, P. (1996). *The teaching portfolio.* Paper presented for the American Council on Education, Department Chairs Seminar, Washington, DC.

Seldin, P. (1997). *The teaching portfolio: A practical guide to improved performance and promotion/tenure decisions* (2nd ed.). Bolton, MA: Anker.

Seldin, P. (July, 1997a). *Improving college teaching: Learning to use what we know.* Paper presented for the International Conference on Improving College Teaching, Rio de Janeiro, Brazil.

Seldin, P. (1998, March). How colleges evaluate teaching: 1988 vs. 1998. *AAHE Bulletin, 50* (7), 1-7.

Seldin, P. (1998a, February). *The teaching portfolio.* Paper presented for the American Council on Education, Department Chairs Seminar, San Diego, CA.

Seldin, P. (1998b, June). *Changing practices in faculty evaluation.* Paper presented for the AAHE Assessment Conference, Cincinnati, OH.

Seldin, P., Annis, L., & Zubizarreta, J. (1995). Answers to common questions about the teaching portfolio. *Journal on Excellence in College Teaching, 6* (1), 57-64.

Seldin, P., & Associates. (1990). *How administrators can improve teaching: Moving from talk to action in higher education.* San Francisco, CA: Jossey-Bass.

Seldin, P., & Associates. (1993). *Successful use of teaching portfolios.* Bolton, MA: Anker.

Sheppard, S. D., Leifer, L., & Carryer, J. E. (1996). Commentary on student interviews. *Innovative Higher Education, 20* (4), 271-276.

Sheppard, S. D., Johnson, M., & Leifer, L. (1998). A model for peer and student involvement in course assessment. *ASEE Journal of Engineering Education, 87* (4), 349-354.

Shore, B. M., et al. (1986). *The teaching dossier* (Revised ed.). Montreal, PQ: Canadian Association of University Teachers.

Shulman, L. S. (1993, November/December). Teaching as a community property: Putting an end to pedagogical solitude. *Change, 25* (6), 6-7.

Sixbury, G. R., & Cashin, W. E. (1995). *Description of database for the IDEA Diagnostic Form.* IDEA Technical Report No. 9: Manhattan, KS: Center for Faculty Evaluation and Development, Kansas State University.

Sorcinelli, M. D. (1984). An approach to colleague evaluation of classroom instruction. *Journal of Instructional Development, 7* (4), 11-17.

Sorey, K. E. (1968). A study of the distinguishing characteristics of college faculty who are superior in regard to the teaching function. Dissertation *Abstracts, 28* (12-A), 4916.

State of New Mexico. (1995, March 18). Legislative Senate Bill 1131, Chapter 150: Requiring a Post-Tenure Review Process.

Stevens, E. A. (1987). *The process of change in college teaching.* Unpublished doctoral dissertation. Palo Alto, CA: Stanford University.

Theall, M. (1998, October 9). Email communication to the Professional and Organizational Development Network (POD) listserv.

Theall, M., & Franklin J. (1991). Using student ratings for teaching improvement. In M. Theall & J. Franklin (Eds.), *Effective practices for improving teaching.* New Directions for Teaching and Learning, No. 48 (pp. 83-96). San Francisco, CA: Jossey-Bass.

Tiberius, R. (1997). Small group methods for collecting information from students. In K. T. Brinko & R. J. Menges (Eds.), *Practically speaking: A sourcebook for instructional consultants in higher education.* Stillwater, OK: New Forums Press.

Tompkins, J. (1996). *A life in school: What the teacher learned.* Reading, MA: Addison-Wesley.

Toward greater excellence in teaching at Stanford. (1995). Final report of the C-AAA Sub-Committee on the Evaluation and Improvement of Teaching. Palo Alto, CA: Stanford University.

Trower, C. A. (1996). *Tenure snapshots.* New Pathways Working Paper Series, No. 2. Washington, DC: American Association for Higher Education.

University of California, Davis. (1993, August 19). *Office of the Provost Memo: Implementing of Five-Year Reviews.* Davis, CA: University of California.

University of Hawaii, Manoa. (1992). *Criteria for Periodic Faculty Review, Department of Economics, April 29, 1992 and Post-Tenure Review, Department of Special Education, 1992.* Manoa, HI: University of Hawaii.

University of Oregon. (1985 & 1993-94). *Post-Tenure Review, Faculty Legislation, April 6, 1977, as amended April 10, 1985 and 1993-94. Teaching Work Group Report: Guidelines for Evaluating and Rewarding Teaching at the University of Oregon.* Eugene, OR: University of Oregon.

University of Pittsburgh. (1995, September). *Faculty handbook,* Article III: General Policies of Appointment and Tenure. Pittsburgh, PA: University of Pittsburgh.

University of Wisconsin, Green Bay. (1996). *Faculty governance handbook.* 69-70. Green Bay, WI: University of Wisconsin.

University of Wisconsin, Madison (1993 & 1994). *Faculty policies and procedures,* 11-106. Policy on Review of Tenured Faculty (1994) and Report of the Planning Committee on Tenured Faculty Review and Development, February 1993. Madison, WI: University of Wisconsin.

US Department of Education. (1991, Winter). Assessing teaching performance. *The Department Chair: A Newsletter for Academic Administrators, 2* (3), 2.

Virginia Polytechnic Institute and State University (1995, December). *Faculty handbook,* Section 2, 10.4; Post-Tenure Review. Blacksburg, VA: Virginia Polytechnic Institute and State University.

Webb, J., & McEnerney, K. (1997). Implementing peer review programs: A twelve step model. In D. DeZure (Ed.), *To Improve the Academy,* Vol. 16 (pp. 295-316). Stillwater, OK: New Forums Press and the Professional and Organizational Development Network in Higher Education.

Weimer, M., Parrett, J. L., & Kerns, M. (1988). How am I teaching? *Forms and activities for acquiring instructional input.* Madison, WI: Magna.

Wergin, J. E. (1992, September). *Developing and using performance criteria.* Paper presented at the Virginia Commonwealth University conference on faculty rewards.

Wesson, M., & Johnson, S. (1989). *Study of post-tenure review at the University of Colorado. Report to the Board of Regents.* Boulder, CO: University of Colorado.

Williams, W. M., & Ceci, S. J. (1997, September/October). How'm I doing?: Problems with student ratings of instructors and courses. *Change,* 13-23.

Wilkerson, L. (1988). Classroom observation: The observer as collaborator. In E. C. Wadsworth, L. Hilsen, & M. A. Shea (Eds.), *Professional and organizational development in higher education: A handbook for new practitioners* (pp. 95-99). Stillwater, OK: New Forums Press and Professional and Organizational Network in Higher Education.

Wilson, R. C. (1986). Improving faculty teaching: Effective use of student evaluations and consultants. *Journal of Higher Education, 57* (2), 196-211.

Wilson, R. (1998, January 16). New research casts doubt on value of student evaluations of professors. *The Chronicle of Higher Education,* A12-14.

Zubizarreta, J. (1994, December). Teaching portfolios and the beginning teacher. *Phi Delta Kappan, 76* (4), 323-326.

Zubizarreta, J. (1995). Using teaching portfolio strategies to improve course instruction. In P. Seldin & Associates, *Improving college teaching* (pp. 167-179). Bolton, MA: Anker.

INDEX